MAX

A Biography of C. Maxwell Stanley
Engineer, Businessman, World Citizen

MAX

A Biography of C. Maxwell Stanley
Engineer, Businessman, World Citizen

ROS JENSEN

Iowa State University Press / Ames

ROS JENSEN spent more than thirty years in newspaper work, including twelve as an editorial writer for the *Des Moines Register*. He has taught in the journalism schools at Drake University, the University of Iowa, and Indiana University. He has degrees in history and journalism from the University of Iowa.

All photos courtesy Stanley family unless otherwise noted. Frontispiece: United Nations / Y. Nagata.

Excerpt from *Old Glory: An American Voyage,* by Jonathan Raban, pp. 151–52. Copyright © 1981 by Jonathan Raban. Reprinted by permission of Simon and Schuster, Inc.

"This is my song, O God of all nations," from *The Methodist Hymnal B.* © Copyright 1964, 1966, by the Board of Publications of the Methodist Church, Inc. Reprinted by permission of the Lorenz Corporation, Dayton, Ohio.

First edition, 1990

Library of Congress Cataloging-in-Publication Data
Jensen, Ros.
    Max : a biography of C. Maxwell Stanley, engineer, businessman, world citizen / Ros Jensen. — 1st ed.
        p.   cm.
    Includes bibliographical references.
    ISBN 0-8138-0598-8
    1. Stanley, C. Maxwell (Claude Maxwell), 1904–   . 2. Engineers—United States—Biography. I. Title.
TA140.S717J46   1990
327.1′72′092—dc20
[B]   89–24416

Contents

Appendices

Max Stanley's Pragmatic Idealism:
A Model of Global Citizenship

Congressman Jim Leach

To understand Max Stanley is to understand the search for peace in the twentieth century. Max was in junior high school when America entered World War I and in high school when Woodrow Wilson proposed the founding of the League of Nations to ensure that Europe's cataclysm would be the war to end all wars. As a college student he watched an isolationist Senate turn down United States participation in the League, and as a graduate engineer and budding entrepreneur he observed a Pyrrhic peace so devastate Germany economically and psychologically that the malignant seeds of fascism were sown—and with it the genocidal events of World War II.

At the end of the second war to end all wars, Max joined a small group of idealistic internationalists who founded the World Federalists. Starting from Einstein's famous quote that "splitting the atom had changed everything except our way of thinking," he and his colleagues dedicated themselves to the task of changing human thinking and institutions so that the scourge of war would be eradicated from the planet.

Max never thought small. He stood squarely in the tradition of small-town, self-made professionals with a progressive social outlook and expansive world view symbolized at various points by fellow midwesterners like Wendell Willkie, Henry Wallace, and Dwight Eisenhower. A native Iowan raised in the rural hamlet of Corning, he possessed a buoyant, almost naive optimism, which was sternly tempered not only by the political events of the day but by the entrepreneurial challenges of carving out a business in the wake of the Great Depression.

While an idealist, Max was never an innocent. Others may have amassed greater fortunes and established larger foundations, but few have used their resources more wisely for a better cause. Forerunner by three decades of today's peace movement, Max Stanley concerned himself with the ultimate political question: how to resolve human conflict without resorting to force. In this effort he was fond of quoting William Graham Sumner, who wrote during 1903 that "a wiser rule would be to make up your mind what you want, peace or war, and then to get ready for what you want; for what is prepared is what we shall get."

That's why Max cared about the United Nations. And that's why he devoted so much of his time to holding conferences for leaders of the international community. Leaders of the West, nonaligned and Soviet Bloc met in what can best be described as "shirtsleeve" settings — in settings which discouraged the cant, political diatribe, and pomposity we often hear on nationalistic podiums or in the U.N. General Assembly. Max created the Stanley Foundation so that committed citizens, policymakers, and scholars could work together in a common forum toward an end at once supremely noble and sublime — a "secure peace with freedom and justice on this fragile planet earth."

Max was acutely conscious that the most fundamental issues in world politics today are, in the first instance, how to contain and restrain weapons of mass destruction, and in the second, how to advance international comity and the rule of law.

In describing his internationalist idealism, Max wrote: "If responsibility and opportunity truly parallel power and affluence — and I believe they do — the United States ought to be the world's leading advocate of a more ordered world without war and the most dedicated activist promoting wise management of critical world issues. Competence, technology, affluence, experience and heritage all combine to equip us uniquely for leadership."

The United States is still very much the leader of the free world. We stand at the brink of an era in which there is good reason to hope that the force of American values and ideals will shine more broadly and brilliantly than ever before.

If a new generation of leaders in America is able to realize the potential for good this opportunity presents, it will be in large measure because of the progressive sense of national purpose nurtured by citizens like Max Stanley.

Max Stanley never led by dint of elective office. He would have found a political career too constraining. In a democracy, where, as

Franklin Roosevelt observed, a political leader could not be more than a half step ahead of the public, Max took on the more daunting challenge of attempting to move the public first and then asking political leaders to catch up.

Eighteen months before his death, in a speech delivered at the University of Dubuque, Max exhorted the student body to pledge themselves to the advancement of the human species. "The problems we face," he said, "are global in proportion, but their solution begins with individuals. I challenge each of you to think and act as global citizens and commit yourselves to educating your friends, family, associates, and students for a greater sense of responsibility concerning this fragile planet we call home."

A United States that remains the active agent of human progress through the exercise of resolute and principled global leadership is Max's legacy to the future. In telling his story, this biography ensures that Max's philosophy of globalism and the brotherhood of man will be commended to a new generation, inspiring young and old to nurture from within the will to support responsible internationalism into the twenty-first century—and beyond.

Acknowledgments

Scores of people contributed to this book. Some brought me into homes and offices for long talks about Max Stanley, others wrote recollections in letters to me (one man sent a cassette tape), and still others answered my questions in telephone conversations. I am grateful to all of them.

The Stanley family deserves special thanks for letting me intrude on their lives, probe their memories, and rummage through family mementoes and Max's journals, correspondence, and collections of talks and articles. Dick Stanley, as president of the Stanley Foundation, worked closely with me and offered helpful advice on many parts of the manuscript. Betty Stanley, always kind and gracious, was unstinting in the time she volunteered for my questions about her husband. Arthur Stanley, Max's brother, welcomed me to his home at Rancho Santa Fe, California, as Byron Stanley, a cousin, did to his home in Corning, Iowa. Donna Buckles, one of Max's grandchildren, offered considerable material she had collected about the Stanley ancestors.

The staff of the Stanley Foundation will always have a warm place in my memories. I am indebted to Kenton Allen, the former administrative director who served as an adviser and critic; Anita DeKock, who edited the manuscript; Jack Smith, the staff patriarch who shared countless memories of Max with me; Dan Clark, who broached the subject of a biography with the family after I mentioned my idea to him one winter day in 1985; Jill Goldesberry, who took care of much of my correspondence.

I am thankful, too, for the help of Wanda Hawkins and Kathleen Johnson at Stanley Consultants, Bob Carl and Dick Johnson at HON Industries, Jane Miller and Linda Thompson at E & M Charities, and Suzanne Lowitt and Bill Silag at the Iowa State University Press.

Before starting work on the book, I sought advice from and received the encouragement of three colleagues: Lauren Soth and Gilbert Cranberg, my editors during twelve years on the editorial page staff of the *Des Moines Register and Tribune,* and Herb Strentz, professor and former dean of the School of Journalism and Mass Communication at Drake University.

Finally, let me express thanks to the members of my family who encouraged this venture, supported me in it, and lifted my spirits when that was needed.

Ros Jensen

MAX

A Biography of C. Maxwell Stanley
Engineer, Businessman, World Citizen

1

A World to Keep

▬▬▬

Max Stanley was like many businessmen who got things done in countless midwestern cities a generation ago. But he was different, too. Beyond his business and civic activities, he devoted much of his life and a large part of his fortune to a dream: "a secure peace with freedom and justice," as he liked to phrase it. A world at peace was not merely a utopian idea, a topic to discuss at endless rounds of scholarly conferences, or a negotiable issue at one summit meeting after another; for Stanley, the dream was a lively possibility and, more important, a human imperative that ought to be realized before the leaders of the superpowers blew humankind's living place into smithereens.

When Stanley converted the dream into a personal mission, he chose to carry it out from his hometown, Muscatine, Iowa, a small industrial city on the Mississippi River thirty miles southwest of Davenport. It was an unlikely place to plant an organization to advance worthy efforts to sustain world peace. But, then, Stanley seemed an unlikely trespasser on the pampered turf of the foreign policy experts. He had engineering and business experience, but he lacked the political, diplomatic, or academic credentials that commonly distinguished those who got things done on the world scene.

Stanley's exceptional skills as an engineer and an industrialist evidently gave him the courage to think as a visionary about global affairs. As a practical businessman he solved numerous problems—production schedules for a new line of office files, the design of an electric power plant, the reorganization of the management staff—so why not apply those skills to the crucial problems that clouded the world's future. If at

3

first he appeared to be a provincial innocent from rustic Iowa, he quickly dispelled such a notion by becoming a knowledgeable authority on the major global issues — a volunteer who earned the respect and admiration of diplomats, foreign policy specialists, and the leaders of organizations working on peace-related matters.

Among his neighbors at home Stanley was honored as "citizen of the world." He traveled to all parts of the world and mingled regularly with the international community assembled at the United Nations. Yet he never moved from Muscatine, apparently never wanted to, and he was at times an outspoken chauvinist about his home state, good-naturedly chiding friends and employees who grumbled about Iowa's extremes in weather or its countrified atmosphere. He spoke as one who had learned to blend comfortable provincial habits with the stimulating appeal to help change the world. So he moved easily from an engineering problem in Muscatine to an arms control conference on the East Coast to a football game in Kinnick Stadium at Iowa City.

As a result, perhaps, open-mindedness characterized Stanley's global outlook, for he was willing to listen to anyone who wanted to talk seriously about world peace. His views, as they matured over the years, were remarkably free of ideological cant, nationalistic presumptions, and the confrontational stridency spawned by the Cold War. With him, all things were possible — an optimistic attitude that was an antidote to cynicism. He was not a creative thinker on world affairs, but he possessed an analytical mind that recognized ideas and propositions that might ease the world's anxieties. To that end he worked vigorously to bring together both the thinkers and the doers who could make a difference in how nations lived with one another. This was his exceptional contribution to the peace process, his legacy to future generations.

By the conventional American standards of measuring success, Stanley's most remarkable accomplishment was HON Industries. Although he did not live to see the company formally inducted into *Fortune* magazine's elite list of the five hundred top companies, he had set the course for the enterprise and then had entrusted it to the capable management of his protégé Stanley M. Howe. HON was a true creation, started virtually from nothing as the Home-O-Nize Company after World War II and, largely by guts and wits, fashioned into one of the country's largest producers of office furniture and equipment. It attracted attention, too, for its innovative "human relations" programs and benefits for employees.

HON made Stanley a millionaire many times over, and all that money made him uneasy. How to make worthy use of his money became a continuing concern; he tended to put the question in religious terms, of how he could be a good steward of God's gifts. When he set out on an engineering career, he did not expect to become rich, and he was surprised when HON, the offshoot of a Sunday afternoon conversation with his brother-in-law, turned into a pot of gold. HON and his engineering company supplied Stanley and his wife, Betty, with a comfortable life-style, including a beach house on Sanibel Island off Florida's Gulf Coast, numerous foreign trips, and a collection of African art that is among the finest in the country. Earnings from HON also enabled the couple to establish the Stanley Foundation, which is dedicated to research and educational programs to help build a peaceable world, and E & M Charities, which provides financial grants to religious, educational, and charitable organizations.

Before there was HON, there was the Stanley Engineering Company, or Stanley Consultants as it became known in 1966. It was plenty for an ordinary man to handle. But Stanley was not an ordinary man. He transformed a two-man operation, which he joined in 1932, into the largest engineering company in Iowa, one of the fifty largest in the country, and one with a significant impact in several developing nations of West Africa. Stanley was trained to be an engineer, fulfilling a boyhood dream, and he always thought of himself, first and foremost, as an engineer. Outside his own company he was active in engineering societies and wrote a book, *The Consulting Engineer,* and numerous articles — ethics was a favorite topic — for engineering publications. By contrast, his interest in business, successful though he was with HON, rarely reached beyond his own company.

Yet Stanley's principal legacy most likely will be the Stanley Foundation, to which he gave most of his time and energy after he stepped down from his leadership functions at HON and Stanley Consultants. He had succeeded beyond his dreams at engineering and manufacturing. His greatest dream was to help influence the ideas and events that would dispel the threat of war from the world. The foundation has been a unique contribution toward that goal. As the first private organization dedicated solely to the search for world peace, it was the inspiration for a number of organized approaches to the resolution of conflict, arms control, and other matters caused by international tensions.

One of Stanley's favorite bits of advice was a quotation from William Graham Sumner: "A wiser rule would be to make up your mind on what you want, peace or war, and then to get ready for what you want; for what is prepared for is what we shall get."

Peace required preparation, and Stanley tried in many ways to broaden public understanding of what peace entailed. Peace was as demanding as war, though probably not as costly and certainly far more beneficial to human well-being. But those bearing olive branches did not always command the attention of those who rattled sabers.

In 1983 Stanley was chosen to be the fourteenth honorary rector of the University of Dubuque. At the installation ceremony on April 27 he talked on "Global Citizenship," pulling together themes that reflected his outlook on international affairs. Given about a year and a half before his death, the address offers a concise summation of the Iowan's worldview.

One of his aims was to puncture a nostalgic notion that the United States could rejuvenate an insular attitude toward the rest of the world. As he briefly reviewed the history of the postwar period, he stressed that the "comfortable isolation we enjoyed prior to and following World War I is but a happy memory," because World War II thrust the nation "into a leadership role from which there is no withdrawal." For economic reasons as well as for military security, the nation is "integrally tied to the rest of the world." In the immediate aftermath of World War II, American leaders from both the public and private sectors put forth creative programs to hasten peaceful recovery in Europe and Asia: the World Bank, the International Monetary Fund, the Marshall Plan, and the Truman Doctrine. American support also was given ungrudgingly to the United Nations and its special agencies. With dismay Stanley noted that nearly four decades after such postwar accomplishments many Americans, "including our current president [Ronald Reagan]," wanted to lessen or reject U.S. participation in cooperative efforts to solve international problems.

"Today our world drifts toward economic chaos and international anarchy because it lacks both a coordinated multilateral response to its problems and determined, innovative leadership—leadership that the United States and other powerful nations fail to provide. . . ."

Stanley identified six major global problems, beginning with peace and security, which had been the predominant concern three decades earlier. Now there were other matters requiring attention and broadening the range of international cooperation. He listed economic order, meaning efforts to achieve equitable relationships in trade, commerce, and development; improving the pace of social and economic development in the Third World; balancing population growth with the depletion of resources; protecting and managing the biosphere; and extending human rights, which he termed the "most fundamental global issue."

These problems became critical, Stanley said, because technology has "compressed the world," expanding human desires and aspirations but also spreading disease, terrorism, and economic inflation. "Local crises," he added, "immediately become global concerns." He deplored the failure of national leaders to deal with international problems and the apathy of the industrialized nations toward the Third World countries as they moved away from their colonial pasts.

"If responsibility and opportunity truly parallel power and affluence — and I believe they do — the United States ought to be the world's leading advocate of a more ordered world without war and the most dedicated activist promoting wise management of critical world issues. Competence, technology, affluence, experience, and heritage all combine to equip us uniquely for leadership. The missing ingredient is a strong national will to provide such leadership. The development of national will depends upon vastly enlarging the American constituency supporting a stronger global leadership role."

He looked for help from schools, colleges, and universities and from the nongovernmental organizations working on matters related to global problems. More and improved educational programs were needed, for adults as well as for children and youth, to provide an international perspective that would motivate more people to influence the course of U.S. foreign policy "toward better management of global problems." He mentioned how dismayed he was by how little "some of our nation's brightest young adults...comprehend or appreciate the United Nations, global problems, or the world itself."

Along with a growing awareness of the world beyond American shorelines, Stanley continued, people would have to change some attitudes about U.S. dealings with other countries. This could mean modifying "our nationalistic spirit with a greater sense of global concern." Among the possible changes, he suggested more cooperation with other nations instead of acting alone and expecting others to follow, a de-emphasis on military power and more emphasis on economic and political assets, and international management of the biosphere.

Possibly the most startling suggestion, to some of his listeners anyway, was a broader definition of human rights. Here is how he put it: "The status of human rights throughout the world is an important yardstick for determining how well other critical issues are being managed. The U.S. approach to human rights worldwide has deteriorated from dynamic leadership to evasive disregard. Rhetoric, yes, but refusal to ratify numerous U.N. human rights conventions and continued support of dictatorial governments which are disregarding human rights are deeds that speak louder than words.

"We value political and human rights — freedom of worship, speech, assembly, and movement, and rights of equal treatment, privacy, dignity, fair trial, and property ownership. We need to expand our definition of human rights to recognize the rights of food, shelter, health care, employment, and education — the needs of those suffering from extreme poverty and malnutrition. We need to include the most elemental and inalienable human right to which every citizen of this globe is entitled — the freedom from the insecurity and trauma of war, terrorism, and barbarism."

Stanley concluded with an appeal for compassionate outreach and for committed individuals:

"Wisdom and intelligence, cooperation and coordination, innovation and determination are all necessary, but they are not enough. We need greater compassion. Understanding, respect, and love are needed to accommodate our differences and unite our efforts to enhance the livability and grandeur of this tiny ball spinning in space. . . .

"The problems we face are global in proportion, but their solution begins with individuals. I challenge each of you to think and act as global citizens and to commit yourselves to educating your friends, family, associates, and students for a greater sense of responsibility concerning this fragile planet we call home."

Had he wished to, he could have pointed to himself as an example of an individual who made an extraordinary, voluntary pledge to work for peace. He could have voiced hope that his contributions to the deliberations on arms control, a law of the seas, environmental concerns, and trade and economic assistance to the Third World nations might have long-range benefits for future generations. He could have mentioned how his work for peace added a gratifying dimension to his life.

To many of the men and women who were acquainted with him, Stanley was an enigmatic figure. He was not easy to know, certainly not on a familiar level, because of the high value he placed on personal privacy. He did not cultivate cronies, and he had few confidants. Yet he had a remarkable array of friends — businessmen in Muscatine; engineers in Iowa and in other parts of the country; schoolteachers and university professors; Methodist bishops, ministers, and laypeople; art dealers and museum curators; congressmen; State Department bureaucrats; and United Nations envoys.

All his friends notwithstanding, Stanley was anything but a social animal. He preferred small dinners, where conversation was intelligible, to large ones, where the talking too often produced verbal chaos; he cared little for cocktail parties, especially the flighty chatter that went with them. He was most likely to linger at the fringe of a crowd rather than move toward its center. By nature he was quiet, almost shy, which some interpreted as haughtiness, yet he was known to have angry outbursts that made some of his employees cringe. He had a wry sense of humor, and he often slipped a witty remark into a conversation, punctuating it with a little smile and a twinkle of his blue eyes. Telling knee-slapping jokes was not for him.

His was an analytical mind that examined problems and possible solutions with meticulous interest, and sometimes with sheer fascination. Former engineering associates still talk about his quick grasp of a design idea and how easily he detected flaws. Once he studied a problem, whether in his businesses or in world affairs, he normally proposed solutions with several steps or options, listed in 1, 2, 3 order, and his articles and talks often contained such numbered lists of propositions.

He was not an imposing figure physically. "Five-eight and a half" was his measure of his height, and he boasted that his trim frame carried only ten pounds more than it had when he was in high school, running the quarter mile. He was unwilling to surrender to old age, so he kept up a middle-aged pace that had acquaintances guessing he was ten years younger than his age. In his last years the most evident clues of advancing age were the strands of gray in his brown hair, deepening facial lines, and heavier pouches under his eyes.

Throughout his working career, Stanley was a self-generating dynamo, spinning off a multitude of tasks in rapid order. Look at 1956, for example. He was leading the Home-O-Nize Company into the highly competitive office furniture market, following several years of financial uncertainty that pushed the company close to bankruptcy. The engineering company was retained to design a diesel power plant in Liberia, which became the foothold for extensive foreign work. As he completed a term as president of the United World Federalists, he and Betty started the Stanley Foundation. His first book on international relations, *Waging Peace,* came off the presses. When Muscatine needed an economic transfusion, Stanley headed the twelve-member industrial commission looking at opportunities for growth. He sat on the Iowa Wesleyan College board of trustees as it planned for a new science hall, for which he took charge of the fund-raising drive the next year. So it went, year after year, even after he let go of the reins at his two companies. The man who thrived on such varied activities prodded himself with the work ethic, a sense of public service, and the firm conviction that the world could be spared the worst destructive impulses of its human inhabitants.

Stanley's versatility and the diversity of his interests were not readily apparent when he began making a mark in Muscatine. Among the memorabilia at the Stanley home was a four-page counseling report from Rockford Plans Incorporated, which had given him and possibly several of his engineering colleagues a battery of aptitude tests in the summer of 1946. Such tests were popular at the time as World War II veterans tried to find their places in the postwar society. As one would expect, Stanley scored high, exceptionally high, in mathematical and mechanical tests; he had lower scores on reading comprehension and vocabulary. On an inquiry of his interests, he showed a preference for social service and computational activities, followed by literary, mechanical, scientific, and clerical activities. Of least interest to him were musical and artistic activities. The report, dated August 28, 1946, concluded that "an increase in executive responsibilities may not be very satisfactory to you if they should greatly decrease your engineering duties."

Stanley went on, whether deliberately or not, to overcome the shortcomings the tests showed. He became a prolific writer on engineering and foreign policy topics, including one book on the former and two on the latter. In his later years he became one of the country's foremost collectors of African art, thus reversing his low marks on aesthetic interests. And, undeterred, he assumed ever-expanding executive responsibilities with Stanley Consultants, HON, and the Stanley Foundation. The test results, it seemed, were a challenge to him.

One thing the tests did not show was his adaptability to changing circumstances. That may have been his most serviceable trait. Change challenged him, not to take a defensive stance, but to take hold of an opportunity to turn new conditions into favorable ones for human well-being. Change was a familiar theme he brought to the audiences he addressed. His own willingness to change was, in many ways, one of his most valuable strengths.

2

Setting Out

————

When he was born on June 16, 1904, he was given his father's name: Claude Maxwell Stanley. He never was called Junior, and when he was addressed as Claude, he politely but firmly said that that name belonged to his father (who had earned renown as a soldier, lawyer, and state official). To avoid confusion, the son chose to go by C. Maxwell Stanley. But he was known to just about everyone from boyhood on as Max, although some of his associates referred to him as CMS, the initials he scrawled on his office memos.

Max Stanley admired his father's success in three careers, and he himself duplicated that achievement as a consulting engineer, a business executive, and a foundation leader concerned about global well-being. To those accomplishments he added activities in civic affairs, education, religion, politics, writing, philanthropy, and art collecting. A deeply rooted sense of public service was a legacy from his father.

His mother, Laura Esther Stephenson Stanley, was a proper lady of old New England stock who wrote essays, liked art and music, and was known for her sewing and beautiful embroidery. She epitomized what the wife of a prominent citizen contributed to the civility and culture of an Iowa town in the early decades of the century. Her example was not lost on her first-born son as he balanced propriety, both cultural and ethical, with the competitive impulses of the American way of business.

Much of what Max Stanley knew about human dynamics evolved from his growing-up years in Corning, a city of about 2,200, the county seat of Adams County, in southwest Iowa. Such small communities in the Midwest exude an egalitarian spirit, but practically all of them are run by a ruling clique to which Stanley's parents, uncles, and aunts belonged in Corning. Claude and his brother Carl were partners in a law practice; each completed two terms as county attorney, and they served as city attorney as well. Carl, older by a year, was the mayor in 1904, the year of his marriage. Claude was president of the school board in the late twenties. Both were Methodists, Masons, members of the Commercial Club, and occasional golfers at the Happy Hollow Country Club. They differed about politics. Carl, an admirer of William Jennings Bryan, decorated his side of the law office with Democratic campaign posters, and Claude posted Republican broadsides on his.[1]

Laura Stanley's brother Walter was an insurance man in Corning, and her sister Estelle was married to Ed Okey, president of the Okey-Vernon Bank, one of three banks in the city in the twenties. Okey caused a stir in 1933 when he refused to close the bank in conformity with President Roosevelt's bank holiday order. This brought banking overseers from Des Moines to Corning to shut the bank's doors. But the next morning Okey had the bank open for business.

When Max was a baby, the family lived in a small, one-story frame house (it still stands, enlarged and with metal siding) at Ninth Street and Grove Avenue, a block from the large brick home of Dan Turner, who was Iowa's governor from 1931 to 1933. The governor was the son of Austin Beecher Turner, a merchant who is revered as one of the city's patriarchs. The Stanleys later moved to a square, two-story house (it, too, still stands) with four bedrooms and a sleeping porch at 606 Tenth Street. The Okeys lived across the street, and Carl and his family were only a block away.

The Stanleys in Corning traced their ancestry through a long line of Quakers beginning with three brothers who migrated to Virginia in the late 1600s after their father disinherited them for joining the Quaker movement in England. Carl and Claude were born near Ackworth, a Quaker settlement in Warren County in south central Iowa. Their parents, Levi Stanley and Rebecca Maxwell, were teachers, but in 1872 they moved to Adams County to start farming. There they had two more sons, Arthur and Harry, and a daughter who died in infancy. After Levi Stanley was elected the county treasurer, the family moved to Corning in 1888. Two years later the Stephenson family, whose youngest member was Laura, moved to Corning from a farm in neighboring Union County, where her father Briant had settled after helping establish

Nevinville, a community made up largely of people who moved to Iowa from New England and upstate New York.[2]

The converging family lines—the Stanleys and Maxwells on one side, the Stephensons and the Emmonses on the other—produced two spirited but diverse sons for Claude and Laura Stanley.

"Max was brilliant, sober, an ideal son, as compared to me," his brother, Arthur, once said. "I was kind of an ornery kid. I had fun. Max studied all through high school. He was always recognized as a brilliant student. . . . He was a model, and my mother often asked me why I couldn't be more like Max."

When his school days in Corning were finished, Max was tied for second with Merle Dillon in scholastic standing; Alma Johnston led the 1922 class of fifty-two, equally divided between girls and boys. Max had a hungry curiosity that was not satisfied with classroom subjects alone. He built a radio receiver, reputedly the first one in Adams County, so he could bring a bigger world to his consciousness. He traveled to Omaha to buy his own nine-volume Steinmetz Electrical Engineering Library. And he read and read and read.[3]

By contrast, Art, younger by four years, preferred sports, playing pool, and driving cars. "I never took a book home," he said, explaining that his indifference to high school studies probably cost him chances to go to one of the service academies at West Point or Annapolis. "But I had fun in high school." He recalled the day a girl his brother had been dating came up to him in the drugstore and said, "Why don't you get that big brother of yours to loosen up a little?"

Serious as he was about his studies, Max had his share of fun in school. He liked track and ran the quarter mile and was on the mile relay team. His close companion, Paul Bliss, was the team's star, usually taking firsts in the broad jump, high jump, and pole vault in which he set a state record of 11 feet, 3 inches in 1922. Bliss was the fullback for the Red Raiders, and Max was the right halfback, with John Riegel at left halfback and Ben Romberger at quarterback (his brother Bob was the coach). Max twisted his right knee and played in only a few games in the fall of his senior year, a season in which Corning claimed the sectional championship after defeating Red Oak 3 to 0 on Thanksgiving Day.[4]

Max liked acting and was cast in the lead role for the senior class play, *What Happened to Jones.* It was a comedy centering on the adventures, or misadventures, of a traveling salesman for a hymnbook publisher who becomes entangled with a number of characters, including a bishop, an anatomy professor, a sanatorium superintendent and an inmate, and a young woman and her fiance. It was typical of the school plays of the time.[5]

While Max was in his early teens, his father was called to military duty, first in the Mexican Border campaign in 1916 and then with Gen. John J. Pershing's American Expeditionary Force in France in 1917 and 1918. (Obviously, Claude Stanley did not subscribe to the pacifism of his Quaker forebears, and neither did Max Stanley, who never tried to draw a connection from his Quaker ancestry to his advocacy of the United Nations, world federalism, and various proposals meant to enhance international harmony.)

A veteran of the Spanish-American War of 1898, the elder Stanley had kept himself militarily fit in the Iowa National Guard. After the United States entered the war against Germany and its allies, the Guard's Third Infantry was mobilized as the 168th Infantry of the Army's 42nd Division, the famed Rainbow Division. Major Stanley (he was promoted to lieutenant colonel shortly before the war ended) led troops in the decisive battles of Chateau Thierry, St. Mihiel, and the Argonne Forest prior to the 1918 armistice.[6]

The divisional chief of staff was Col. Douglas MacArthur, who usually wore a cap, not a helmet, and a turtleneck sweater when he strode among the trenches with Stanley and other officers. It was MacArthur, then a general and the commander of the 84th Brigade, who recommended Stanley for the Distinguished Service Cross for conspicuous gallantry and heroism during fighting near Verdun (the Meuse-Argonne offensive) in mid-October 1918. Several years later, MacArthur and his wife visited Corning, coming by train, and stayed overnight with the Stanleys. That was the talk of the town for days.

Max Stanley was proud of his father's military record, which never was diminished in the son's mind by his absorbing interest in later years in peace and disarmament proposals that drew fierce opposition from many military leaders. When Max wrote to his father, the envelope ordinarily was addressed to Colonel Claude M. Stanley (he was in the Infantry Reserve after the war). When he died in 1965, at the age of ninety-three, his sons saw to it that he was buried with military ceremony while a soldier played "Taps."[7]

Soldiering was not Claude Stanley's only claim to fame. In 1932, bucking the Democratic trend that year, he was elected to the state senate. His legislative service is best remembered for his work on the 1936 law that established the Iowa Employment Security Commission and provided means to tax employers for a compensation fund to aid unemployed workers. He then accepted an appointment as the employer representative on the commission when it began functioning in 1937 and served there for twenty-two years.

Ten years before his successful legislative run, Stanley was drawn into a high-stakes political game over a seat in the United States Senate. William S. Kenyon gave up the seat to accept an appointment from President Harding to the Eighth Circuit Court of Appeals. Representative Smith Brookhart, who had emerged as the radical spokesman for the small farmers and other victims of a worsening Farm Belt depression, was considered the odds-on favorite to win the Republican nomination. Stanley was one of five men who challenged Brookhart in an apparent move to throw the nomination into a party convention where the Republican Old Guard was likely to manipulate the choice. Under Iowa law a party convention chose the nominee if the top candidate did not get 35 percent of the vote. But Brookhart won easily, with 44 percent of the vote, and went on to defeat Democrat Clyde L. Herring in the general election. Stanley finished sixth in the Republican voting.[8]

The year of that election, 1922, was a threshold for Max Stanley. In addition to graduating from high school and getting a first-hand view of politics, he left home to enroll in the engineering college at the University of Iowa. He had decided on an engineering career in the eighth grade, remembering his interest in the construction of a reservoir near Corning several years earlier. The lock and dam on the Mississippi River at Keokuk left a memorable impression, too, after a family trip to eastern Iowa.[9]

The nation was passing through a period of change and upheaval. Much of the upheaval occurred in the Farm Belt where a depression, especially severe in Iowa and the Dakotas, caused forced farm sales, bankruptcies, and foreclosures. Substantial improvement was not evident until later in the decade, only to be followed by the collapse of the thirties. To help distressed farmers, Congress passed the Cooperative Farming Act, or Capper-Volstead Act, to permit agricultural producers, cooperatives, or associations to buy and sell in interstate commerce without transgressing antitrust laws. The law opened more opportunities

The father, Claude Stanley (1918), soldier, lawyer, public servant. (Haight Photo)

The mother, Laura Stephenson Stanley (1918), a proper lady of New England stock. (Haight Photo)

*Max and his mother
(1904) when he was
twenty-nine days old.
(Tinsley's Studio)*

*Max at six months.
(Tinsley's Studio)*

The house at 606 Tenth Street in Corning, where the Stanleys lived when Max was growing up. (Below) Lake Okoboji beckoned the Stanleys in the summer of 1910.

Funny, yes? Max and brother Art.

The two brothers, ready for winter in 1914.

A year after graduating from engineering school, Max worked in 1927 on the design and construction of the University of Iowa's Hydraulics Laboratory on the Iowa River.

Max, center, with faculty members in the Testing Laboratory at the University of Iowa College of Engineering, 1928.

The young engineer on a surveying job, 1930.

for the co-ops, including participation in the rural electrification program that would be crucial to Stanley's success in the thirties.

Beyond the Farm Belt, economic and social changes brought new vitality to the cities. Business was riding a tide of prosperity, overcoming a two-year deflationary trend. Following the lead of Henry Ford, major manufacturers began converting factories to assembly-line production. On the West Coast, moviemaking, which would drastically alter popular entertainment and affect American living modes, was booming and making "stars" of such favorite actors as Charlie Chaplin, Mary Pickford, and Rudolph Valentino.

Books of three writers with midwestern roots won critical acclaim in 1922: Willa Cather's *One of Ours,* Hamlin Garland's *A Daughter of the Middle Border,* and Sinclair Lewis's *Babbitt,* two years after his best-selling *Main Street.* The books mirrored, albeit from different angles, a growing sensitivity to the tensions brought on by the transformation of society from an agrarian, small town culture to an increasingly urban one. In education, John Dewey was leading the chorus for change from country-school methods. Naturalism and realism were the trends in literature, drama (Eugene O'Neill was the celebrated master), and in art. Louis Sullivan and Frank Lloyd Wright held sway over architecture.

The Washington Disarmament Conference, which opened late in 1921, concluded early in 1922 with an agreement to limit future naval buildups and to scrap parts of existing fleets. All the great powers except the Soviet Union, which was not invited, took part in that attempt to reduce the threat of future wars.

In an atmosphere reverberating with change, Stanley arrived in Iowa City to start purposeful preparations for an engineering career. Not much time passed before he caught the attention of his professors and once again earned the reputation of a brilliant student. He was elected to Tau Beta Pi and Sigma Xi, honorary engineering societies. After he was graduated in 1926 with a degree in general engineering, he became a structural designer for Byllesby Engineering and Management Corporation of Chicago. As a student he took special interest in hydraulics, the branch of engineering concerned with the movement of water, other liquids, and gases, particularly as a source of power. So in 1927 he took a job to work on the design and construction of the University of Iowa's Hydraulics Laboratory on the Iowa River, and in 1930, after a year of graduate study, he was awarded a master's degree in hydraulic engineering.[10]

By then Stanley was married, a father, and working at a new job. His marriage to Elizabeth M. Holthues took place in November 1927, about five months after she was graduated from the university in Iowa City. The following spring Stanley joined Management and Engineering Corporation, and the couple moved to Dubuque, where their first son, David, was born in September. The company transferred Stanley to Chicago after he completed his graduate work and assigned him mainly to hydroelectric and waterworks projects, although he spent some time on diesel power problems.[11]

Floyd A. Nagler, who stimulated Stanley's interest in hydraulics, was instrumental in attracting his former student to Muscatine in 1932. (Two years later Stanley was invited to give a memorial tribute to Nagler at an open house in the new Hydraulics Laboratory at Iowa City. He spoke of his former instructor as a leader in the development of hydraulic technique and referred to the laboratory as the fulfillment of Nagler's dream.)[12] Nagler had advised Stanley of an opportunity to buy into Central States Engineering Company. The impressive name meant nothing, for the company was essentially Charles Young, the engineer who had started it in 1913 but was looking toward retirement. Nonetheless, the little setup was appealing to Stanley, who was weary of morning and evening commuting in Chicago and who also guessed that Management and Engineering was in for rough times because of deteriorating economic conditions. The engineering operation was a subsidiary of a utility company and did not survive the Depression as money vanished for major power installations. In later years Stanley described his departure from Chicago as "one jump ahead of the pink slip."[13]

With savings and financial help from his brother, Stanley bought a 49 percent interest from Young, became a principal in Young and Stanley Incorporated, and assumed the duties of general manager. At the end of the first year, actually about ten and a half months from the time the new company was formed, the firm grossed $6,200 and showed no profit. Bleak as the outlook seemed, Betty said many years later, she and Max were happy to be back in Iowa, and soon after their return they welcomed their second son Richard, or Dick as he usually was called. Their daughter Jane was born four years later.[14]

Stanley was soon forming a staff that would be capable of diversified work. When he came to Muscatine, the firm concentrated mainly on drainage problems along the Mississippi River and its tributaries. Eight or nine engineers were on the staff in 1936, and they were expected to be generalists, drafting, surveying, and designing for different kinds of work. A major project was the renovation of the High Bridge across the Mississippi at Muscatine. The company's first power contract was for the municipal diesel generating system at Corning.

Stanley's brother, who completed his engineering studies at the University of Iowa in 1931, joined the company in 1934. He had moved to different assignments with the Iowa State Highway Commission until funds for road building ran out before the summer of 1933. Art worked for his brother that summer, then took a job with the State Board of Control at Clarinda in the fall. Soon after the first of the year, Art moved to Muscatine, feeling certain that the little engineering company offered more stability than the state agencies. He became a partner after Young retired in 1938. The two brothers bought Young's remaining interest, and in 1939 they named their enterprise Stanley Engineering Company.[15]

Employees numbered seventy, reflecting the rapid growth of the company's power projects, many of them spawned by the Rural Electrification Administration (REA), which had been set up in 1935 as part of President Franklin Roosevelt's New Deal. Simultaneously, the Stanley brothers traveled about Iowa to meet with city officials who were interested in building or expanding municipal electric plants through a state law that was conducive to such developments.

Stanley by then felt confident about his future in Muscatine, confident enough to draw plans for a new home. He and Betty were settling into life in the old river city, and he was beginning to make his influence felt in the civic organizations controlled by the city's old families. In 1940 Betty and Max and their three children moved from a small frame house on Iowa Avenue to their new home on Sunset Drive. It was a large two-story, buff brick house surrounded by about eight acres of ground (even more land in later years) on which there was a stand of tall elms, which fell victim to Dutch elm disease twenty-some years later. The structure, built for about $30,000, had a simple, spare design that evoked the influence of both Frank Lloyd Wright and the German Bauhaus school.

Both the design and the structure of the house caused considerable interest in Muscatine. The cinder block construction, deviating from the conventional reliance on a wood skeleton, stirred the most curiosity as the house took shape. One Sunday when Stanley was checking on the building progress, he heard several people analyzing the project on the other side of the block wall from where he stood. Their conclusion was that he must be crazy to put up a house like that.[16]

The house included a number of innovative features: a dishwasher, radiant heat, indirect lighting, and cupboards and closets that were more spacious than common at the time. Stanley had an office next to the entryway, and the children had a large playroom, which included a child-level water fountain. Four bedrooms were upstairs. This would be Stanley's home until he died.

Thirty years after he moved to Muscatine, Stanley reminisced for his associates at the annual conference of Stanley Consultants, as the firm was then known, mentioning reasons "why the organization started then couldn't succeed":

> In the first place, the time was wrong—it was the depth of the depression. Next, we were all wrong geographically. Whoever heard of a successful engineering firm located in a town of 20,000? How could we succeed in the international arena when we were located in the isolationist Midwest? It wasn't possible (was it?) in one firm—and it was a small firm to start with—to do a diversity of work. How could we be experts in all these areas? Wouldn't we become jack-of-all-trades and a master of none? . . .
>
> And then I've heard, even down to the moment, the suggestions: How can we grow and develop if [we] haven't an exact plan and program which we wanted to follow; goals that we wanted to reach a few years ahead? . . . By any standards you wish to apply objectively, this organization has been successful. . . .
>
> I'll stack up against the best professional engineers any place in the world the top professional people we have in this organization today. We have gained a stature, I'm sure, in that field.[17]

Much of that stature could be traced to Stanley's decision to take advantage of a New Deal rural electrification program that furnished government loans to the farmer-run cooperatives to extend electrical power to rural areas. This often led to clashes between co-ops and private utility companies. Thus do life's ironies surprise, for Stanley was a stalwart Republican and a devout believer in the free enterprise system. Yet the promise of success brightened for him when he joined in the Depression-era effort to help improve living conditions in rural areas. This was to become typical of him, for he accepted opportunities as life offered and, more often than not, found some public good as well as private gain in what he achieved.

3

REA Pioneer

Max Stanley's engineering company needed work badly in the midthirties, so he was eager to be part of a national effort to bring electricity to rural areas. Aside from the expected financial gains, however, he recognized it as a pioneering venture that would bring dramatic changes to farm life.

As a teenager, Stanley had spent a summer on his uncle's farm in Missouri. That was enough to convince him that he did not want to spend his life raising livestock and growing corn.[1] Farming was a hard life, nothing that his practical mind could romanticize. Small-town boy though he was, he was to become attuned to the urban pulse of a nation destined for astonishing transformations after World War II. A continuing string of rural electrification projects, beginning in the last half of the thirties, gave him a chance to see the possibilities of change on a broad scale and to play an important part in bringing urban advantages to rural residents. It was a time when most of the nation was hooked up electrically, evoking from coast to coast a growing desire for all sorts of power-operated gadgets—radios, electric irons, refrigerators, vacuum cleaners, electric washing machines, toasters, and, of course, the electric lights that replaced kerosene lamps in house and barn. It was a new frontier drawing the skills and visions of scientists and builders. It was an exciting and productive time for the young engineer in Muscatine, whose notes in his daily journals charted his eager pursuit of electrical power projects.

When Robert A. Caro went to the Texas Hill Country to collect memories of Lyndon Johnson for the first part of a three-volume biography (*The Path to Power*), he heard over and over, "He brought the lights. No matter what Lyndon was like, we loved him because he brought the lights."

Recalling that experience, Caro said, "They were talking about the fact that when Johnson became congressman from the Hill Country in 1937, at the age of twenty-eight, there was no electricity there. And by 1948, when he was elected to the Senate, most of the district had electricity." Caro added that the full significance of this development had eluded him for a time, because he was a New Yorker for whom "electricity was always just *there*." In the Hill Country he learned "what electricity meant in the lives of impoverished farm families, or what their lives had been like in this isolated and remote region without it. . . ."[2]

Had Iowans — and many other Midwesterners, for that matter — been inclined to venerate those who brought them their lights, they most likely would have given homage to Max Stanley and Ken Brown. The engineering firms led by those two — Stanley's in Muscatine and Brown's in Des Moines — had much to do with spreading electricity to vast stretches of the rural Midwest. They saw to it that the new systems were laid out in an orderly and efficient pattern, that the poles were put up and the lines strung.

The extensive rural electrification effort was a key part of President Franklin Roosevelt's New Deal economic recovery plan. Trying to crack stubborn unemployment, Roosevelt asked for and got $100 million for rural electrification as part of a $5-billion public works bill. To carry out the plan, he set up the Rural Electrification Administration by executive order on May 11, 1935. Morris L. Cooke, the REA's first chief, soon met with top leaders of the privately owned utilities and asked them for a proposal on how to proceed with rural electrification. In July the companies submitted a plan to let them take the entire $100 million in REA funds to connect 351,000 rural customers, 247,000 of them farmers. One company representative observed that "there are very few farms requiring electricity for major farm operations that are not now served."[3]

Cooke was outraged. He had estimated potential REA customers at 5 million farms. In short order the REA was turned into a major lending agency to assist organizations that wanted to operate electric power systems. It was a way of sidestepping the big utilities, but, with the National Grange and the American Farm Bureau Federation favoring federal action to get light and power to rural areas, the administration felt it had popular support among the nation's farmers. By December of 1935 farmer-run cooperatives had become the main force in developing electrical systems in rural areas.[4]

Carl Hamilton, former Iowa State University vice-president who was an assistant administrator of the REA in the 1940s, has recalled the fierce battles and devious maneuvers that often engaged the cooperatives and the private utilities:

> REA employees and farmers alike would be thrown into a frenzy of anger and activity when, just as a loan application had been put together, a utility "spite line" would be built—sometimes within a matter of hours. It would skim the cream out of the cooperative's plans. There were records, too, of instances in which utility representatives, posing as farmers, would infiltrate cooperative organizational meetings and raise questions about the integrity of the "promoters" of this new socialistic scheme. These activities were actually counterproductive from the utility standpoint; they only further energized REA employees and their farmer friends. But a good many cooperative plans were thwarted in those early days.[5]

In August 1936 the REA approved Stanley's specifications for the Boone Valley Electric Cooperative. It was the first REA project in Iowa to come up for bids. Three months later Stanley received his first check from that project—$600. By the end of 1936 Stanley learned that the REA had approved spending $185,000 for a steam power plant to generate electricity for rural customers in Calhoun, Pocahontas, and Humboldt counties. Stanley's firm was picked to do the engineering work.[6] In 1937 the cooperatives in those counties, plus Buena Vista, would form the Central Electric Federated Cooperative Association, commonly known then as Central. That same year five cooperatives joined to operate the Federated Cooperative Power Association, based at Hampton and serving Franklin, Hardin, Butler, Wright, and Grundy counties. Ten years later the two associations consolidated and took the name Corn Belt Power Cooperative. Stanley's company was closely involved in planning the expansion, particularly on additions for the power plant at Humboldt, with a generating capacity of nearly 75,000 kilowatts. Corn Belt eventually furnished electrical power to more than 30,000 farms and rural residences in twenty-seven northern Iowa counties.[7]

"In 1938 the company had so many REA line contracts, Max and Art realized they needed to hire more people," Sanford K. Fosholt remembered. "They decided to hire electrical engineering graduates and give them a six-week course in line work and then put them in charge of staking crews." Fosholt, fresh from his courses at Iowa State College, was one of those hired, along with a classmate and two Iowa graduates. The recruits were paid $60 a month and promised $120 after they took charge of a crew and $200 after a year, provided they had not been let go by then. Marking places to put electrical poles was rudimentary work for a graduate engineer, but Fosholt, later to become a partner and then an officer in the Muscatine company, felt lucky to have a job in those lean years.

After his training, Fosholt was put in charge of a three-man crew that traveled the country roads of Grundy County to stake a cooperative's system. That job done, he went to Mitchell County, adjacent to the Minnesota border, driving every road in the county, in a pickup truck, so he could lay out a map for an REA project. Then he was assigned to Estherville with a crew of seven men to stake out another REA system. Projects in southern Illinois and northern Missouri followed before Fosholt was sent to Corning, the Stanley brothers' hometown, to help the Adams County REA. From there Fosholt was transferred to Muscatine to start working on power plant projects, which for years to come would be the company's bread-and-butter work.[8]

Stanley Engineering Company figured in the early development of more than a dozen major cooperative power systems in the Midwest and several in other parts of the country. Among these was the Dairyland Power Cooperative, based at LaCrosse, Wisconsin. Plans for it caught Max Stanley's interest as the REA began reviving from a dormant spell in World War II. He traveled to LaCrosse late in March 1945 to try gaining the favor of the board formed to oversee what was to become one of the largest diesel generating plants in the REA network, with a 5,000 kilowatt capacity. He returned home disappointed, and possibly a little bitter, after learning that his company was the board's third choice. The first was a Wisconsin firm. "Politics & price seem to be main consideration," Stanley complained to his journal.[9]

What a surprise, then, when he learned a few weeks later that his company had been retained — "after long controversy," his journal notes — to design the diesel plant, which would be built at Baldwin, near the Mississippi River between Chippewa Falls and the Twin Cities. Two days later he was in Milwaukee to confer about the plans for what he called a "rush job." Early in May he visited the plant site and attended a board meeting. "Making progress on selling selves to board," a journal entry reads. "Believe we can make grade if we can carry Baldwin job through satisfactorily." On June 1 he reported completing the plant design, "45 days — on schedule." The following year he was awarded the contract for Dairyland's transmission lines.[10]

Stanley gained "a feather in his cap," as Fosholt put it, when he successfully negotiated the engineering work for the East Kentucky Rural Electric Cooperative Corporation.[11] This system furnished 1,180 miles of transmission lines for a 25,000 square mile area. It engaged the company's attention for much of the fifties and sixties.

In the late fifties the company was retained on a Missouri River Basin study, which was aimed at pooling the generating and transmitting capabilities of cooperatives serving about two-thirds of Iowa, one-third of South Dakota, and a portion of Minnesota.

The big regional projects — Corn Belt, Dairyland, East Kentucky, Alabama Electric, Colorado-Ute — were the offspring of much smaller power-plant projects for cities in Iowa in the latter half of the thirties. In 1931 the Iowa Legislature passed what was known as the Simmer Law, which granted municipalties the authority to buy power plants with the income from electrical service. At a special session three years later, the legislators amended the law to permit cities to issue bonds for power plants. That was a signal for Stanley and his brother to start traveling to all parts of Iowa to meet with city councils that had shown interest in building power plants.

These notes from Stanley's journal for January 1935 chart his bustling pace: second, "Drove to Des Moines for meeting with Lamoni council. . . . Manning contract signed." Third, "Drove to Waukon in afternoon for council meeting." Fourth, "Drove from Waukon to Corning for mass meeting re coming franchise election." Fifth, "Started work at Manning. . . ." Eighth, "Received wire from Waukon employing us on preliminary for electric plant." Ninth, "Started work on Des Moines River Valley project." Fourteenth, "Galesburg, Ill. — wild goose chase after diesel job." Seventeenth, "Drove to site on Des Moines River in afternoon and on to Boone. Art has work in good shape." Eighteenth, "All day in Boone on electric plant job. . . . [Ralph] Esmay came over from Manning for conference." Twenty-fourth, "Drove to LaPorte with Betty for talk at mass meeting." Twenty-sixth, "DD#13 [drainage ditch] meeting at Wapello."

Over the years more than fifty Iowa communities invited the Stanleys to provide engineering services for steam and diesel power plants and distribution systems. At the same time the firm completed similar projects in Illinois, Indiana, Michigan, Missouri, Minnesota, Nebraska, Wisconsin, and the Dakotas.

As Stanley Engineering Company earned its favorable reputation among city officials in the Midwest, the scope of its work broadened. By the late thirties and 1940, Max Stanley's journal contained references to a swimming pool at Greenfield, street lighting at Savanna, Illinois, water mains at Galesburg, Illinois, streets at Audubon, a reservoir at Bedford, sewers at Urbandale, a levee at Muscatine, sewage disposal at Lamoni, water treatment at Sac City, and waterworks at Fort Madison.

But the company's success with the cities and the cooperatives won little popularity for Stanley among the private utilities. Grudging respect, maybe, but not friendship—and no business. Not until the seventies did Stanley start getting contracts for work with a few utilities, although by then the Stanley name was recognized across the country as one of the foremost consulting firms on power systems. As early as the spring of 1952 Stanley, his partners, and key staff engineers talked about approaching the utilities. A year later Stanley reported a "discouraging trip" to see power company executives. Late in 1966 engineers for a utility company came to the engineering offices in Muscatine for what Stanley described as a "look-see," but nothing developed from the visit.[12] When some projects finally materialized, they were minor, by Stanley standards, except for a coal-blending facility for Commonwealth Edison of Chicago and a series of high-voltage transmission lines for Interstate Power of Dubuque.[13]

The animosity of the utility companies toward Stanley was traceable to his frequent court appearances on behalf of cooperatives and cities that competed with the utilities. In franchise or territorial disputes, Stanley often was called as an expert witness to refute a utility company's arguments. To the utilities he was a hostile witness. On a few occasions, his brother recalled, Stanley was asked by lawyers for a cooperative or a city to question utility company witnesses. That was sure to infuriate company executives. On one occasion, goes family lore, a utility company lawyer attacked Stanley's testimony and said he was not yet dry behind the ears. When the verdict went against the utility, Stanley dramatically pulled out his handkerchief for the lawyer to see and started wiping behind his ears.[14]

Although Stanley wanted work from the private utilities, he was not disposed to soften his criticism of their conduct. In a 1956 talk to the managers of Iowa's electric cooperatives, he traced the rapid growth of the rural systems. When rural electrification began in earnest, he observed, the cooperatives had tried to get power from the utilities, only to learn that such power was "available only at a prohibitive cost or not available at any cost."[15] Three years later, in an article for *Public Utilities Fortnightly,* Stanley appealed for less confusion in utility rate-making procedures, contending that "some of the claims made by utilities involve weird contortions of past practices and theories." He offered five proposals that would tie rates to the original cost of a utility's facilities and operations. Stanley argued that uniform adoption of original cost standards would reduce disputes over such elusive factors as "fair value," "prudent investment," or "cost of reproduction."[16]

The REA signaled a revolutionary turn in rural living, with unexpected social and economic consequences. Carl Hamilton observed that the "first loans, with a lot of blue sky thrown in, were projected on the basis that farmers might use as many as 75 kilowatts a month! Quicker than anyone could believe it, many farmers were using 1,000 a month. It was obviously a rich market." Then he added, "Rural electrification did more to change rural America than any other single thing."[17]

Stanley touched on this in a paper distributed by the American Institute of Electrical Engineers in December 1950: "The growth of load on these rural distribution systems has been spectacular. It is not unusual to find cooperatives which have loads today that are ten to twenty times the 1938 or 1940 demands. This increase has resulted both from enlargement of the systems and from greater consumption." He stressed the need for the cooperatives to concentrate on providing more reliable service, pointing out that farmers who used electricity for poultry brooding or refrigerating milk lost money from a power failure of any length.[18]

The thirties were a watershed period in Max Stanley's life. He was tested, of course, by gloomy economic conditions, but he had the knowledge, the skills, and the self-confidence to master the technical problems put before him. It was a time, as well, for him to test what he had learned—growing up in a small town, studying at a university, beginning work in a big city—against the stubborn problems that gave rise to disillusionment and self-doubt. He must have watched with satisfaction as the REA projects set off a flurry of welcome activity throughout a region stricken with hard times.

Nearly thirty years later he would tell an audience at the University of Iowa: "If you are to lead, you must cope with change in a positive fashion. You cannot hang back or seek to avoid it. You cannot ridicule or resist it as the work of radicals, crackpots, or starry-eyed idealists. You must meet change head-on, taking it as a normal and expected way of life."[19]

From his own experiences in the Depression years, Stanley was giving shape to an essential ingredient of his personal philosophy. He was not one to succumb to despair. Ever the optimist, even in hard times, he saw in the flourishing growth of the REAs and the municipal companies fresh signs of hope, not only for the survival of his fledgling company, but for the recovery of a region. It was not a time for tentative minds.

4

Home Front Warrior

On the day the Japanese attacked Pearl Harbor, December 7, 1941, Max Stanley left this reaction in his journal: *"War with Japan!* Which means with Germany also — Relief that the uncertainty is over. Doubt that it will be as easy as many people think. Expectation that it will be long and hard, with near elimination of our business."

Nine days later, uncharacteristically, he was brooding: "Very discouraged & despondent. Ten years of building an organization only to face the necessity of seeing it disintegrate because of war. Must throw off this mood and get to work in search of some military construction."[1]

By the time America joined the war, the engineering staff of the Muscatine company was already depleted. Art Stanley, holding an ROTC infantry commission, was ordered to duty with the Army Air Corps as a captain in mid-July 1941. Seven others were called to military service by the end of August and two had left for war industries.

Stanley wasted no time in trying to line up military projects for what remained of his staff. Four days after the attack on Pearl Harbor, he was soliciting work from the Army Corps of Engineers at Rock Island. Later there would be a trip to Chicago and a telephone call to Washington, neither of which produced immediate results.

As 1942 began, he was restless. He realized that the fate of his company was dependent on military work. Suddenly, that was about all there was to do. A talked-about merger of big Iowa power cooperatives did not come about. REA projects were put on hold in Washington. While he fretted about the company, he wondered whether he should apply for a commission in the Army or the Navy (he had relinquished the ROTC commission he had received at the University of Iowa). In mid-February he registered for the draft.[2]

Betty Stanley recalled him feeling that "maybe he should get involved" and he talked about it with his father, the old colonel from the Rainbow Division. If the son thought he might satisfy a paternal expectation by marching off to war, the father quickly disabused him, advising the son that he belonged at home with his family.[3]

Still, patriotic urges lingered, no doubt in part because the war had taken on the aura of a crusade to stamp out fascism. Dave Stanley, who turned eleven in 1939, the year the German armies struck against Poland, said his father was certain that "we were going to be in it, that we couldn't avoid it, that Hitler had to be stopped. It wasn't that he liked war; he didn't look forward to it, but he just saw it as something that had to be done."[4] If not an outspoken interventionist, Stanley recognized that the United States could not turn its back on Europe, as the isolationists pretended. From war, a sense of global interdependence was being reinforced.

It is tempting to try forcing that thought, to imagine the war as Max Stanley's wilderness experience from which he emerged with dedication to a special mission of proclaiming peace to a nation mesmerized by the rectitude of military power. But in 1942 Stanley was not ready for that, and he left no evidence intimating that he had serious qualms about the Allied conduct of the war. Rather, sketchy notes in his journal reveal a continuing internal struggle over how best to serve his country.

Kenton Allen, former administrative director of the Stanley Foundation, remembered Stanley telling him that in the late stages of the war he thought seriously about going into politics, most likely to try getting a seat in the U.S. Senate. "He was appalled by the devastation of the war," Allen said, "and recognized that supposedly civilized nations could not keep doing this to one another every twenty or twenty-five years. The world wouldn't last." Yet he realized his dilemma: To be a Senate candidate in the postwar period, to have even a chance to work in Congress against future wars, he would need a record of war service, which he did not have.[5]

Stanley's thinking on politics at the time no doubt was inspired to a large extent by that of Wendell L. Willkie, the small-town Indiana boy who had become one of the country's influential business leaders and then was chosen by the Republicans in 1940 to run against President Roosevelt, who was trying for a third term. Willkie lost on election day, but he left a lasting impact on the Republican Party, particularly on what was called the moderate or progressive wing. "I still remember how enthusiastic my parents were about Wendell Willkie," Dave Stanley related. "Here was a businessman running for president. At that time my dad thought that was a very good idea, that somebody with business experience would really be helpful in government. Willkie struck him as a person with imagination and some new ideas, somebody who could get the mushrooming government under control and also had some imagination in world affairs."[6]

Anticipating a theme he would explore more fully in his book *One World,* Willkie wrote in an article in the April 1940 *Fortune* that the modern globe was so small that foreign affairs must influence domestic politics. "It makes a great deal of difference to us — politically, economically and emotionally — what kind of world exists beyond our shores." He argued that freer international trade in a free world was a way to stimulate the American economy.[7] They were words with strong appeal for Stanley.

But in 1942 Stanley focused his attention on the war. On March 14 he recorded his frustration: "For two months have been diligently trying to connect with war work — without avail! Always seems close but never materializes. Many competitors (no better qualified than we) are getting jobs. Quite a problem to know what to do."[8]

A week later he got a call from Washington advising that his company had been picked to work on the design for an Air Corps technical school for about 15,000 men at Sioux Falls, South Dakota. It was to be a joint engineering and architectural project with a Sioux Falls firm, Perkins and McWayne. On April 3 he was in Omaha negotiating a contract with the Corps of Engineers and learning how busy he was going to be. A journal entry reads: "Tough schedule — 33 percent completion by June 15. Much confusion." Two days later, a Sunday, he was in Sioux Falls working on preliminary plans and calling Muscatine to round up a staff. On the seventh, the Corps gave the start-work order. The next day Stanley set up an office in a Chevrolet garage building and started hiring men. He was upset because he had learned that the Sioux Falls firm had no employees other than a stenographer. Then one of the partners, probably sensing Stanley's anger, went home sick for several days.[9]

Day by day the short notes in Stanley's journal reflected the rising tempo of the work. He was excited. He was in charge. He was "in the field," doing what engineers are supposed to do. For a while he would forgo city council meetings and sessions with a cooperative's directors. He and his crew worked eleven to twelve hours a day. Then he went "home" to a room in the Blackstone Hotel. Betty came to see him late in April, and he went back to Muscatine for a weekend early in May. "A day of rest seems like a luxury," the journal echoed him. Two days later, when he left, "Dreaded going back as I was really tired and 3-day letup was too short." Then the next day, "Into the grind again."

The technical school, a training center for radio mechanics, was to have six large classroom buildings, shops, and warehouses, as well as housing for the men, administrative offices, and a hospital unit. In addition, the project would enlarge the municipal airport with new runways and a lighting system. The cost was estimated at $1.2 million.

Under Stanley's prodding, the design work was completed by May 11, well ahead of schedule. Soon, seven contractors put construction crews at the site, and five more were there by the end of the month, building what amounted to a small city. Stanley supervised the bustle, which kept more than three hundred workers busy. By the end of June, half the construction was finished, and on the second of July two troop trains pulled in with the first trainees.

Stanley wrote long letters to his brother reporting on the developments at Sioux Falls. In one, dated April 17, Max began by congratulating Art, "For an Infantry Reserve Officer to be promoted to a Major in the Air Corps at the ripe old age of 33 is definitely progress." Then he told of his activities, the enthusiasm spilling out on the pages:

> I have never in my life worked half as hard as I did between April 3rd and April 12th. . . . We now have about 120 employees on the payroll. Since April 12th, the organization has been functioning smoothly and we are really turning out some work. . . . Decisions have to be made on the basis of judgment rather than analysis. Speed is the essence of the work and quality comes second, but Art

you would be tickled to death to see the way our gang has stepped into things and have speeded themselves up to meet these requirements and believe me, as a whole, they measure up with the older more experienced men they are placed with. . . . Needless to say, I feel that I am doing something definite to contribute to the war effort of the country. I am doing so much more than I could possibly do as an officer in the Army that at the time being I am under no temptation to get back my reserve commission. . . . we are going to live up to our end of the schedule and should be able to set ourselves quite a record by doing so. . . . [10]

In a letter a few weeks later, Stanley complained that too many of the employees "are clerks, etc. to take care of government red tape." Two paragraphs later he added, "The biggest trouble, of course, is that someone higher up is always changing their mind. For instance, we released the hospital for bids last Saturday night, bids being due on May 7th and now today [May 2] we receive a copy of a letter from the Chief of Engineers, dated the same day we released the plans and specifications, wanting to change types of structures, numbers of structures, arrangements, etc., but after the first dozen or so of such changes, you develop a philosophy and a sense of humor and the changes do not bother much from then on out."[11]

Journal entries from the end of August and into October mention a series of disagreements between Stanley and a Corps of Engineers officer recently assigned to oversee the Sioux Falls project. In one Stanley refers to a "Two hour trip of criticism" with the officer, and in another he tells of being chastised for "procrastination."

Closing a letter to his brother, Stanley wrote: "On the whole I am having a lot of fun. I have always wanted to tackle a big sized project and I really have it this time. If only the family were a little closer or could be here, I would be perfectly happy . . ."[12]

As the Sioux Falls training school moved into the last stages of construction, Stanley went to Omaha to talk to Corps officers about other projects. In July Stanley Engineering was retained for the architectural and engineering work on a satellite airfield at Watertown, South Dakota. Late in August the firm got the contract for a similar project at Pierre, South Dakota. About one thousand men would be stationed at each base, to practice takeoffs and landings. Both would be rush jobs; the Corps wanted construction completed before winter.

Two days before the end of the year, Stanley negotiated a contract for work on a prisoner-of-war camp at Scottsbluff, Nebraska. After Stanley's staff finished the project by the following May, the Corps had another in mind, an expansion of the internment camp at Fort Robinson, Nebraska. But negotiations broke down when Stanley and the Army could not agree on a fee—"$25,000 vs $30,000," as he recorded in his journal.

He got his last war contract in May 1944, an expansion of the air base at McCook, Nebraska, which was being upgraded from a satellite field to a heavy bomber training base.

Whatever satisfaction Stanley derived from those achievements, it was not enough to quell the nagging disquiet about the value of his part in the war effort. In his mind apparently his work did not measure up to that of military service. In September 1942, when he was hurrying from job sites in Sioux Falls to Watertown to Pierre, he wrote to his brother that he was thinking about getting into the Navy Civil Engineer Corps or the Army Specialist Corps. Never mind that Art had advised him in an earlier letter, "I would suggest that if you can keep busy with defense jobs that you do it. I know, and lots of others know, that you will be doing a lot more for the present cause in your present capacity than being a First Lieutenant in some engineering company."[13]

Stanley's ambivalent feelings were understandable in a nation brimming with patriotic fervor. Newspapers were full of dispatches from battlefronts, popular magazines struck militant themes, jukeboxes blared songs about soldiers and sailors and the sweethearts they left at home, and the leading men in motion pictures usually wore khaki or navy blue. Bob Hope's weekly radio show was broadcast from military installations, and one radio program signed off with "Bye-bye, buy bonds." On the home front, civilians traded ration stamps, gave up Sunday pleasure drives, and practiced blackouts. There were two forms of sacrifice, and Stanley wasn't sure his was worthy enough.

To his wife and children, Stanley might as well have been in military service. He was gone from home for most of the year. Betty took Dick and Jane with her, traveling by train to Sioux Falls, to see him for a few days in mid-June, and Dave spent a week with him in August, a visit that included a couple of outings with surveying crews.

In the last journal note of 1942 Stanley characterized the year's accomplishments as "war service." Yet when Art returned to Muscatine on leave the following August (he was a lieutenant colonel by then), Max wrote in his journal that his brother was "more mature and has had real experience & responsibility. I envy him his war duty."[14]

Art Stanley had a commendable record of Air Corps service, though it did not match the heroic dimensions of his father's exploits along the western front in World War I. After Pearl Harbor, he was transferred from Luke Field, near Phoenix, Arizona, where he had been a training officer, to the headquarters of the Western Flying Training Command, near Santa Ana, California, where he headed the buildings and grounds department. This meant overseeing the location, layout, and design of air bases, with the work subsequently involving sixty bases. In 1944 he had orders to go to England as a liaison officer to the Corps of Engineers, which was expected to rehabilitate captured airfields in Europe after the D-Day invasion. But he never got there. Instead, he was ordered to the Harvard Business School for an accelerated twelve-week course in management. Then he was sent to San Diego as a contracting officer at Consolidated Vultee, now part of General Dynamics. He remained there, after a promotion to colonel, until June of 1946, helping wind up military contracts with the manufacturer. Nearly ten months after the war ended, he returned to Muscatine.[15]

Almost a year after VJ-Day, Claude Stanley wrote a letter to his older son, handwritten on Employment Security Commission stationery. It is among the letters Max Stanley saved, keeping it with other mementoes at home rather than in a correspondence file at his office. The first paragraph reads: "You did a trying job during the war years and did it in fine shape when a more glamorous position could have been had by going into the army." The letter is signed, "With lots of Love — Your Dad." It was an old soldier's blessing on a home front endeavor.[16]

As the tide of the war changed in the Allies' favor, Max Stanley began thinking about the opportunities peace might bring. The Rural Electrification Administration was ready to let loose numerous projects in 1944, and Stanley expected to resume where the company had been when the war began. Midwest cities would be trying to catch up on delayed public works, including power plants. Stanley had a hint of things to come early in 1943 when the company received a contract for sewer work in Milan, Illinois. At home in Muscatine there was a survey at a government alcohol plant that was to be transferred to private ownership. Grain Processing Corporation would become one of the city's major employers. There was also a design job for the Carver Pump

Company, which had a contract for a sewage treatment plant in the Soviet Union. By the summer of 1945, Stanley Engineering had more than seventy employees, the highest number yet, and they needed more working room.

Stanley's year-end note for 1942 sounded a bold theme, "Stanley Eng Co. has come of age and is 'rearing' to go." He had proved this convincingly with his military work. Not that *he* doubted his firm's capability, but others had. War projects were slow in coming, he indicated in his journal, because the Corps of Engineers considered the company "light" on its municipal experience, lacking the big, varied, complex projects that some high authority had decided were suitable preparation for military work.

The Sioux Falls technical school was a test, and Stanley and his crew passed it masterfully. Afterward he wrote proudly in his journal, "Well received in District office [Corps at Omaha] — we rate."[17] Although he did not realize it at first, the military projects permitted Stanley to prove his company as well as himself. By so doing, he showed that he could lead effectively. He silenced the doubters and earned new respect.

5

Engineering Here and There

Many of the trends Max Stanley observed in the aftermath of World War II pointed to dramatic changes in the way Americans were going to live, with clear signs of an industrial boom that would generate explosive urban and suburban development. Such a changing society would require new and bigger power systems, new and improved streets and highways, more factories, more schools, expanded sanitation systems — and the list ran on and on. What a promising time for an engineer, especially one as energetic and imaginative as Stanley. Much of his success and that of Stanley Engineering Company (SEC) can be traced to his ability to convert trends into profitable opportunities. The desire to capitalize on another postwar trend, an expected housing boom, figured in the decision by Stanley and his brother-in-law, Clement T. Hanson, to start the company that became HON Industries. This was what being an entrepreneur was all about.

Taking advantage of the prewar REA experience and the reputation that followed, Stanley soon piled up contracts for an array of power projects. By the midfifties the company counted more than sixty-five steam systems and more than fifty-five diesel systems for both cooperatives and municipalities. The flourishing power work accounted for about 40 percent of the company's work. That it did not take up a larger proportion was evidence of growing diversity. Thus as some activities declined, as work on electrical power systems did after the sixties, SEC shifted to other undertakings, such as sanitation and sewage projects, which increased as the public became more concerned about environmental problems.[1]

One opportunity Stanley sidestepped was nuclear power. He recognized its potential and paid lip service to what was then the popular notion that nuclear reactors would supply homeowners with energy costing only pennies. But such cheap power, Stanley and his associates surmised, would require costly systems. Engineering designs were part of that initial equation. To assure adequate safeguards in a design for a reactor would require a specialized staff, including nuclear physicists. So the company was content with other opportunities rather than plunging into unpredictable currents.[2]

Company growth took several forms. The work force rose steadily, reaching four hundred by 1970 and more than seven hundred by 1980 before a slumping economy and declining power demands forced a series of staff reductions. Fees for services brought in more than $3 million in 1961; twenty years later income exceeded $40 million. Stanley Engineering Company became an employee-owned corporation in 1961 (when employees were designated as members), and within ten years nearly a hundred on the staff had become shareholders. Five years later the company name was changed to Stanley Consultants Incorporated (SCI) to reflect expanding endeavors that included consulting services in architecture, planning, and management as well as engineering. By then the company was numbered among the fifty largest engineering and architectural firms in the United States. It was, though operating in a city of not quite 25,000 population, the largest engineering company in Iowa.

Stanley opened an office in Chicago in 1953 and installed as his representative Frank Edwards, an engineering school classmate who had been teaching at Illinois Institute of Technology. The company later opened offices in Atlanta, Birmingham, Cleveland, Indianapolis, and Washington. When Stanley accepted a project in Liberia in 1956, he was drawn into a new opportunity that would extend company activities to more than thirty countries and lead to the formation of two foreign subsidiaries and several branch offices overseas.

Spotting talent was another of Stanley's gifts. He liked to hire aggressive, innovative engineers who would come up with new ideas, yet he had difficulty dealing with bright men who might challenge his dominance and his need to be right. Consequently, many capable engineers chose to handle their assignments as effectively as possible without crossing the boss, and they became a cadre of "yes men" who gratified his whims. Stanley had a low tolerance for fools and those who proved incompetent. Anyone who questioned his judgments with flimsy reasons was destined for hard times in the company. His highest esteem was reserved for a few individuals whose competence not only was in a league with his, but who had the self-confidence and courage to challenge and correct his thinking when that was needed. Appreciation was sometimes shown grudgingly, for he was loath to concede that someone else might have a better idea.

The company acquired an enviable reputation both for integrity and performance that attracted bright, energetic engineers. In the early years most of the staff came from the engineering schools at Iowa and Iowa State, but in the postwar period a number of top positions were filled by graduates of Purdue, MIT, Illinois Institute of Technology, Indiana Tech, Texas Tech, North Dakota State, New Mexico State, and Penn State.

Roy Vanek was a key addition to the firm in 1950, and he quickly earned not only Stanley's respect but his trust. Coming from positions in both private and public power companies, he took charge of major power projects and subsequently, as senior vice president, managed most of the firm's domestic work, freeing Stanley to concentrate on international business. Meanwhile, CMS's brother Art took charge of projects with the Iowa State Highway Commission and the Army Corps of Engineers. As the firm broadened the scope of its operations, Stanley put together a staff of specialists who gained professional recognition for their accomplishments. Among them were Ralph Esmay, whose knowledge of electrical transmission systems went back to the REA program; Hank Godeke, who had taught at the University of Iowa engineering college before moving to Muscatine as a power plant specialist; Al Garvik, project manager on power systems; Gene Lister, chief electrical engineer who previously taught at Iowa State; Frank Swengel, a creative designer and developer though he lacked an engineering degree; Dimitri Nesterenko, a former city engineer in Warsaw, Poland, who came to the United States after World War II and eventually became the company's chief structural engineer; Al Dunton, a brilliant project analyst and later the company treasurer; and partner H. Sidwell Smith, who led the firm into sanitary work, then left to teach at Iowa, later becoming dean of engineering at the University of Utah.

The energy of the organization was disturbed from time to time by disagreements among the partners. A partnership implies a cooperative or shared control, but Stanley wanted to have final authority over all operations and was not hesitant about asserting his position as the senior partner with the largest financial stake in the firm. The year-end entry in his 1946 journal is revealing: "S.E.C. beginning to operate more smoothly & efficiently. Art, Marvin & Sid taking hold well but none seem to 'drive' as I used to. I am unloading some but not enough." Within twenty years those partners—his brother, Marvin O. Kruse, and Sid Smith—had moved on, leaving only Sanford K. Fosholt, who was taken into the partnership in 1950. Fosholt endured partly because he and Stanley took to passing memos during the cooling-off periods after blowups.[3]

Stanley was a demanding boss, but as demanding on himself as he was on others, and when he saw errors or misjudgments, his temper flared. The storm usually dissipated as quickly as it had blown up, and the hardier engineers learned to tolerate the outbursts as part of the Stanley personality. They also learned that he did not admit error easily, and doing so often required a roundabout explanation of why different circumstances or new data had impelled him to change his mind. "He would go through hell to keep from being wrong," his brother observed. For all his domineering posture, Stanley agonized at length over decisions to dismiss or demote staff members and frequently sent a trusted aide to convey the bad news. As the years passed Stanley mellowed (the word used almost universally by family and friends) and showed more understanding of the faults and foibles of the men and women he worked with—and possibly his own. He could be generous and compassionate to those who were passing through personal crises caused by money problems, poor health, or a marital breakup. "Things tended to be black and white with Max, and it wasn't until the last years that he could see shades of gray," Ron Barrett said. "People who only knew him in those last five or ten years couldn't believe what they heard about him in his forties and fifties."[4]

The International Division was Stanley's pet. The foreign operations began almost incidentally from work with Republic Steel Company in this country. In 1956 SEC was retained to design a diesel power plant adjacent to a mine Republic owned in Liberia. As the project moved ahead and after talking to Liberian and U.S. government officials (Congress had voted to extend technical assistance to Liberia), Stanley was convinced that Liberia and possibly other African countries were lands of opportunity for his company. Early the next year he called his partners together and got their agreement "to proceed aggressively on overseas work in Liberia."[5]

In the May 1957 issue of *Compass,* SEC's employee publication, Stanley gave these reasons for "a challenging venture in Africa":

>   1. We believe overseas work can be profitable once we have passed the development period. It can add volume and diversity which will have economic benefits to us.
>   2. We believe it will enhance our reputation in the United States. There is a real glamour or prestige factor which is associated with work in foreign countries.
>   3. We believe it offers a real opportunity for service. It is important that the new nations of Africa develop their economies as free nations and that they avoid the perils of totalitarianism and communism. American engineering and know how can help.

Norman Thorn was sent to Monrovia, the Liberian capital city, to open the SEC office in the fall. On December 2 Stanley learned that the company had been awarded the contract to modify the design and supervise the construction of a harbor to accommodate large vessels at Greenville. Next came a study to develop a countrywide electric power system. That led to planning for a $25 million hydroelectric plant for which the Iowa firm was given start-to-finish supervision, with a fee of more than $2 million. It was one of the company's largest projects up to that time, and Fred Reusswig, a hydroelectric specialist, was hired to direct the work. Stanley was overjoyed the following fall when the company won a contest for the design of the executive mansion in Monrovia. In March 1959 he and Betty were invited to a state dinner at the Liberian embassy in Washington—the first of many formal affairs that signaled government recognition of the company's contributions to African autonomy. He was honored by the Liberian government and awarded the medals of Grand Commander, Star of Africa, in 1963 and Grand Commander, Humane Order of African Redemption, in 1967.

With work in Liberia progressing rapidly, and with engineers in Muscatine vying for overseas assignments, Stanley sent Bill Gilliam to start work in Ghana, but then pulled him out when Prime Minister Kwame Nkrumah turned Communist and set up a dictatorial government. It was no more than a momentary setback, for Gilliam was soon in Nigeria, followed by an English engineer, Geoffrey Smith, whom

Stanley hired to run a new branch office at Lagos. Meanwhile, Stanley scanned the globe for places to stake new outposts. In the sixties his journal contained references to work in Tunis (Tunisia), Kingston (Jamaica), Nassau (Bahamas), Nairobi (Kenya), Lima (Peru), St. John's (Antigua), San Martino (Argentina), Kampala (Uganda), and many other places. The result was an array of new power plants and electrical systems, highways and bridges, deep-water harbors, airfields and hangars, schools and hospitals for Christian missions, warehouses and service stations for oil companies, office buildings, and a plant in Antigua to remove salt from seawater. At their peak, foreign projects accounted for a quarter of the company's business, more than was gleaned from Iowa.

Stanley opened an office in Washington in 1961 and appointed H. Peter Guttmann as his representative there. It was a deft move. Guttmann and his successors were links to U.S. government officials, particularly in the State Department and the Agency for International Development (AID), to international financial institutions, and to representatives of foreign nations where the engineering firm had work or might want to work. Guttmann, a graduate of the University of San Carlos in Guatemala, traveled extensively in South America cultivating business for the Iowa company.

But the overseas boom for American companies did not last. The new nations of Asia, as they moved farther from colonial paternalism and dependence on foreign financial aid, trained their own people to supply many essential services that foreign companies had provided. That happened as well in the developing countries of Africa and Latin America. So American companies had to look continually for new opportunities, often extending their lines farther from the home base at ever higher costs. As successful as Stanley Consultants was (ranked twenty-fifth in volume of international work in the early seventies among sixty-five American firms with extensive overseas projects), it did not grow rich on foreign contracts. When Stanley relinquished the company presidency in 1971 and with it the control of the International Division, Ron Barrett, who was put in charge of overseas work, began cutting costs, curtailing future work, and closing some branch offices. By then, too, the luster had vanished from overseas work.

Barrett, who was Stanley's right-hand man on African work for twenty years, pointed out that a combination of humanitarian motives and an internationalist outlook supplied enough justification for Stanley to continue the foreign activity. To the irritation of his brother and, later, the frustration of Roy Vanek, Stanley did not always measure the worth of an undertaking by profit-loss standards. The company had to bear substantial financial losses on the work for the executive mansion in Liberia — "a fiasco" to Art Stanley — but gained advantageous attention — "prestige" to Max Stanley — among architects, engineers, financiers, and leaders of other African nations. Had Stanley wished to build huge profits from foreign work, Barrett said, he would have done better by getting into the postwar Marshall Plan developments in Western Europe; instead, he concentrated on projects in the Third World. "Max genuinely wanted to do some good for people, and he was caught up in this international thing from the United World Federalists [which he joined in 1947]."[6]

Stanley was proud of the company's accomplishments in foreign lands, not only the bridges and highways and buildings but the less visible benefits: using steel to reinforce construction, washing sand and gravel for concrete, training surveyors, and raising the voltage of power systems to make refrigeration and air conditioning possible. The company, quite simply, improved the quality of construction in many countries and, as a result, the quality of life of many people. At the same time the International Division gave engineers in Muscatine, including more than three-fourths of the managerial level staff, a chance to travel overseas and to work with the people in undeveloped countries. For some it was drudgery, for others an exhilarating experience, and for all a sample of the boss' philosophy in action. Among them was Gregs Thomopulos, a native of Nigeria, who eventually became head of the International Division and then, in 1987, Dick Stanley's successor as president of Stanley Consultants.

A continuing series of rifts between Max and Art led finally to a falling out in 1966. They were, to begin with, two different personalities. Outside the office, Art was outgoing, sociable, a regular at the country club. His older brother tended to be reserved, not one to go out with the boys for a beer. In the office, though, Art was the cautious, tight-fisted treasurer, while Max often forsook his normally prudent ways to follow a daring course. They differed over Max's obligations to Home-O-Nize and the money he borrowed from SEC to keep the new company afloat. The decision to start engineering work in West Africa caused further tension, Art seeing the move as a potential drain on domestic operations, both financially and in key manpower. Art was upset, too, about the time his brother spent with the United World Federalists and later with the Stanley Foundation.

Dick Stanley joined the company in June 1955 after graduating near the top of his class at Iowa State with degrees in both mechanical and electrical engineering (later he earned a master's degree in sanitary engineering from the University of Iowa). He visited several engineering and manufacturing firms before deciding he could "make it on my own" at SEC. From times in his father's Boy Scout troop, the son knew not to expect favored treatment, but to be held to a higher standard of performance. From the beginning the younger Stanley, who had done a number of part-time jobs around the company since he was in junior high school, was looked upon as a likely successor to his father. In the fall Dick joined the Army, to fulfill his ROTC commitment, and served two years as an officer with the Army Corps of Engineers at Fort Belvoir, Virginia. After returning to SEC in October 1957, he advanced rapidly to higher positions — without apparent favoritism from his father — and confirmed the promise of his outstanding student record.[7]

Strained feelings between the brothers reached the breaking point as the result of a management study by Batten and Batten, a Des Moines consulting firm. Max referred to the consultants' conclusions as a "startling set of recommendations, fully substantiating [the] seriousness of personnel problems with which I've struggled unsuccessfully for several years." Art was incensed by the findings, many of which appeared directed at him and in his mind even cast doubt on his loyalty to the company. The upshot was that Art, after lengthy talks with his brother, agreed reluctantly to move to California as the company's western representative. He left Muscatine convinced that he had been exiled so he could not block the accession of his nephew if Max died unexpectedly or became disabled.[8]

Bonds between the brothers remained frayed for many years. On one occasion after Art had been in Muscatine, Max confessed that he was "chagrined at my failure re our personal relations." When Art returned in the spring of 1970 for a retirement ceremony and dinner with the company directors, Max wrote in his journal: "Art departed without saying goodbye — still very resentful and complaining, gripes at my dominance but gripes at being out! Maybe time will heal?" Before leaving,

Art stopped at his brother's office, but Max was not there. Time passing apparently did have beneficial results for cordiality was restored between the brothers.[9]

On February 22, 1971, at a dinner for the company's officers, Stanley announced that he planned to turn over the presidency to his son and become chairman of the board, a position the directors had created for him. "This decision has not been easy," he said. "For nearly forty years Stanley Consultants has been the major interest in my life, excepting only my family and home. HON Industries, though interesting and profitable, has always been secondary to Stanley Consultants. My many outside activities, centering now on the Stanley Foundation and international affairs, have been avocations — absorbing, and at times demanding, but yet secondary to my professional career with Stanley Consultants."[10]

The change, although under consideration for about two years, was a traumatic one for Stanley when it finally happened. He confided to his journal that he was "despondent at being on sidelines" and felt "some irritation at pressures and criticism of international," a reference to internal suggestions that he ought to start letting go of the corporate reins (he was sixty-six at the time) and to quit coddling the International Division. But by year's end he had dispersed his gloom and had become "well adjusted to the role of chairman."[11]

The reduced responsbilities at SCI gave him more time to examine questions stirring discussion among the professional engineering groups, and he soon stepped up his output of articles for engineering magazines and his talks at conferences. Trendspotter that he was, Stanley was drawn to the growing concern about pollution and environmental neglect, and he urged fellow engineers to recognize a responsibility not only to protect the environment but to help manage it so that the quality of life could be sustained. In an article for *Civil Engineering,* he observed:

> Engineers in general, and civil engineers in particular, like to believe they have had a favorable impact on environment over the years. But the public may not see it this way. From their point of view, engineers are the designers of internal combustion engines that create smog, industrial plants that dump wastes into the river, transportation systems that congest our cities, power plants that spew fly ash and gas into the atmosphere, and other polluting mechanisms. It

is in our self-interest to overcome any doubts by whole-hearted ac-
ceptance of our environmental responsibilities.[12]

At the same time Stanley took a close look at SCI's record on
environmental questions, concluding that the company had a "strong
position" from which it could broaden its opportunities by acting as a
consultant on environmental problems and by forming a separate environmental department or group. But economic setbacks in the seventies stymied such expansion.[13]

Professional consciousness was rooted deeply in Stanley's sense of
who he was. To him engineering was a form of public service and as
honorable a calling as the law, medicine, or the ministry. He was a fellow
or a member of ten professional organizations and was the recipient of
three awards from the Iowa Engineering Society, two from the American
Society of Civil Engineers, and one from the National Society of Professional Engineers. He was especially pleased in 1984, when he was eighty,
to be selected "Engineer of the Year" by *Consulting Engineer* magazine
(the Steinmetz Award recognizing a distinguished career as a consulting
engineer).

Milton Carlson, who was in the Stanley crew at the Sioux Falls
airfield in World War II, recalled an example of CMS's professional
dedication:

> For several months we all literally worked night and day. At
> dinner one evening in a local restaurant, Max told us of his interest
> in a special structural problem—completely unrelated to the Air
> Corps project—and that he had prepared an engineering paper on
> the subject during the past few weeks! I will never know how in that
> particular time he could have managed to do this. For him, ap-
> parently, this problem was simply a release and a diversion from the
> pressures of the Air Corps project.[14]

A decade or so later it was not unusual for Stanley to keep two or
three or even four ideas dancing in the air at the same time. He slipped
adroitly from engineering to manufacturing to international affairs to
community development, effortlessly shifting his concentration from
one matter to another. It was in such a vibrant atmosphere that Stanley
fit in his writing on *The Consulting Engineer,* an important contribution
to his profession. The book, first published in 1961 and then revised for
an updated edition in 1982, supplied advice to many aspiring engineers
about client relations, contracts and fees, accounting practices, person-

nel management, and other functions. In a review Hunter Hughes, then managing director of the American Engineering Consultants in Washington, D.C., suggested that the book might have been titled *What Every Young Would-Be Consulting Engineer Should Know* and that "15,000 of these fair-haired boys . . . should get a copy of this book and read it at least twice."[15]

Beginning the year after he was graduated from engineering school, Stanley wrote forty-three articles for engineering journals and prepared thirty-four papers for conferences, all of which were published. As a leading authority on power systems, he was invited to talk to such organizations as the American Waterworks Association, the American Institute of Electrical Engineers, the Midwest Power Conference, and the Iowa Rural Electric Cooperative Association. By the sixties his articles and talks diverged from engineering's benefits and promise to his growing fascination with management and an assertive stance on ethics.

He found a forum in *Consulting Engineer* magazine, where ten of his articles appeared from 1961 to 1979. He warned against a trend to nonprofessional ownership, meaning the takeover of consulting engineering firms by contractors, investors, or conglomerates. He was against government requirements for bidding by engineers, insisting that fee negotiation was proper when professionals were involved. When the resignation of Vice-President Spiro Agnew in 1973 revealed that he had taken payoffs from contractors and engineers while he was governor of Maryland, Stanley not only decried unsavory dealings with politicians but criticized the engineering profession for being "lamentably slow in policing itself with enforcement and deterent policies." In a later article he rebuked the anonymous author of "I Gave Up Ethics—To Eat," a confession by an engineer who bribed his way to profits from government contracts, and again he appealed for courageous disciplinary action by engineering societies and state engineering examiners.[16]

Stanley was not simply clutching a trendy theme when he wrote about ethics. As early as 1940, fourteen years removed from engineering school, he presented a paper on ethical codes to the Iowa Engineering Society, and the next year he helped write such a code for the organization. Ethical concerns and professional standards were given prominence when Stanley became president of the society in 1949. Henry M. Black, for twenty-six years the head of the Mechanical Engineering Department at Iowa State, and A. F. Faul, who held a number of positions in a long career with the Iowa State Highway Commission, worked with Stanley on society affairs, and they told how he traveled about the state trying to build up membership and promote a sense of professional responsibility among the engineers with whom he met.[17]

An ethical test for Stanley came in 1955 when SEC was in line for a design contract on a $4-million section of the Calumet Skyway in Chicago. Frank Edwards, who was negotiating with the Chicago planners, informed Stanley late in March that the contract would be signed as soon as the company forwarded a political contribution of a sizable but unspecified amount. Stanley was outraged and, after conferring with his partners, pulled out of the project. Reports of the incident soon circulated among engineers, and SEC became known as a company that would not play money games with politicians.[18]

Early in the Liberian venture Norman Thorn bought two cases of 12-year-old Scotch, one for delivery to President William Tubman and the other for distribution to high-ranking government officials. Stanley was furious when he heard about it and was only partly mollified when a few associates reminded him that Christmas was near. He frowned on wining and dining clients, and, of course, he steadfastly refused to cut deals with bribes and payoffs, which became common preliminaries to business negotiations in several African nations as the former colonies gained independence. Stanley's unbudging attitude meant, in effect, that the company forfeited opportunities to work in places where under-the-table palm-greasing determined who was eligible to compete.[19]

Questions of another kind arose for Stanley as a result of his activities with the world federalist movement, the Stanley Foundation, and the United Nations. The most notable incident took place late in 1969 after SCI was chosen for the design work on an antiballistic missile site near Great Falls, Montana. San Fosholt had been soliciting the Corps of Engineers for new business and, to Stanley's astonishment, had landed the ABM project, one of the biggest the company had been offered. Lucrative as the project would be, Stanley wanted no part of it. He was opposed to the ABM program, arguing that it was an escalation of the arms race at a time when the superpowers should be curtailing new weapons systems. When the matter came before the four-man Executive Committee, Stanley voted against it, Fosholt and Roy Vanek voted for it, and Dick Stanley was left with the deciding vote. Although his feelings about the ABM were not much different from his father's, he voted for the project. He had three reasons for agreeing to the project: Since the contract resulted from a company initiative, which his father endorsed, SCI would lose credibility by suddenly pulling out as a protest against U.S. foreign policy; the government policy, whether good or bad, was not going to be changed by SCI's decision to accept or reject an ABM contract; if the missile site was to be built, it should have a superior engineering design, which SCI could do. Stanley accepted defeat graciously and then explained the decision, pro and con, in a memo to SCI members.[20]

Over the years Stanley had emphasized internal growth for the company, relying largely on his staff's ability to take advantage of new opportunities. For the most part, the key men in the organization had moved up through the ranks. After he was settled in as board chairman, Stanley began looking at the possibility of growth by acquisition. HON Industries had gone that route in the seventies, gaining corporate strength, increased sales, expanded product lines, and greater manufacturing flexibility. Stanley encouraged his son to consider a similar strategy for SCI.

Middle West Service Company of Chicago was acquired in 1981 and was brought under the umbrella of the Muscatine management. Three years later Stanley was excited about the possibility of obtaining Mettee-McGill-Murphy Incorporated of Phoenix, which would give SCI an extension into the growing Sun Belt. However, Stanley died shortly before arrangements were completed to make the Phoenix firm a subsidiary of SCI. Two years later, in 1986, SCI acquired two companies in West Palm Beach, Florida.

Thus a new pattern began taking shape to prepare the company for changing circumstances. With subsidiaries in fast-growing parts of the country, the Midwest-based company would be less vulnerable to regional uncertainties, such as the Farm Belt recession of the seventies. By broadening the range of its American activities, SCI could offset part of the diminishing activity in foreign lands. Once again, the company moved to capitalize on changing trends.

6

Joining the Business Elite

HON Industries, Max Stanley's leap of faith, qualified for the Fortune 500 in 1985 (reported in *Fortune* magazine's issue of April 28, 1986). Although he did not live to celebrate this achievement with HON's executives and employees, he was aware before his death in 1984 that the company soon would be welcomed to the elite rank of American business. Corporate Secretary Robert L. Carl recalled how Stanley "was very tuned to that," regularly checking HON's sales, production, and financial figures against those of companies on the magazine's select list.[1]

In forty-one years HON had become the country's third largest manufacturer of office furniture and equipment. Actually, the company's rise happened in about thirty years, following early struggles that brought Stanley and his partners close to bankruptcy. Making office products was the offshoot of a manufacturing sideline started when a postwar steel shortage thwarted plans to produce kitchen cabinets.

HON expanded rapidly in the seventies by acquiring other companies with production facilities in different parts of the country, and it enhanced its status by gaining entry to the "A Grade" (or premium price) market for office furniture. In addition to a standard metal desk costing about $200, HON then could offer customers a luxury executive model made of high-grade wood and priced at more than $2,500. No longer could HON's competitors try to laugh it off as a Corn Belt upstart.[2]

When Home-O-Nize, as the company was originally known, first recorded sales above $1 million in 1953, office products accounted for only a third of the business. Two years later sales of those goods alone topped $1 million. In 1965 the company's sales passed $10 million, and

57

twenty years later, when admission to the Fortune 500 was assured, sales exceeded $470 million.

Stanley knew, of course, that he had been riding with a corporate success for thirty years, but the prospective recognition by *Fortune's* editors would be distinctive confirmation of HON's feat, begun in a refurbished pearl button factory in a small Iowa city. The recognition would be a tribute, too, to his entrepreneurial spirit, which had not flagged despite the early setbacks—two severe floods and a bad fire as well as critical financial difficulties and fitful progress making different products for other companies. Stanley was an engineer, after all, whose plunge into manufacturing owed more to a sense of adventure than to a carefully plotted corporate strategy. Largely self-taught in managerial techniques, he dared to blend new skills with trusted instincts to nurture a homegrown industry that provided more jobs in Muscatine, attracted talented executives, and rewarded longtime shareholders.

Stanley's experiences along the road to industrial success supplied the framework for what was meant to be his fourth book, which he gave the tentative title "The HON Story." He commenced the project in 1977, not only recording his own memories but soliciting recollections from veteran employees and reviewing company records. The work proceeded spasmodically when Stanley had free time from other responsibilities, and much of the writing (dictated to a recorder actually) was saved for solitary interludes at the beach house on Sanibel Island. When he died, he had finished twelve chapters and had three others in draft form. James H. Soltow, professor emeritus of history at Michigan State University, was engaged by the company in 1986 to complete the book.

Stanley's story began with a scene from a pleasant Sunday afternoon in June 1943 when he and Clement T. Hanson, who had married Betty Stanley's sister Sylvia, were relaxing in the backyard of the Hanson home in Moline, Illinois:

> We had known each other since college days, having courted, and later married, sisters. As was customary at our family gatherings, the kids were playing, the sisters were chatting and clearing the remains of a hearty meal, and Clem and I were solving the world's problems. Our discussion ranged broadly. We talked about the progress of World War II, the nation's political and economic challenges, and anticipated postwar problems. We returned, inevitably, to a topic of common interest. We had often observed with disdain the

mediocrity of management in many manufacturing companies, particularly the management of corporate relationships with employees, customers, and communities. . . .

Over the years, Clem and I had discovered many common opinions on public policy, business organization, and industrial management. We shared similar ideas about human relations. We both believed there was need in our country for more enlightened approaches to employer-employee relations. . . . Clem and I were worried, as many people were, that employment would be a major problem when, at war's end, the country converted to a peacetime economy.[3]

The conversation finally inspired a vision of the two of them running a manufacturing concern. Stanley had his engineering background plus organizing and administrative skills; Hanson, an advertising executive, was equipped to take care of sales and marketing. Hanson suggested that they invite a mutual friend, Wood Miller, to join them, adding knowledge of products and design. "Our confident enthusiasm," Stanley recalled, "was matched only by our considerable naivete about the difficult problems and obstacles ahead."[4]

Foreseeing a postwar building boom to relieve a housing shortage, the three partners quickly focused on the home market and then specifically on the kitchen. Miller, who had been a consulting designer for an appliance manufacturer, had a number of innovative ideas for kitchen cabinets, such as extendable modular units and upper cabinets that could be raised or lowered electrically. Home freezers and possibly other appliances were part of the plan, too.

Home-O-Nize was chosen for the company name, mainly because of its suitability for slogans, as in "Economize with Home-O-Nize" and "Modernize with Home-O-Nize." Hanson and Miller designed a logo with two musical notes inside the capital O.

Since none of the three had experience in industrial production, they looked for an associate who was familiar with sheet metal fabricating. They found him—or thought they had—in Albert F. Uchtorff, who ran a company in Davenport that manufactured a wide variety of metal products, including conventional square-cornered kitchen cabinets. Uchtorff was enthusiastic about the Home-O-Nize plan, and the others invited him to join the embryonic enterprise.

The company was incorporated in January 1944, a few weeks after a small second-floor office in Davenport was rented for $10 a month.

Hanson ("with some trepidation," in Stanley's memory) agreed later that year to become the company's first fulltime employee at a salary of $400 a month. He was to explore sales prospects and develop marketing programs. Meanwhile, Miller designed kitchen cabinets in his spare time, and Uchtorff built models, at least one of which was transported to Stanley's garage for what was termed "a consumer test." By late November the partners were ready to present the "Lyric" and "Duet" lines of Home-O-Nize kitchen cabinets. They had a working model and artist's sketches to show a group of Midwest distributors who were invited to Davenport early in December. But before that happened, Uchtorff abruptly pulled out of the company, leaving the firm without a production plant.

"Our planned approach to manufacture was scuttled," Stanley wrote. "We were compelled for the first time, but not the last, to deal with adversity, rise above abject disappointment, and move ahead, albeit on an altered course."[5]

After getting $100,000 through a government loan program, the remaining partners took over a vacant button factory in Muscatine and began converting it for manufacturing kitchen cabinets. But an unanticipated steel shortage blunted their hopes. Increasing demand for consumer goods, particularly automobiles and home appliances, exceeded the productive capacity of American steel manufacturers and, in the aftermath of war, foreign steel was unavailable. Desperately, Stanley and his associates turned every which way to get work. Stampings Incorporated of Davenport gave them a contract for stamping and packing housings for bottled gas tanks, commonly used at rural homes. Later Home-O-Nize made combine pickup attachments for John Deere, cabinets for the Herman Nelson Division of American Filter, and, under a subcontract with Bell Aircraft, fairings for B-47 bombers produced by Boeing.

In July 1948 the officers signed a $540,000 contract with Associated Manufacturers of Waterloo to produce a newly designed corn picker. That surely was the long awaited stroke of good fortune. It turned out, however, to be the "greatest fiasco" (Stanley's words) of Home-O-Nize's history. The one demonstration picker tested in a cornfield near Muscatine failed under the critical gaze of the banker who had been asked for a loan to back production. Stanley did not get the loan. Numerous design changes did not improve performance, and the Waterloo firm went bankrupt, leaving the Muscatine firm on the brink of financial disaster.

The old U.S. Button Company building in Muscatine furnished a home for the fledgling Home-O-Nize Company.

The logo for Home-O-Nize and the emblem designed for its giant offspring, HON Industries.

Stanley Howe, who would succeed Max as head of HON Industries, checks with his mentor on construction progress of a HON addition. (George T. Henry)

Honored at a HON Industries celebration were the three founders: Clement T. Hanson, Wood Miller, and Max.

Liberia's president, William V. S. Tubman, welcomes Max to Monrovia in 1957. (Below) Max spoke in the Liberian capital in 1979 at the dedication of a bridge designed by his engineering company. President Tolbert, with white hat, is at left.

Throughout those early years Stanley, Hanson, and Miller were beset with a seemingly endless series of financial troubles, and in 1949 operating expenses, debts, and losses diminished the company's strength by more than $100,000. The factory workers picking up their paychecks on Saturday often were asked to wait to cash them until Monday so that Fred Winn, the secretary-treasurer, could get sufficient money into the bank. Some employees at times accepted stock in lieu of salaries. William Newsom, hired ostensibly to generate product sales, spent much of his time trying to sell shares of stock. Some debts were settled with stock instead of cash. Stanley borrowed funds from the engineering firm, and he persuaded his parents, his mother-in- law, and other relatives to invest in the company. But not his brother.

"HON should never have been," Art Stanley said four decades later. He declined his older brother's invitation to invest in Home-O-Nize after returning to Muscatine from military service in 1946, and he was irritated by his brother's repeated requests to borrow money from Stanley Engineering and to spend more working hours trying to save the fledgling manufacturing company. "Max pulled it off with his determination and ability, but he didn't care who he walked on to get there," the younger brother said. "Stanley Engineering almost failed because of it."[6]

Even Betty Stanley balked when her husband suggested mortgaging their home to get money for Home-O-Nize. "I cried," she said, "which was not a very good response, but at any rate he dropped that immediately and never brought it up again."[7]

The company was in a precarious situation in 1949. Lenders were wary because of the corn picker disaster; suppliers shipped materials only COD; spreading rumors of a shutdown all but ended sales of stock. Late that year Hanson was ready to quit.

"But calling it quits was something I would not do," Stanley wrote, although he confessed to being sleepless many nights because of the worsening situation. "Too many people had invested in Home-O-Nize because they had confidence in me. Even if I had reconciled myself to failure and personal loss, I could not let them down."[8]

The turnaround for Home-O-Nize began unexpectedly the next year as a result of Stanley's friendship with George H. Olmsted, the retired army general and Des Moines insurance executive who was active in the world federalist movement. Olmsted sat on the board of Bell Aircraft, which wanted to dispense with production of an engine-powered wheelbarrow called the Prime-Mover. Through negotiations initiated by Olmsted, Bell sold its Prime-Mover operation to Home-O-Nize and promised the Muscatine firm up to $125,000 to help pay for start-up costs. Functioning as a separate division, the Prime-Mover Company became a stable, if unspectacular, part of Home-O-Nize and gradually expanded its line of materials-handling equipment.

An unexpected discovery was the potential profit in scrap. The aluminum leftovers from the stampings for the bottled-gas housings were saved, rather than sold for scrap, to be used in making file boxes for 3 x 5 and 4 x 6 cards, useful for collecting recipes, addresses, research notes, and many other things. As quantities of steel became available, the company began producing a combination storage and filing cabinet called a Unifile. In short order a variety of office products — as many as forty-two in 1953, more than ninety in 1955 — were rolling out of the Muscatine factories. But not one kitchen cabinet was assembled. The early dream faded as Home-O-Nize concentrated on penetrating the crowded and competitive office products industry.

The company landed in what was called "the middle market" where the buyers expected sturdy, functional, and economical products without costly frills. Soon it was turning out a large volume of durable desks, chairs, filing cabinets, and bookcases, which attested to efficient production and consistently good workmanship. It set up its own sales organization, rather than relying on manufacturers' representatives, to improve the reliability of distribution. It further strengthened sales opportunities in 1964 when it began supplying Sears, Roebuck and Company with a separate line of files and cabinets. Then in the seventies and early eighties the company, now named HON Industries instead of Home-O-Nize, acquired six office furniture manufacturers, increasing productive capacity and adding luxury wood furniture lines.

As their company flourished, the backyard visionaries, Stanley and Hanson, realized the goals that had motivated them in 1943. One had been to provide jobs to help offset an anticipated shortage of work when men returned to civilian life from World War II. Reaching that aim was delayed for Home-O-Nize by the steel shortage, but employment rose in the fifties, exceeding 200 in 1956, at a time when Muscatine languished in the economic doldrums. A decade later the company had more than 500 workers in Muscatine. After the expansion of the seventies and early eighties, HON's employment throughout the country totaled more than 5,300.[9]

Stanley probably took greatest pride in achieving the goal of building a company dedicated to harmonious relations between the workers and their bosses. Home-O-Nize in 1947 began adjusting worker wages in line with the federal Cost-of-Living Index, becoming one of the first companies in the nation to adopt that practice. Two years later the company introduced a profit-sharing program for employees, which caused an uproar at the annual meeting because the shareholders had yet to receive any dividends on their stock. Subsequently the company added other benefits, including a retirement fund and incentive bonuses for executives.[10]

But monetary benefits were only part of what Stanley and Hanson had in mind. Both stressed employee participation, and they instituted a series of regular meetings at which company executives talked to the workers about company matters and then answered questions. This practice was introduced at other plants the company acquired through expansion. Referring to employees as "members" was another widespread practice (at Stanley Engineering, too) because, as Stanley said, the term "projects a greater sense of belonging and participation." To that end, members sat on committees writing safety rules, developing a health insurance program, and planning the company picnic.[11]

Worker rejection of union organizing appeals in Muscatine validated for Stanley the effectiveness of his "human relations" approach to gaining blue-collar loyalty. The Teamsters lost an organizing vote in 1963. Then the Machinists union began an organizing drive the following year, and the company forced the issue in 1965 by petitioning the National Labor Relations Board for an election, which the union lost. The Machinists tried again in 1971 and again failed to win majority support from the workers.[12]

More troublesome was a bitter, sometimes violent nine-week strike by Machinists union workers at the Corry Jamestown Corporation plant at Corry, Pennsylvania, in 1975, three years after HON acquired the company. The dispute ended with the two sides agreeing to an hourly wage settlement only three cents higher than the company's original offer. A shorter strike broke out in 1978 when workers rejected a contract proposal negotiated by the union bargaining committee and company representatives. After two weeks the striking workers accepted the contract.[13]

A third impulse moving Stanley and Hanson in 1943 was the "challenge to creating and managing a manufacturing company." Dissatisfied with his job, Hanson was looking for new opportunities; Stanley was searching for a diversion to satisfy his restlessness—"a new world to conquer," as he put it. Hanson, as Stanley did, divided his time between Home-O-Nize and another business, the advertising agency he started in 1945 in Moline. He was secretary-treasurer of the Muscatine company until 1952, when he became vice-president, an office he relinquished in 1965 to take a seat on the board of directors. Stanley, as president, assumed much of the management burden until 1964 when he entrusted the presidency to Stanley M. Howe and became chairman of the board; he was consulted regularly about major corporate decisions—not merely asked to ratify them—until his death.[14]

As for the shareholders, they received their first dividends, $5 per common share, in 1955. Growing and thriving, the company attracted increasing attention from investors, and in the ten years before 1985 the total return to HON's investors was the eightieth best among the Fortune 500. Sixty persons held some of the original $100-a-share stock issued four decades earlier; each share was worth $59,292 in 1985 and provided more than $1,100 a year in dividend income. Stanley drew personal satisfaction from learning that stock bought by some of his Muscatine neighbors in the forties and fifties had built new homes, put children through college, or provided retirement nest eggs.[15]

One unforeseen result of HON's success was the fortune Stanley gained from it. Stanley Engineering made him comfortably rich. HON made him a multimillionaire, one of the wealthiest men in Iowa. At the time of his death his estate was estimated between $15 million and $20 million although the actual value probably was considerably higher. His earnings from Home-O-Nize allowed Betty and him to start the Stanley Foundation in 1956, and the stock they endowed to that fresh venture grew in value to more than $20 million, providing continuing income for a variety of activities related to the peaceful solution of disputes among nations. Earnings from HON also permitted the Stanleys to help support many other causes through E & M Charities, a second foundation they formed in 1979.[16]

"We are here today only because of his tenacity," Stan Howe once said of the man he succeeded as Home-O-Nize president in 1964.[17]

"He was one heck of a persistent fellow," Arthur E. Dahl remarked of the man who first hired him as a draftsman at Stanley Engineering and then promoted him to the higher echelons of the company that became HON Industries. "If he hadn't been, that company would have gone down the tubes so fast."[18]

Stanley hated to lose. To some who knew him, including his brother Art, the tenacity and persistence others saw was really stubbornness. This dogged willfullness, by whatever term it goes, was a dominant trait in Stanley. His associates differed on whether it was a virtue or a flaw. In most of his endeavors, however, it was more of an asset than a liability. It affected not only his dealings with his associates but motivated his private assessment of himself. Behind HON's success was Stanley's determination to understand business management, and in this his tenacious self-discipline came into play, for most of what he knew about business he had learned on his own, as he had learned earlier about electrical power systems. He enjoyed managing. The product or service did not matter so much to him as the continuing test of bringing together the resources—workers, raw materials, manufacturing capacity, distribution and sales techniques—to satisfy the needs and wishes of a fickle public.

Stanley had the instincts of a gambler. Good Methodist that he was, he did not bet on horses or visit the casinos in Las Vegas, yet many of his accomplishments began as risky undertakings that more timid persons would have shunned. "Max was a true gambler" to Edward E. Jones, a HON executive who had bumped against a few gaming tables. "The true gamblers are not in Vegas; they are the risk-takers in business." Howe acknowledged that Stanley was not afraid to take long chances, such as proposing a HON move into Africa, which Howe opposed and the board blocked. Stanley's daring usually was of the calculated sort, following a logical analysis of foreseeable pluses and minuses.[19]

Choosing capable executives to lead HON's different operations probably was Stanley's most important contribution to the corporation's long-term well-being, especially for the period of expansion in the seventies. Foremost among them was Howe. He was a Muscatine boy who had been in Stanley's Boy Scout troop and Sunday School class and had worked at summer jobs at Stanley Engineering while he was an engineering student at Iowa State College. He won a scholarship to attend the Harvard School of Business. When he came home with his M.B.A. in 1948, Stanley persuaded him to join the young, struggling Home-O-Nize because he would have a chance to move up rapidly.

"Not much of a company. Not much of an office. Not much of a job. It had to be Max," Howe said by way of explaining his confidence in Stanley.[20]

Others who figured prominently in the expansion included Dahl, who headed the Prime-Mover division; Jones, who overhauled the sales system and became the first chief operating officer of the Muscatine-based HON Company when it became a corporate division; Rex Bennett, the production expert who eventually took charge of operations at the Holga Corporation in Van Nuys, California, after it was acquired by HON in 1971; Frederick S. Winn, secretary-treasurer; Phil Temple, who headed product engineering; Max Collins, who managed the various human relations programs; and three younger executives, John Axel, Ralph Beals, and Gene Waddell, who became officers in later years.[21]

They helped turn Stanley's adventure in business into an affirmation of the free enterprise system in which he believed so ardently. As he wrote in "The HON Story," the American business system "allows entrepreneurs to venture, but it does not guarantee success. It is no wonder that so many ventures fail. Success requires many things, including a marketable idea or product, competent and committed people, and good management. It also demands of entrepreneurs the dedication to overcome difficulties and the financial resources to see the new ventures through to profitability. Finally, an element of luck, or perhaps timing, is often involved. . . ."[22] Actually, luck did not figure significantly in HON's success. More important, Stanley backed his daring with perseverance and his never-say-die attitude with unwavering self-confidence. He knew how to use the force of will.

7

Finding a Cause

—

The United World Federalists gave Max Stanley growing space for the internationalist ideas he had cultivated long before World War II altered the nation's role in world affairs. For nearly two decades this relatively unknown engineer and businessman from a little city in Iowa was in the forefront of a significant postwar movement that espoused a form of international government modeled on the American federal system. Brimming with self-confidence, he moved up quickly and easily in the organization, relishing the give-and-take of the challenging company of an elite group of rich and powerful citizens. He was president of the United World Federalists (UWF), the American branch of the movement, from 1954 to 1956, and chairman of the council of the World Association of World Federalists from 1958 to 1965. He led the UWF a second time from 1964 to 1966.

Stanley gave credit to his son Dave for introducing him to federalist ideas in 1947. While Dave was at the University of Iowa, he had joined the Student Federalists and was drawn to the federalist approach to world peace. On a trip home to Muscatine he took along a copy of *The Anatomy of Peace* by Emery Reves and suggested that his father read it. Stanley did and was profoundly impressed by Reves's arguments for a world governing body with the power to enforce international law and safeguard peace, and he took seriously the author's warning that, without such a governing body, nation-states surely would soon start a war that would annihilate humankind.[1] (Jacques Leprette, long the French ambassador to the United Nations, remembered fondly the first time he met Stanley at a foundation conference at Vail, Colorado, and discovered they were "on the same wavelength," one or the other having uttered the name of Emery Reves and his book.)[2]

Stanley confirmed his new faith in October 1947 when he traveled to St. Louis for a meeting of the United World Federalists, which had been organized in February at Asheville, North Carolina, by the merger of five small groups with common convictions on a federal design for some form of world government. Cord Meyer, Jr., a former Marine captain, was elected the first president by acclamation. "Very stimulating," Stanley wrote in his journal of the St. Louis meeting. "Am convinced that U.W. F. need supporting & has fair chance of accomplishing its ends. I'm ready to go to work for it."[3]

What he would work for—always ardently, often tirelessly—was the proposition that the United Nations should be given sufficient power to prevent aggression and to control armaments. The idea of such a world-wide governing authority frequently was misunderstood, or misinterpreted. Critics contended that building up the United Nations was the first of an insidious series of moves to strip independent nations of their sovereignty. UWF, sometimes defensively, emphasized that it sought a narrowly defined prescription for strengthening of the United Nations for peacekeeping purposes; it did not believe that the international body should have power to regulate currencies, tariffs, immigration, or national domestic matters.[4]

The UWF members backed these suggested changes in the U.N. Charter: eliminate the veto power of members of the Security Council; allow eventual universal U.N. membership for all nations; establish U.N. police and military units for inspection and enforcement of disarmament; provide a more realistic and equitable voting system to replace that of "one nation, one vote"; assure that the United Nations would not interfere in the internal affairs of a nation or deprive its citizens of their national rights.[5]

Stanley was full of zeal for his new cause, and so were others in his immediate family. As he commented in a journal entry at the end of 1947, "Probably biggest news of the year is the Stanley family's all-out campaign for U.W. F."[6]

As a new year began, Stanley plunged into UWF activities: a talk to the Burlington Commercial Club; a national executive council meeting in New York; an Iowa council meeting in Iowa City; a chapter meeting in

Muscatine at which son Dave and Michael Flak of Czechoslovakia spoke; starting plans for a World Government Week in Muscatine at the end of May, an event that brought Cord Meyer to town.[7]

Art Stanley did not share his brother's enthusiasm for either world government or UWF. He was upset because his brother was spending so much time on this cause — time, as Art felt, that should have been spent with the engineering company. Art, who kept watch over the firm's financial condition, had complained earlier that Max's work with Home-O-Nize deprived the engineering operation of his services at a time when postwar construction opportunities, after the wartime hiatus, were growing dramatically. UWF became an added intrusion.

The younger brother was upset when two FBI agents came to his hotel room in Kansas City during an engineering society meeting. As he recalled the incident, the agents said the FBI was monitoring UWF as a Communist front organization, "and they were asking if Max Stanley was a commie." He assured his inquisitors that his brother "was not a subversive in any way, but the kind who gets involved in causes." Art recalled the incident as "kind of a bitter blow," reinforcing his fear that Max's UWF could be costly to the firm.[8]

UWF was never cited by any government department or agency as a subversive organization, although it remained a suspect group to some Americans when McCarthyism was considered a high form of patriotism. One UWF member, Fern Bruner, a California schoolteacher, brought suit in 1953 against a radio commentator and publisher of a Hollywood gossip magazine after he charged she was a Communist through her federalist connections. She won the case and was awarded $55,125 in damages.[9]

Stanley once demanded, and got, a published retraction from the commander of the American Legion because one of the publications of the veterans' organization had labeled UWF as "red" and "subversive."[10]

In April 1950, two and a half years after Stanley joined the federalists, he was elected president of the Iowa affiliate (he and Betty had helped start a chapter in Muscatine), and in October he was elected to the National Executive Council and then was chosen its chairman. His first meeting as presiding officer was early in December, and it was, by his account, "stormy and frustrating." He saw the members divided: "Pessimism vs optimism. Despair vs hope. Universalism vs patriotism.

Words vs action. Continued action vs war restriction." But with new leaders and a growing membership, the federalists soon experienced brighter days, more united in both spirit and mission.[11]

On his fiftieth birthday, June 16, 1954, Stanley flew to Washington, D.C., for the opening of that year's UWF assembly. Three days later he was elected president, succeeding Norman Cousins, the writer and editor of *Saturday Review.* He was reelected the next year, and he confided in his journal that he was moving in "Fast company."[12] That he was. Along with Cousins, he was rubbing shoulders with Oscar Hammerstein II, the lyricist; Robert E. Sherwood, the dramatist; Walter P. Reuther, the labor leader; Grenville Clark, a confidant of old New Deal leaders; Alan Cranston, a rising political star who would become a senator from California; and George H. Olmsted, a fellow Iowan, a former Army general, and an influential figure in the insurance industry. The National Advisory Board was made up of thirty-one prominent individuals, including a governor, a federal judge, two bishops, plus representatives from business, industry, labor, education, and the arts.

In his leadership years with the UWF, Stanley watched the organization grow to 700 chapters with 50,000 members, and with the growth came increasing respect for the organization from many government leaders. He was asked to testify in 1955 before a Senate subcommittee considering proposed revisions in the United Nations Charter. He was invited to a White House conference on "Foreign Aspects of U.S. National Security," at which the speakers included Presidents Eisenhower and Truman, Vice-President Nixon, Adlai Stevenson, Secretary of State John Foster Dulles, and his predecessor Dean Acheson. Stanley traveled to London, Paris, Amsterdam, and Copenhagen to visit federalist groups in Northern Europe and to exchange ideas with their leaders.

News reporters covered his talks, interviewed him, and sought his opinion on developments in foreign affairs. The *Seattle Times* printed a report in December 1954 in which Stanley commended President Eisenhower for submitting to the United Nations a dispute over eleven airmen held by the People's Republic of China, thus avoiding an international collision with the Communist regime. In a talk the next month in Clearwater, Florida, he invoked the name of his father's old Rainbow Division commander, noting that General Douglas MacArthur's appeal to "disarm for peace" coincided with the main goal of the UWF. In Denmark two years later, *Berlingske Tidende,* a Copenhagen daily, carried Stanley's view that the precipitate seizure of the Suez Canal by Great Britain and France, to thwart nationalization of the waterway by Egypt, had set back hopes for world government even though a U.N. emergency force was sent quickly to the region to displace British and French troops.[13]

All of this must have been heady stuff for Stanley. Yet he kept his equilibrium, no doubt because his journeys always ended in Muscatine, where he would be quickly pulled from a rarefied atmosphere by a new engineering project, a financial crisis at Home-O-Nize, or lunch with businessmen who focused on the city's well-being. He was content to keep Muscatine as the center of his universe, but he was impelled to reach beyond the provincial boundaries to satisfy his interest in the world's well-being. The federalist movement was a godsend, for it gave him a noble cause with fresh opportunities to stimulate a nimble mind.

Without the UWF experience, Stanley might not have felt motivated to start an organization to amplify many of the federalist goals, along with some of his own. The overseas work of Stanley Engineering Company, begun in 1956 in Liberia, is partly an outgrowth of the world outlook that deepened after he joined UWF. He owed much to the federalists, many of whom became fast friends as well as allies in a cause. From their meetings he learned much about group dynamics, which would be beneficial when the Stanley Foundation began underwriting conferences and educational projects on world affairs.

Most important, perhaps, the federalists gave Stanley the chance to prove his worth among a group of influential people. That, too, would be important to the development of the foundation, which directed most of its policies, especially in the early years, toward people who could have an influence on U.S. foreign policy and on U.N. affairs.

Before receding into the shadows as a federalist elder statesman, Stanley gave his presidential report to the organization's twentieth General Assembly in Washington on June 17, 1966. The world he looked at on that day was not a comfortable place, and certainly not a peaceful one. It was, in fact, dangerous, and possibly even self-destructive. It had not heeded the freely given advice of men and women of goodwill, like Stanley himself, who proffered plans for bringing a collection of unruly nations under a rule of law.

Three parts of the report merit special attention. First, there is his view of the world two decades after the end of World War II and the formation of the United Nations Organization:

> . . . The fragile unity of the great powers at the close of World War II has collapsed, weakening the foundations of the United Nations. The great powers are divided by ideology and cold war. The collapse of western colonialism has given birth to many new nations, each jealous of its sovereignty. Flames of nationalism are fanned by ideological and racial hatreds. Numerous wars have been fought in the last two decades. Asia is in an uproar with war in Vietnam and a surging China with nuclear devices. Americans fight and die on that far-off continent. Millions of men bear arms. Nuclear stockpiles are rated in terms of overkill. Nations can neither keep peace nor guarantee security. The United Nations is impotent against the great powers, and its peacekeeping efforts among lesser powers are shackled by financial and procedural differences. The world's population explodes. Poverty and hunger persist, spawning unrest and revolution in their wake. Economic and social development stagnates in many of the new nations while the world pours $140 billion a year into military establishments. Indeed it is a different world, and the outlook is grim and ominous.[14]

The words could be transformed without difficulty into a litany of the despairing. What had happened to the confident expectations inspired by the founding of the United Nations? Why had the leaders of the great powers engaged in confrontation rather than cooperation? Why were the old national prejudices allowed to trample reasonable arguments for enforceable world law, arms control, and a strengthened United Nations?

The federalists did not need to look far for reasons to feel discouraged. The 1960 presidential campaign had intensified Cold War anxieties, with John Kennedy pounding away at Richard Nixon over a nonexistent "missile gap" in the Eisenhower administration's defense policy. (As William L. O'Neill has wryly observed, "It was typical of President Eisenhower that his greatest achievements were all negative. He ended the Korean War, entered into no new ones, and kept military spending down. People were grateful for the first, took the second for granted, and, often as not, attacked him for the third.")[15] By the midsixties, U.S. intervention in the Vietnam War had spawned not only political turmoil in this country but social unrest and cultural alienation. What was loosely called a peace movement was actually a chaotic alliance of anti-war groups, some of which wanted U.S. troops withdrawn from South-east Asia, while a few sought an accommodation with North Vietnam, and others demanded the impeachment of government officials responsi-ble for carrying on an "illegal" war. Few of these groups had any long-range goals for attaining international peace, and seldom did they join forces with such old-line organizations as the American Friends Service Committee or the Women's International League for Peace.[16]

After letting his fellow federalists sample despair, Stanley pointed them toward the familiar UWF goals, stressing that "the urgency to replace anarchy with law is as desperate as ever. Nothing that has oc-curred since World War II has lessened it one iota. On the contrary, events since World War II have harshly underlined the need." He reminded them that nationalism, racial prejudice, religious hatred, ideological conflict, and war are products of human devising. "What man has wrought, man can overcome — if possessed of adequate wisdom and determination," he said before calling up visions of a peaceful planet with disarmed nations served by a world parliament and world courts.[17]

Finally, Stanley offered advice to help rejuvenate UWF, both in terms of its activities and in its appeal to a younger generation. Flexibil-ity was one injunction: Let loose of rigid, doctrinaire positions. Only recently, he said, had UWF "grudgingly" acknowledged that the United Nations might be strengthened and improved by evolutionary develop-ments rather than by amendments to its charter. He suggested that arms control proposals should not be dismissed out of hand merely because they did not satisfy UWF's aim of general and complete disarmament.

Next in importance to eliminating war, he continued, was social and economic development, a subject virtually ignored by UWF although it drew increasing attention among U.N. leaders. He was critical, too, of the organization's "narrow, national" view of global changes, especially a hesitancy "to challenge our government's archaic China policy." And, he asked, while holding aloft the prize of world peace, "May not security and freedom be important and compelling benefits?"

The talk, or report, is important not so much for its content as for what it shows of Stanley's way of approaching global problems. His analysis of the world's troubles was not original, nor was it particularly incisive on critical developments. Yet it furnished a backdrop for ad-vancing or endorsing possible solutions, some of which leapt UWF con-sensus, State Department policies, and the conventional wisdom of the

Eastern foreign policy establishment. Many persons who are familiar with Stanley's views on international relations called him a realistic idealist, or an idealistic realist. Others spoke of his pragmatic nature. The three elements were evident in his status report to the UWF: the realistic appraisal of unpleasant world conditions, the idealist's fidelity to the organization's first principles, and the pragmatic willingness — perhaps even desire — to seek new or different solutions within the federalist framework, which for him remained structurally sound.

Stanley may have felt a strong urge to reaffirm UWF goals because many of his allies from the early days of the federalist cause had given up on the organization (his son Dave was one of them, dropping his membership in 1964). Stanley never left, although he became less active in later years as he concentrated more of his time and energy on the foundation he and his wife had set up in 1956. His will left $50,000 to the World Federalist Association.[18] In the foundation's formative period he occasionally devised ways to link the two organizations on certain endeavors, but he dropped such connections when the foundation gained a desired stature of its own while the American federalists lost vigor and influence in the seventies.[19]

He was distressed, of course, by the decline of UWF or, as it later was called, the World Federalists USA. Speaking to the 1971 assembly of WFUSA in Boston, he said bluntly that the organization was "feeble and faltering." He was upset by "dissension," and he suggested that the remedies proposed as a cure "are no more than pills and ointment when surgery may be required." Yet he kept the bond, insisting at the end of his talk that "the goal for which the United World Federalists was created twenty-five years ago remains vital and essential."[20]

8

To Fulfill Visions

Willard D. Archie, the longtime editor of the *Shenandoah Sentinel,* once spoke of Max Stanley as "audacious," mentioning his activities with the United World Federalists and the international conferences sponsored by the Stanley Foundation.[1] It was an apt description of a native of little Corning (as Archie was, too), who had by the force of his own will become an esteemed figure among influential American and United Nations diplomats and many others who strove for the causes he supported or advocated.

An audacious person is a daring sort, one most likely to delight in improvising, and Stanley did a great deal of that as he led the foundation to a respected place among the many organizations, committees, and other groups concerned with the multitude of issues related to peacekeeping. In this way, as Bill Wickersham observed, Stanley was instrumental in "legitimizing and developing programs for the study of peace," which spawned growing interest in what now is called conflict resolution, dealing with disputes on a community scale as well as among nations. Wickersham, once a foundation staff member and later the executive director of the World Federalists Association, attributed Stanley's influence not only to a broad knowledge of peace-related subjects but to being both "the meticulous engineer and manager" and "the visionary planetary citizen."[2]

Lauren Soth, retired editor of the editorial pages of *The Des Moines Register,* likened Stanley to Paul Hoffman, David Rockefeller, and a number of other prominent business executives who divided time after World War II between government assignments and their corporate responsibilities. With them, Stanley stood in the progressive wing of the Republican Party, which advocated greater international trade and cooperation among nations. But in the immediate postwar years Stanley was unknown in the higher political circles in Washington, so he set his own course—unique for the times—through the Stanley Foundation.[3]

More than Stanley Consultants or HON Industries, the foundation was an extension of its leader. He was in full command there, something that was harder for him to be as the two corporate enterprises grew in size and scope, requiring the dispersal of day-to-day operating authority. At the foundation he could run the show completely, choosing the topic for a conference, selecting the guests, and picking the wines for the dinners. Or, if he preferred, he could delegate all or part of the responsibilities to the staff. It was an enjoyable avocation.

Two passages in Max Stanley's life mark the evolution of the foundation he and Betty established in 1956 to generate more informed interest in various matters that could sustain a peaceful world community. One was a diversified appeal from the original concentration on "the decision makers and the opinion shapers," as the foundation staff came to categorize them, to a broader program that included "grassroots" projects. The other was his own philosophical journey from the American post-war ideology—the good guys vs. bad guys mindset of the Cold War period—to a more flexible, less dogmatic attitude on international relations, especially with regard to the Soviet Union and its satellites. This change is most noticeable when comparing the two books he wrote on U.S. foreign policy and international problems, *Waging Peace: A Businessman Looks at United States Foreign Policy,* published in 1956, and *Managing Global Problems,* published in 1979.

Even as the Stanley Foundation's programs expanded, they reflected his vision of the world as he thought it could become when nations recognized that they needed one another. The conferences, published reports, educational programs, and eventually Stanley's own commentaries for newspapers were largely products of his thinking or his reactions to the thinking of others. From all this one can surmise that he believed it was possible for a single individual to do something about evil in the world, whether evil was perceived as an arms buildup, disrespect for international law, or indiscriminate pollution of the environment. The power and influence of one person was an idea he often talked about in appearances before college students.

Whether motivated by an expansive ego or simply assertive self-confidence, Stanley built a forum of his own devising, one organizational consensus, where he could follow his curiosity along new paths. He had felt increasingly frustrated working with the United World Federalists: the organization had admirable objectives but a scattershot method of trying to influence political decisions. He wanted to have a more direct impact on those who made policy, and through the foundation he opened new channels for dialogue on global issues.

The foundation, which took form from a suggestion by Stanley's son Dave, was dedicated to research and education in international relations, particularly on policy issues affecting peace. In the simplest terms, the foundation stood for "a secure peace with freedom and justice," a phrase Stanley recited like a petition in a familiar prayer. He and his wife and three children made up the foundation's board of directors, which met for the first time on December 24, 1956. (Board membership still is composed of Stanley family members.)

The foundation was begun with $250 in cash from Stanley and 160 shares of Home-O-Nize common stock (valued at about $10 a share). When Stanley died in 1984, the foundation had accumulated assets of nearly $20 million, thanks to the success of HON Industries. (The foundation's net worth was nearly $30 million at the end of 1987.) Although Stanley realized tax benefits by establishing the foundation, he maintained that "economic motives were not the impelling reason for starting it."[4]

In its early years the foundation concentrated mainly on giving scholarships to high school and college students and donating funds to a number of charitable, educational, and religious organizations with international programs.

Through friendship with Tom Slick, Stanley saw opportunities for influence by sponsoring conferences that would bring together government officials and prominent citizens to talk about world affairs. Slick, who had made a fortune in oil, was acquainted with numerous leaders in both business and politics, and he suggested that Stanley join in arranging a conference to discuss a long-term "strategy for peace." Plans for such a meeting in 1958 failed, but Slick succeeded two years later in gathering eighty-some participants at Arden House in Harriman, New York. This was the first Strategy for Peace Conference, which was to become a staple of the Stanley Foundation after Slick died in an airplane accident in 1962.[5]

World federalists from many nations met in San Francisco in 1965 in conjunction with a twentieth anniversary celebration for the United Nations. Stanley, who was president of the American federalists, planned a conference to focus on the United Nations of 1975, and he invited world leaders and scholars to talk about the world body's strengths and weaknesses. This was the origin of the foundation's annual meetings on the United Nations of the Next Decade.

In time, the foundation sponsored from six to eight conferences a year, most of them involving persons who were decision makers and opinion shapers. Such conferences were, and still are, the cornerstone of the foundation's activities. They gave Stanley and his family occasions to become acquainted with many of the people who figured in the outcome of international political decisions. They were representatives to the United Nations, State Department officers, congressmen, scholars familiar with the U.N. or with U.S. foreign policy, and business executives, educators, editors, and directors of other foundations with special interests in international affairs.

These meetings, over which Stanley usually presided, were commonly moved forward in an informal style, without prepared speeches or papers. Through open discussion Stanley hoped the participants would come up with fresh ideas to break diplomatic deadlocks or to surmount sterile nationalistic thinking. "Misinformation is dangerous," he once said. "Let's clear up the misunderstandings."[6] To relax his guests' inhibitions, Stanley promised them anonymity when their comments appeared in the published report of a discussion. The settings helped, too, removing participants from workaday surroundings and bringing them to secluded conference centers, college campuses, or resorts with scenic vistas.

The foundation occasionally joined forces with like-minded organizations to sponsor seminars pointing to mutual goals. One such session was a foreign policy forum in December 1983 with the Kennan Institute for Advanced Russian Studies. Later the same month the foundation lent backing to the Iowa Inter-Church Forum for a conference of religious leaders who prepared a "pastoral message on the challenge of peace" for members of their churches. In the preceding year the foundation joined the medical and nursing schools at the University of Iowa for a conference on nuclear war and health. Over the years Stanley also was willing to arrange special meetings to help generate support for particular proposals coming before the United Nations General Assembly.

The gatherings produced an ongoing series of reports that were mailed to congressmen, government officials, editors, educators, and others deemed influential. In addition, the foundation published other materials, most notably a series called Occasional Papers, most of which were written by scholars and other specialists in international relations. The series was begun in 1972 after four publishers rejected an article Stanley had written to propose U.N. management of the environment, so he published it through the foundation.[7]

As the years passed and the great powers continued their ideological posturing, Stanley realized that he should stretch the scope of the foundation's activities. It was not enough to reach influential people, many of whom had become tied to the status quo, so Stanley sought to broaden the potential audience for the foundation's messages.

From 1969 through the midseventies the foundation helped arrange several student conferences in Iowa. None produced the continuity Stanley hoped for. His main push was for the World Order Studies program at the University of Iowa, for which the foundation supplied $200,000 in "seed money." In 1975, after a three-year experiment, the foundation withdrew its financial support because the university had not integrated the program into its administrative structure and its course offerings.[8] (During the same period Stanley did not fare much better with his personal appeals to United Methodist bishops, administrators, and educators for church-sponsored peace programs.)

The foundation had more success with Project Enrichment, which stemmed from an idea of Betty Stanley's. It began modestly in the late sixties in the Muscatine school system, with the foundation providing money to buy books and films on international relations. The foundation also sponsored a visit to Muscatine by astronaut Scott Carpenter. Over the years, first under the direction of Carol Lowthian and then Jan Drum, Project Enrichment was developed into a model program for schools and community organizations to help children learn about the world, its peoples, and the need for international cooperation.

Outreach, a program with broad possibilities for cooperative ventures with other organizations, took form in the early eighties. Stanley saw it as a way of building public support and interest in the Midwest while working with business, labor, educational, and religious groups, as well as with organizations avowedly dedicated to peace, disarmament, and related causes. By then the foundation had the resources, both in money and in staff, to expand its activities to a wider public, especially in the Midwest.

Stanley's entry into mass communications was a dramatic and unexpected turn in foundation activities, since he had no experience and little knowledge of publishing and broadcasting. His intimate involvement in his son Dave's political campaigns evidently had heightened his awareness of the mass media impact on public opinion. It was knowledge that served him well as he expanded the orbit of foundation activities.

"Serendipity," he once wrote, brought him to publishing through the renewal of a friendly relationship with Alfred Balk, who had been an Eagle Scout when Stanley was the scoutmaster of Troop 127.[9] He came to Stanley's attention again in the late sixties when he was feature editor of *Saturday Review,* the magazine edited by Norman Cousins, Stanley's friend from the United World Federalists.

In 1973, after four years as editor of *Columbia Journalism Review,* Balk was part of a syndicate trying to resurrect *Atlas World Press Review,* which had died of financial ills two years earlier. Balk approached Stanley about helping finance a revived *Atlas* so that interested Americans could continue reading articles, editorials, and book reviews condensed or reprinted from foreign publications. Stanley agreed to join a group of investors and promised to put up $50,000. The magazine resumed publication in May 1974 under the direction of John A. Millington, who had held several positions in the business operations of Time Incorporated. By the year's end *Atlas* was again in financial trouble, and Balk was called upon to try negotiating a takeover by Stanley.

As 1975 began, Max and Betty Stanley became owners of a magazine, which they eventually called *World Press Review,* dropping Atlas from the name. They paid a token $10,000 for the magazine while agreeing to assume substantial debts, and if they turned it into a profitable venture (not likely, in Stanley's estimation), they would pass on to the former owners a 20 percent cut of pretax earnings from the first four years.[10] Balk was named editor and publisher. Three years later ownership was transferred to the Stanley Foundation, permitting tax and postal savings because of its nonprofit status. The magazine has continued to operate from offices in New York, separate from other foundation functions directed from Muscatine.

"It was phenomenal that the Stanleys did this when there was no rush in the East to save the magazine," Balk said. The magazine offered

Stanley a new challenge, and he soon was thinking in terms of turning it into an international magazine, rather than concentrating on an American audience. But both he and Balk underestimated the amount of money that would be needed, and neither foresaw the severe financial jolts an economic downturn would cause in the publishing industry.[11]

Writing in the tenth anniversary issue, Stanley summarized his reasons for backing the magazine:

> Years of study and activity in foreign affairs persuade me that extreme provincialism greatly inhibits efforts to maintain a strong, enlightened U.S. foreign policy responsive to the problems and opportunities of our increasingly interdependent world. Most of our citizens as well as many of our officials have little knowledge of the countries beyond our borders—their peoples, cultures, resources, problems, and aspirations. *World Press Review*'s role is to shrink this information gap and thereby overcome our tendency to see others as we see ourselves.[12]

Balk said Stanley never intruded on the editorial side of *World Press Review* and never sought to use the magazine as a platform for his own views. "He believed strongly in what we tried to do," Balk added. "He felt there was a need for it. He, as I, was disappointed when the old *Saturday Review* died, living on in name only. He felt that *World Press Review* would help fill the void."[13]

But the magazine was a financial drain on the foundation, although circulation rose gradually from 100,000 to 150,000 and advertising revenue improved. Stanley was willing to cover losses of $400,000, but he was distressed when the subsidy—the difference between expenses and revenue—exceeded $750,000, as it did in 1982 and two years thereafter. To help offset losses in the summer of 1982 he sold 20,000 shares of HON stock at $13 a share, only to see the price start to rise, eventually reaching $45 a share. In a conversation with James Towers in 1983 Stanley said, "If we had it to do again, I'm not so sure we would have done it. There was more subsidy involved than we anticipated. We didn't know what a tough job it would be to get it where it could be self-sustaining, and it isn't there yet. . . . Why did we do it? Because we felt there was a far greater need for people in the U.S. to know what was happening in the foreign media."[14]

Stanley never backed away from the magazine's problems. There might be a retreat, but not surrender, even though success eluded him.

He was preparing for a trip to New York on Friday, September 14, 1984, the last day he wrote in his journal. One of the items: "WPR *[World Press Review]*—Face difficult situation." He and Balk conferred several times before laying out a plan to increase subscription rates to deliberately force a reduction in subscribers, possibly to about 100,000, and to consider joining a combine of magazines to improve the chances of getting more advertising.[15]

Radio was added to the foundation's activities in 1979 after a brief experiment suggested by Gordon Anderson and John Redick, both of whom were working on research projects for the foundation. Anderson, who had worked for a radio station in Kansas City, consulted the Johnson Foundation in Racine, Wisconsin, about its radio series, "Conversations from Wingspread." At the 1978 Strategy for Peace Conference, Anderson taped four interviews and sent them to fifty radio stations. About half the stations used the tapes, enough to satisfy Stanley that radio was a promising tool for reaching more people. In 1979 the foundation produced seven tapes and again got favorable results.[16]

Jeffrey Martin, who had been news director of station KWPC in Muscatine, joined the foundation in 1980 to take charge of the radio series, which was given the name "Common Ground." Broadcasting started on a regular basis that fall with thirteen half-hour programs, to which another thirteen were added before the first anniversary. To facilitate distribution Stanley agreed to put a recording studio into the lower level of the foundation building. Martin recalled how he approached Stanley one day with a request to buy about $6,000 in production equipment. Asked if that was enough to do quality programs, Martin said that what he would like to have would cost about $20,000. Without hesitating, Stanley told him to buy what he wanted. "There was no halfway measure with him," Martin said.[17]

Through satellite transmission and a tie-in with National Public Radio, "Common Ground" became available to more stations at a lower cost to the foundation. In 1983, when the number of stations carrying the series topped one hundred, the foundation spent about $52,000 on the radio operation.[18]

Most interviews and discussions aired on the series were taped at foundation conferences, a ready source of experts on foreign policy issues. To broaden the range of topics, interviewers frequently taped programs in other settings with persons familiar with refugee programs, terrorism, or world trade. Late in 1983 the series focused on presidential aspirants prior to the Iowa political caucuses the following year.

For a man who liked to keep control of most things done in his name, Stanley was easygoing about "Common Ground." As long as the programs furnished the public with different points of view, Stanley was willing to give considerable leeway to the producers. He appeared twice on "Common Ground," both times in 1981, once for an interview on his foreign policy views and then in a discussion with Representative James Leach of Iowa and a Soviet diplomat.[19]

Not until ten years after the foundation was organized did Stanley appoint an executive director. He was Thomas B. Manton, who had earned a Ph.D. in Asian studies and who had lived several years in Burma. It was a fortunate choice for Stanley because Manton was acquainted with U Thant, the Burmese representative who was elected the U.N. secretary-general after Dag Hammarskjold was killed in a plane crash in 1961. Manton helped open doors for the foundation at the United Nations.

Stanley was impressed with his new associate and, faced with some vexing internal problems at SCI, he said it "is tempting" to give more attention to the foundation and Manton. But the relationship started to sour in the spring of 1968 after Manton revealed he wanted to head the Muscatine County campaign for Senator Robert Kennedy, who was seeking the Democratic presidential nomination. Stanley was deeply involved in his son Dave's campaign to gain the Republican nomination for a U.S. Senate seat. After "hours of counseling," as Stanley wrote in his journal, Manton gave up his political plans, apparently agreeing to Stanley's wish to keep the foundation free of partisan activity. But it was only a temporary concession. The two clashed in the fall when Manton showed interest in working for the Democrats (Kennedy had been assassinated in June). In one journal entry Stanley wrote, "Tom wants pay to Dec. 31 for commitment not to campaign in Iowa." Stanley, with his son in a heated contest with Governor Harold Hughes, undoubtedly was in a partisan frame of mind himself and fired Manton late in September.[20]

Three years later Manton, then in New York as chairman of the United Nations Committee for New China Policy, wrote to Stanley saying he "would like to bury the hatchet." Acknowledging the "mutually unpleasant and painful" incidents of 1968, Stanley replied, "I have never made a practice of nursing grudges against any individual, and I have none against you." He added that he saw no reason why they could not work cooperatively "if the occasion rises."[21]

To replace Manton as the foundation's executive director, Stanley selected Jack Smith, who had been HON's personnel director four years. Smith, who had a B.A. in economics ("without one hour in political science, without one hour in international relations," he once said) may have lacked Manton's academic background and his U.N. connections, but he quickly formed an effective bond with Stanley. Referring to himself as an "untried manager," Smith said Stanley was "the one who put more confidence in me than any one in my life."[22]

Smith helped lead the foundation through an expansive period and remained in the director's post until Stanley decided to reorganize foundation functions in 1983. Smith then became senior associate director assigned to external relations, Susan Koehrsen became associate director for project management, and Jeffrey Martin became associate director of policy and issues. Two years earlier Stanley had brought in Kenton Allen, a former executive director of the Iowa Republican Party, as administrative director.

Stanley did another audacious thing when he wrote a book about international relations, *Waging Peace: A Businessman Looks at United States Foreign Policy.* It was published in 1956, the same year he and Betty set up the foundation. At the time Stanley was a relatively obscure Iowa engineer and manufacturer who thought he had some things to say to the nation's political leaders and foreign policy experts. Many of his world federalist friends agreed with his thinking, and UWF chapters throughout the country helped promote sales of the book, which was praised in publicity blurbs by Senator Hubert Humphrey of Minnesota, editor Norman Cousins, John Cowles, publisher of the *Minneapolis Star and Tribune,* and other prominent men.

Waging Peace revolved around a seven-point program that, in Stanley's words, "could provide a powerful long-range national policy for the United States." The points were:

> 1. Maintain military strength. Continue our present program which has been identified as a "posture of strength." It involves maintenance of adequate military strength, in cooperation with our allies, to deter communist expansion and aggression. . . . It cannot be abandoned until we have achieved a rule of law in the world and have provided other methods for preventing aggression.

2. Lend a helping hand. Continue and expand our support of programs aimed at building a better world and creating a stronger world community. Broaden our efforts to include activities of private enterprise, nongovernmental organizations, our government, and the United Nations. Commit a portion of potential savings from disarmament to an expanded program of technical assistance and economic development.

3. Use the United Nations. Decide that the responsibility for maintaining a secure peace must be delegated to the United Nations. Use and support the present United Nations to the maximum even as we seek changes to improve it.

4. Establish a rule of law. Recognize law as the keystone of order, peace, and freedom. Make the United Nations responsible for establishing a rule of law adequate to control all armaments, prevent aggression, and aid peaceful settlement of disputes.

5. Obtain universal enforceable disarmament. . . . Recognize that enforceable disarmament and world law are intertwined, and that each needs the other.

6. Strengthen the United Nations. Revise the Charter. . . . Give the United Nations the powers and the structure to administer and enforce a rule of law to control armaments and to prevent war. . . .

7. Speak for man. Champion the eternal principles of individual freedom and demand an end to the wanton and stupid destruction of war. . . . [23]

Stanley's propositions furnished familiar themes for the participants at foundation conferences, particularly points 4, 5, and 6 which, put together, called for a United Nations with the power to make binding laws, to enforce disarmament, and to protect individual freedom.

Stanley's analysis of world conditions was influenced by the realities of the Cold War of the fifties, which inspired ominous fears of East-West confrontations. The book is dotted with harsh criticism of the Soviet Union while President Dwight Eisenhower is praised for having "done more than any other American to assure the world of America's peaceful intentions." Stanley advised against any relaxation of military supremacy, he expressed anxiety about an "atoms for peace" policy that easily could be turned into "atoms for war," and he warned—a year before the Soviets launched their Sputnik—about the military threat of space satellites. [24]

Stanley's views had changed dramatically and matured considerably by the time he wrote *Managing Global Problems,* which was published by the foundation in 1979. By then he had seen Hiroshima, which to him was a silent, somber rebuke of the great powers as they accumulated their vast stores of nuclear weapons. Putting ideological arguments behind him, he examined U.S. policies as critically as he did those of the Soviets and was not hesitant about praising the Kremlin leaders when he felt they deserved it. In one passage, for instance, he commended them for demonstrating "a desire for arms limitation, if not reduction," a desire that he did not find so evident in Washington.[25]

In the interval between the two books Stanley had met many representatives of the Soviet Union at the United Nations and at numerous conferences. He came away from the 1969 Dartmouth Conference with the feeling that the Soviets, who had fourteen participants there, were "willing to cooperate more," especially on arms control and Middle East problems. He and Betty traveled to different parts of the Soviet Union during a three-week trip in June 1972, and they returned home with happy memories of the people they had met, including members of a Moscow peace organization who invited Stanley to give a talk at one of their meetings.[26]

Managing Global Problems shows a breadth of concern that appeals for recognition of "today's predicaments." Stanley had not forgotten about peace and security, but he insisted that developing methods of settling international conflicts had to be integrated with workable solutions to the other challenging tasks he saw: improving the world economic order through expanded trade and commerce; broadening economic and social development in the Third World; stabilizing population growth to better manage the earth's resources; protecting the biosphere; extending human rights to all peoples.[27]

Stanley pointed out that the resolution of all international problems, even under a U.N. umbrella, was dependent on the political decisions of national governments. But he was not hopeful about affirmative American responses. He warned:

> Nationalism unduly influences our policies and those of nearly all nations. But in the United States, excessive nationalism takes on larger dimensions. It combines with our great economic and military power, long-standing self-sufficiency, self-righteous conviction that we are chosen people, and an unbridled national pride sometimes resembling arrogance. We have little confidence in world organizations and are extremely hesitant to admit the need for more global and regional solutions. . . .

Two typically American attitudes also handicap our leadership. One is our frustrating tendency to export our political, economic, and social systems without suitable adaptation to local conditions of other nations. The second is our insistence upon instant solutions; we overlook the vital importance of pursuing objectives patiently.[28]

The second book supplied the foundation with a broad agenda for the years beyond his lifetime. At the United Nations, William B. Buffum, while he was under-secretary-general of political and General Assembly affairs, kept a well-thumbed copy near his desk as a prospectus of what might be.

9

Global Causes

Max Stanley was an outsider on the inside of the United Nations organization. From the midsixties on, he was a respected figure at the U.N. headquarters on the East River in Manhattan largely because of the conferences he arranged to generate an interplay of ideas on various international causes. His friends there were truly a global blend, not only from the Western countries, but from the Eastern bloc, the Arab world, the Orient, Africa, and Latin America. He was invited to address the General Assembly, to testify before committees studying specific issues, and, as former Under-Secretary-General William B. Buffum put it, "to provide a unique contribution to greasing the wheels of U.N. diplomacy." By that Buffum meant that Stanley often was enlisted to help expedite progress on a particular concern, usually by setting up special conferences outside the U.N. structure for key diplomats.[1]

Stanley was unswerving in his devotion to the United Nations, even when he was doubtful about some of its actions, and he was unstinting in his support of the delegates who worked diligently trying to attain global cooperation and understanding. From its founding, the United Nations remained a beacon for him — the clearest, steadiest light by which men and women of goodwill could be guided on the path to world peace. He voiced his hope for the United Nations — for the idea as much as for the institution — in a toast he gave at a United Nations of the Next Decade Conference at Vail, Colorado, on June 15, 1974:

> May it grow in accomplishment.
> May it cope more successfully with our many global problems.

> May it become a true center to harmonize the actions of na-
> tions.
> May it strengthen the bonds of friendship and cooperation
> among all peoples even as the spirit of friendship has permeated this
> conference.
> May we each, in our own way, but in common spirit, contribute
> to these ends.

"He was genuine, he was independent, he was committed," said Buffum, who was in charge of the United Nations' political and General Assembly affairs. "You couldn't go to one of these conferences without knowing that here was a man who believed in international coopera-tion. . . . He had a very down-to-earth quality that lent weight to what he had to say about international cooperation. It was not theory. It was an attempt to use management skills to help find solutions to global problems."[2]

Jeremy J. Stone, director of the Federation of American Scientists, saw Stanley personifying "the Middle West view of international rela-tions in which the U.S. could, and should, do its bit to straighten the world out, no matter how hard the task and how painfully slow. Perse-verance was Max's strong suit."[3]

"I think the U.N. was Max's church," said John R. Redick, a Uni-versity of Virginia professor who formerly was the Stanley Foundation's research director. "I think he looked upon the U.N. as a religion. . . . He was a believer, deeply. Sometimes believers don't see the weaknesses of the institution, but I think he did see the weaknesses."[4]

These comments furnish the dimensional characteristics of Stanley's approach to the United Nations, and to the resolution of international disputes. His managerial skills had served him well, and he was con-vinced they could help cut through the layers of diplomacy that often blurred reality. He always carried his midwestern traits with him, and he liked to remind his friends, "The world is made up of thousands of Muscatines," presumably meaning that community-style give-and-take could solve global problems.[5] His convictions about the United Nations and its goals owed as much, perhaps more, to his personal faith in it as to the perceptible successes he saw in its deliberative work.

Stanley's conferences were unusual because of an emphasis on "fu-turism," as James Towers observed in his study of the Stanley Founda-tion. The outsider from Iowa tried to stay several steps ahead of matters on the U.N. agenda—on the proposed treaty to govern the seas, for instance, and on major disarmament initiatives—and encouraged conference participants to take a long view. Thus the foundation did not merely react to events but attempted to induce planning to prepare for foreseeable problems. Homer A. Jack, a Unitarian-Universalist minister who represented the World Conference on Religion and Peace at the United Nations throughout the seventies and early eighties, credited Stanley with projecting "frontier U.N. issues" from the foundation to other like-minded nongovernment organizations. "And without much fanfare or publicity," Jack added.[6]

Trying to evaluate the foundation's impact on international relations is an ambiguous task, as are most attempts to assess the effects of diplomacy generally. "It was frustrating to him, never finding a way to measure success," Jack Smith of the foundation staff said of Stanley's own efforts to grade the conferences. "It was too imprecise. There was no way to quantify. That was difficult for an engineer and a businessman. He got good feedback though. Participants told him how important it was to have good relations with so-and-so, how important it was to discuss such-and-such. Finally, he realized that change would be slow."[7]

Foundation conferences preceded, and apparently had an effect on, the formation of the U.S. Arms Control and Disarmament Agency; the creation of the U.N. Environment Program; the lengthy negotiations over the proposed Law of the Sea Treaty; citizen and congressional efforts to promote the peaceful uses of outer space, long before "Star Wars" aggravated international tensions; and General Assembly deliberations on Global Negotiations, a proposal that sought to improve the economic balance between the industrialized nations and the Third World.[8]

Jacques Leprette, representing France, was party to the knotty negotiations preceding the United Nations' first special session on disarmament: "Everything that could be said on the subject of disarmament had been. All that remained was to convince those who were running the show. A seminar organized by the Stanley Foundation . . . offered the opportunity to do so. It was at the end of a series of long and friendly discussions . . . that I found myself amongst a small group that drafted the principles which served as an introduction for the final act of the Assembly. The situation was partially unblocked."[9]

The introductory statement, adopted by the General Assembly on

June 30, 1978, points to a "final objective" of "general and complete disarmament under effective international control," but recognizes that "the immediate goal is that of the elimination of the danger of a nuclear war and the implementation of measures to halt and reverse the arms race and clear the path towards lasting peace."[10]

A year before the U.N. special session, participants at the foundation's United Nations of the Next Decade Conference in San Juan del Rio, Mexico (Leprette was there), discussed multilateral disarmament and how it might be dealt with in the General Assembly. (Kosta Tsipis, an international security specialist at the Massachusetts Institute of Technology, considered Stanley one of the best informed Americans on disarmament matters, but one of the least known because "he wasn't flashy.")[11] In his opening remarks Stanley left no doubt about what the result should be:

> Nothing less than a world without war is an acceptable, ultimate goal. The death, destruction, and trauma of war and the costs of preparing for it are no longer tolerable. Even though it seems far removed, general and complete disarmament (GCD) is the only disarmament objective consistent with a world without war. With GCD, national armaments and military establishments would be reduced to levels consistent with internal security needs.

He prefaced those remarks by pointing out that nations were spending

> . . . nearly $400 billion (U.S.) annually on military establishments. The needs of developing nations and the mounting domestic needs of the more developed countries go unsatisfied. Scientists create new weapons systems to better exterminate people, devastate cities, and jeopardize survival of the human race. Meanwhile, vital research and technology are shortchanged — how to cope with shortages of energy, food, and other resources; how to protect and enhance the environment; and how to contribute to a higher physical quality of life. . . . Future historians will no doubt describe these early decades of the nuclear era as a time of hazardous folly.[12]

The assembly's "final objective" and Stanley's "ultimate goal" remains elusive to the nations of the world. Despite the setbacks and frustrations, Stanley "never despaired," said Leprette, who had fond memories of his friend from the American Midlands. "No difficult situation, no discouraging turn of events, dissuaded him from an absolute confidence in the capacity of human beings to find solutions to problems, as long as the intellect is informed and the character well formed. Pessimism did not interest him. Hesitant people and professional skeptics tired him."[13]

The proposed Law of the Sea drew Stanley's attention throughout the seventies. Early in 1972 he submitted his views to Congressman Donald Fraser of Minnesota, who headed a House subcommittee studying the matter. Appealing for United Nations supervision of ocean management, Stanley observed, "The coming age of massive development of the resources of the seabeds could precipitate a competitive scramble not unlike the colonial exploitation of Asia, Africa, and the New World by European powers. The ocean bed could be segmented by the major industrialized maritime powers in a pattern similar to the present partitioning of land surfaces."[14]

He had broadened his concern by the time he opened a foundation conference on "Ocean Management and World Order" at South Egremont, Massachusetts, in July 1972, where most of the participants were from foreign countries. "Slowly the world awakens to the urgent needs of its oceans," he said. "The realization grows that the fragile marine environment is now damaged by pollution and enlarging demands for its natural resources. Exciting potentials for the use of oil and other mineral resources of the seabeds have been unveiled by modern technology. The nuclear confrontation has given new dimensions to the oceans' military uses. The oceans can no longer be taken for granted. Our common interests call for rational ocean management."[15]

The foundation followed up with another oceans management conference in January 1974 at Airlie House, near Warrenton, Virginia. Most of those invited to that meeting were U.S. senators, congressmen, and members of congressional staffs. Among the others were Samuel Levering, a member of the U.S. Advisory Committee on the Law of the Sea and the secretary of the U.S. Committee on the Oceans, and Louis Sohn, then teaching international law at Harvard. Later, Levering and Sohn joined to urge Stanley to set up a special meeting to focus on the economic effects of deep-sea mining of manganese nodules. The foundation arranged that meeting for January 1976, and it became the first of five special meetings touching on different parts of the negotiations for an oceans accord. Six months later, another group of conferees explored the problems expected from the formation of an international seabed authority, including the distribution of voting power (the Western powers were opposed to a one nation–one vote plan). How an international authority might control development of the oceans' riches was the subject of meetings in February 1977, followed in December by a broader range of topics facing the negotiators. A conference the next month centered on financial arrangements: Who will get what and how much from the seas?

After seven years of steady and sometimes painful progress, the Law of the Sea negotiators put together an acceptable treaty, which was set for a vote early in 1981. But after President Ronald Reagan took office in January, the U.S. negotiators from the Carter years, headed by Republican Elliot L. Richardson, were dismissed abruptly and replaced by a new team, which apparently had no purpose other than to vote against the treaty. The Reagan administration's repudiation of the oceans treaty was the first in a long series of broken agreements affecting international relations.[16] Without American cooperation the treaty would be a hollow document. To an exasperated Max Stanley, the outcome confirmed his dark suspicion of how President Reagan might cause upheaval in foreign affairs. After more than three decades of open diplomacy in the United Nations, the United States appeared headed for an interval of insular excess in which the United Nations would be either quietly ignored or loudly abused.

Although Stanley was willing to carry water for U.N. causes, he never relinquished control over the foundation-sponsored conferences on U.N. matters. After conferring with associates at the foundation and friends at the United Nations, Stanley chose the conference topic, set the agenda, and picked the participants, whose expenses were paid by the foundation (spouses were invited to the United Nations of the Next Decade Conferences). When a conference was under way, Stanley gave the opening remarks, presided over the roundtable discussions, and wrote the "Chairman's Observations" for the published report. Singapore's Ambassador T. T. B. Koh was impressed "by how much homework Max had done, by his grasp of the subject, by his ability to synthesize different points of view and to suggest practical solutions to some of them."[17]

Max and Betty were hosts at the dinners, for which the conferees and their spouses were rotated so all dined at least once with the Stanleys. For the most part, though, the conferences were conducted in a casual manner that was meant to remove the participants from their normal turf. The United Nations of the Next Decade (shortened to UNND among the foundation's staff) was moved, and still is, to a different remote place each year in late June or early July; it has been held in Communist countries (Yugoslavia and Romania) as well as in Western Europe, Canada, Mexico, and various sites in the United States. The meeting places usually have swimming pools, hiking trails, tennis courts, and possibly nearby golf courses. The conferences on United Nations Procedures (now broadened to United Nations issues) are held every spring, usually at a site within easy driving distance from New York City.

Although Stanley ran structured discussion sessions, governed by his agenda, he tried to encourage informality, with the participants dressing in casual clothes. They were urged to enter into the discussions as individuals, not as representatives of their nations (the conference reports distributed by the foundation list the names and titles of the participants, but do not identify who said what during discussions). Rikhi Jaipal, India's U.N. ambassador, once mentioned how grateful many conferees were for the chance "to shed our official skins and express our personal views free of the restraint of official instructions." What Stanley tried to do, he added, was "make us all realize that we have far more in common than might appear to be the case at the United Nations conferences. That is indeed a great and desirable and necessary achievement."[18]

Stanley's efforts may be measured, to some degree, by the character of the men and women who came to his conferences. Many have become high-ranking leaders of their governments, several have earned distinctive honors or international esteem, and still others have been presidents of the U.N. General Assembly or have assumed direction of a U.N. agency, such as UNICEF's James Grant. President Corazon Aquino of the Philippines accompanied her husband, Benigno, opposition leader of their country's Senate, to a 1970 conference at Fredensborg, Denmark. (When he was assassinated in 1983, Stanley wrote a "Dear Cory" letter of condolence to her.) The Aquinos were introduced to Stanley by his friend General Carlos Romulo, the Philippines foreign minister, often a guest at Stanley meetings. Another at Fredensborg was Congressman John B. Anderson of Illinois, who would become Stanley's favorite presidential candidate ten years later. Kurt Waldheim, Austria's president, attended the 1983 United Nations of the Next Decade conference after he stepped down as the U.N. secretary-general. Others who rose to national posts include Peter Jankowitch, Austria's foreign affairs minister; Zulfikar Ali Bhutto, who was Pakistan's prime minister; Zhao Nan, vice-minister of foreign affairs for the Peoples Republic of China; Esmat Abdel Meguid, Egypt's foreign minister; Salim Salim, who has been both prime minister and foreign minister of Tanzania; Endelkachu Makonnen, Ethiopia's prime minister; and Vladimir Petrovsky, deputy foreign minister of the Soviet Union.

John Redick told of suggesting to Stanley that he invite Alfonso Garcia Robles, the brilliant, widely admired Mexican diplomat to a foundation conference. Stanley was reluctant, doubting that he would come. But when Stanley invited him to the sessions planned for Sinaia, Romania, in June 1971, Garcia Robles accepted. During the discussions, Redick said, there was a subtle, wary duel going on between the two men, both of whom could express strong opinions, buttressed by stubborn defenses and substantial egos. But their interplay, when it happened, inspired respect, which led to admiration and then to friendship.[19] Eleven years later Stanley felt pride when his friend Garcia Robles shared the Nobel Peace Prize with Alva Myrdal of Sweden for their efforts to promote disarmament.

Usually mixed with the diplomats at UNND conferences were a number of specialists in the subject under discussion. Arvid Pardo, co-author of *New International Order and the Law of the Sea,* took part in the conference on "Ocean Management and World Order." So did Mihai Bacescu, director of Romania's National Natural History Museum in Bucharest. James A. Van Allen, world renowned physicist at the University of Iowa, was a participant at the 1978 conference on "Cooperation or Confrontation in Outer Space." Others at the meeting included Herbert Scoville, Jr. of the Arms Control Association and Robert Rosenberg of the National Security Council. In short, Stanley tried to get a diverse range of knowledge and opinion to stretch every participant's thinking.

After a foundation conference on nuclear nonproliferation initiatives in Vienna early in 1980, Stanley wrote in his journal, "Much good will. Too bad we haven't decision-making power."[20] Such hopeful endings fed his desire to preside over a conference limited to U.S. and Soviet participants. What an achievement that would have been, to bring together leaders from Moscow and Washington and then watch them begin to thaw. He saw improving relations between the United States and the Soviet Union as the linchpin of world peace and security, while the nuclear arms race loomed ominously as the crucial and persistent problem of this age.

The flawed records of the superpowers in international peacekeeping furnished Stanley with a continuing theme. At the 1983 conference at Burgenstock, Switzerland, Stanley reminded the conferees that "the arms race continues unabated. Soviet-U.S. bilateral negotiations to limit or reduce nuclear weapons are now at a stalemate. The spirit of detente has given way to increasing tensions and harsh rhetoric. . . ." Those attending the conference later had an unexpected sample of the latter when a series of sharp exchanges passed across the table — uncommon behavior at a foundation conference — between Georgiy Arbatov of the Soviet Union and James Malone from the U.S. State Department while the others in the room sat in astonished silence. Stanley finally gaveled the two into silence and told them that they, along with the nations they represented, had better learn to cooperate because they had to live together on this planet.[21]

Although Stanley himself had not always refrained from the ideological cliches of the postwar period, his experiences with U.N. representatives moderated his outlook, and he began showing impatience with U.S. leaders who resorted regularly to Cold War rhetoric to inflame political feelings. That was a motive he saw for the conduct of Daniel Patrick Moynihan when he was the chief U.S. spokesman at the United Nations. Stanley complained to a friend at the State Department late in 1975 that Moynihan was "using the United Nations as a podium to talk to the conservatives of the United States rather than to deal with international affairs." Such political posturing, Stanley added, "is most detrimental to ongoing relationships of the United Nations and moderates of the Third World and our friends of the developed world." He urged that Moynihan be replaced. When the U.N. representative left voluntarily early the next year, Stanley noted the event in his journal and added, "HOORAY!!!"[22]

Over the years Stanley maintained good relations with representatives from the Soviet Union, nineteen of whom attended at least one foundation conference. But periodic moves to arrange a superpowers meeting bumped into obstacles on one side or the other, sometimes both. If only Stanley could have had his wish, if he could have succeeded in sponsoring a series of superpower meetings with a substantive consensus on disarmament and peace issues, surely he would have been nominated for the Nobel Peace Prize, which his old friend Louis Sohn said he deserved anyway.[23]

A few U.S. senators tried in the late seventies to reward Stanley with an appointment as ambassador to the United Nations, but the move was aborted when he made it clear he did not want to become embroiled in a political tempest stirred up by archconservatives.[24] The absence of diplomatic rank was no hindrance to the dauntless peace activist from Iowa. By then he had demonstrated convincingly that a person with the determination, energy, and money to work patiently and persistently for a world without war was warmly welcomed at the United Nations. Baron Rudiger von Wechmar, long the U.N. ambassador from the Federal Republic of Germany, said of him, "He will be remembered by many of us as Mr. World Peace and someone who was willing to share his time, his thoughts, and his money with others and become their spiritual leader."[25] Yes, *Mister* World Peace, and the distinction probably would have suited the bearer better than *Ambassador* Stanley. Given diplomatic credentials, Stanley would have had to surrender the freedom and independence that permitted him to be an extraordinary citizen with a personal mission to lift humanity's hopes for a secure peace with freedom and justice.

10

Community Builder

"Although Max Stanley truly was a citizen of the world, he helped build the community of Muscatine and enriched it in untold ways," the *Muscatine Journal* said in an editorial the day after his death.[1] The structure of the sentence permits a reader to infer that what Stanley did in and for Muscatine was done on time borrowed from his international interests — the afterthoughts of a man whose mind normally was focused on matters far from home. It would not be surprising to learn that many of his Muscatine neighbors perceived him mainly as a globe-trotting do-gooder bent on reforming a wicked world — a zealous evangelist of world government and international law.

Stanley, to be sure, devoted much of his time — an increasing proportion in his last fifteen years — to the Stanley Foundation and to the various offshoots of its activities. He was invited to testify before congressional and United Nations fact-finding committees. He was asked to advise or assist other nongovernmental organizations working on international issues. Yet his home remained in Muscatine, and much of his life centered on the day-to-day rhythms of the old river city. Even in his later years, when a good book and a comfortable chair must have been nightly temptations, he and Betty attended the Elks Chanters concerts, the Geneva Country Club luau parties, and the Madrigal dinners at the Muscatine Art Center. They were at the Muscatine Community College the night the Bob Roach Little Theatre was dedicated to honor an old friend, and Stanley was among the speakers at an appreciation dinner for Norbert Beckey, an insurance agent and civic leader who had been stricken with the crippling Lou Gehrig's disease. Such events are repeated year after year with slight variations in hundreds of communities throughout the Midwest. They were neither boring nor demeaning to Stanley.

In its editorial the *Journal* commended Stanley for "his leadership of the Muscatine Industrial Corporation and his and Betty's gift of the Stanley Gallery and their support of the Community Health Center." The writer added that Stanley had contributed greatly to the city through his church activities, his work with the Boy Scouts, and "through the solid examples of the good life he lived."[2]

He needed Muscatine — or a place like it. It was an anchor for him. He had not been satisfied with life in Chicago, especially the commuting by train from the suburbs to the city. When he and Betty moved to Muscatine, they soon had friends to play cards with, to go to dances with, to see at church functions.[3] Muscatine was an enlarged extension of Corning, his boyhood home, where his father and two uncles were part of the power structure, as ruling groups are now known. Stanley slipped easily into that group in Muscatine. By the forties he was a leader in the annual Community Chest campaign and was general chairman in 1945, a year in which a special War Chest was included. The next year he promoted the hiring of summer workers to supervise the city's playgrounds, and with help from the Muscatine Club he arranged a benefit basketball game that raised more than $1,100 to cover the added expenses of activity supervisors.[4] He was a regular at the Muscatine Club, later the Rotary, and at the 33 Club, where members took turns presenting papers on favorite subjects (Stanley's were usually on world affairs). He enjoyed the camaraderie of the I Club, the University of Iowa's athletic booster organization, although he once complained about the bawdy jokes of the master of ceremonies at one meeting.[5]

In Muscatine, as many persons have said, Stanley was a big fish in a little pond. In all likelihood he would have been an influential citizen in whichever city he had chosen to live. He was not one to sit on the sidelines watching others exert complete control over events that affected his life. Muscatine was small enough that he could extend the force of his personality and his thinking over a broad range of interests. There were fewer human obstacles to contend with, fewer jealousies to try to placate.

Jonathan Raban, a Londoner who was fascinated by Mark Twain's adventures on the Mississippi, stopped at Muscatine on a three-month, two-thousand-mile journey down the river from Minneapolis to New Orleans in the fall of 1979. Many of the things that impressed Raban—worthy of including in his book *Old Glory: An American Voyage*—can be traced to the farsighted accomplishments of the Muscatine Industrial Development Corporation, which Max Stanley helped organize and which he led as president in its first five years, from 1958 to 1963.

After Raban nudged his sixteen-foot boat into the Muscatine marina, he had a look around:

> The town shelved gently down to the river, an intricate, substantial place of oxblood brickwork and terra-cotta streets. One could tell at first sight that Muscatine had class. . . . a nineteenth-century river town that was in remarkably good working order. . . .
>
> Clearly, Muscatine was in possession of some secret of survival which had escaped almost every other town its size I had visited. I had assumed that slow dereliction and depopulation were the inevitable fate of such places, doomed now to squat and scrape a bare living in the long shadows of their ambitions of a century ago. There must, I thought, be something peculiarly boneheaded about Muscatine in its failure to grasp the basic principles that should have ensured its decline.
>
> The old city had aged gracefully, letting the ivy grow up its walls. At the same time it had managed to absorb a clutch of big new industrial plants which, along with the buttons, the grain elevators and the truck gardens and fruit farms on the town's rim, gave Muscatine its air of being comfortably, unflashily rich. Most towns on the Mississippi had been outfaced by the river. They'd had their boom, and then they'd dwindled, looking shabby and temporary beside the enormous drift of water at their doorsteps. Muscatine, though, had the pride of a place that had always got along fine with the river, able to match it on equal terms. . . .[6]

The next morning, under a clear blue sky and with a brisk breeze stirring the river, Raban went walking instead of sailing. On the bluffs overlooking the Mississippi he discovered an architectural treasure—an array of houses that were "glorious imaginative flights of unbridled nineteenth-century ambition." There were English Georgian homes and others that reminded him of a Byzantine onion dome, a Roman villa, a German Gothic cathedral, a Florentine palace, and something he called Steamboat Corinthian. "Geography and history," he wrote, "had been no object for the builders of Muscatine: they had cheerfully looted the world for the best and showiest of everything, from everywhere and put it up higgledy-piggledy on this wooded hill. . . . a fantastic and exhilarating display of cosmopolitanism run riot."[7]

Twenty-five years earlier Raban might have passed by, consigning Muscatine to a pile of shabby, dwindling river towns. In the early fifties the city was on an economic downslide as one pearl button factory after another closed. The city was famous for buttons, which were made of clam shells harvested from the Mississippi, but a thriving industry was losing out to plastics. Unemployment rose to 18 percent.

Attempting to reverse the erosion, the city council in the summer of 1955 approved the appointment of a twelve-member industrial commission to study opportunities for new economic growth. Stanley was named chairman. Two years later the commission carried out a fundraising drive that brought in $132,000 to finance a proposed development corporation. Although the drive fell short of its goal by about $18,000, Stanley and his associates moved ahead with plans to strengthen and diversify the city's industrial base.[8]

He persuaded Harold Ogilvie, who had owned and operated the city's first supermarket, to become executive director of the new development corporation. Working out of a basement office in the Muscatine Hotel, Ogilvie sent letters promoting the city to the heads of the Fortune 500 companies. One inquiry, from the Monsanto Corporation in St. Louis, led to the start of an ammonia fertilizer plant in 1961. Begun with forty employees, the plant had a work force two decades later of more than five hundred producing herbicides and plastics.[9]

Prospect Park, an industrial area south of the city, originated with the purchase of 200 acres by the development group. Within a few years a half dozen small businesses and industries had located in the area, which later was enlarged to about 240 acres. Many existing companies, sometimes with financial help from the corporation, bought land for expansion, put up new buildings or additions, or obtained new equipment. By the early seventies unemployment in Muscatine was under 2 percent. The city was thriving, and several home-grown firms — Bandag, Grain Processing Corporation (GPC), HON and SCI — had gained national attention, along with Monsanto and Heinz, which had big branch plants in the city.[10]

The Muscatine Chamber of Commerce honored Stanley, Roy J. Carver, L. Ransom McKee, and S. G. Stein III at a Salute to Industry dinner in the fall of 1974. Those four supplied the momentum for an economic turnaround that has been called "the industrial revolution in Muscatine." Stanley, in addition to spurring the industrial development programs, expanded Stanley Engineering and Home-O-Nize (HON). Carver turned Bandag Incorporated, a tire-retreading operation, into major competition for the old-line tire manufacturers. McKee, a teacher-turned-businessman, was a banker and organizer of three firms that processed feeds and grains. Stein, also a banker, was a founder, with Gage Kent, of Grain Processing Corporation, which grew from a World War II government alcohol plant and merged with Kent Feeds.

Muscatine, for its size, was fortunate to have industrial giants of the stature of those four men. They were responsible for turning Muscatine into a stable, industrialized community. Grain Processing Corporation was the biggest employer in the city after World War II until Home-O-Nize began rising in the office furniture market. By the late seventies the three companies — GPC, HON, and Bandag — were counted in the upper class of Iowa's and the country's industries.

Stanley and Carver attracted the most attention, at least outside of Muscatine. Both engineers, they rose from the brink of bankruptcy to convert dreams, Home-O-Nize (HON) and Bandag, into remarkable success stories and personal fortune-builders. They were as different as night and day: Stanley was reserved, taciturn, anything but a social lion; Carver was exuberant and lavish, with a free-wheeling life-style. Both were generous contributors to University of Iowa projects.

The Muscatine Health Center was an example of how the business leaders added to the city's assets. The center was proposed as a solution to a critical doctor shortage. Started as a nonprofit organization, it brought physicians into the community with the help of the University of Iowa College of Medicine, which offered adjunct faculty appointments to them. John L. Parks, a physician who was Stein's son-in-law, promoted the project with the medical college and solicited support from area doctors. Carver gave a grant to the university to finance study and planning for the center. Stanley was influential through the university foundation. His son Dick, Stan Howe, and Norbert Beckey enlisted the support of Muscatine business leaders and served on the health center board in its early years, before it became a for-profit practice.[11]

The industrial revolution in Muscatine was more than larger profits, greater productivity, and higher employment. The growth in manufacturing had beneficial results on retail trades and consumer services, a common offshoot of thriving industry, and there were cultural consequences as well. The city's flourishing plants and new businesses required an increasing proportion of skilled and professional workers. Many of them had both the incomes and the interests needed to restore the old houses that Raban admired on his brief stay in Muscatine; they backed a concert series, campaigned for better schools, helped build a new library, and worked for more recreation programs.

In such an atmosphere Betty and Max Stanley felt comfortable leaving another legacy to the city. This was the Stanley Gallery, a three-level modern structure added in 1974 to the old home on Mulberry Street that was converted into the Laura Musser Museum in 1965. The two buildings comprise the Muscatine Art Center, a complex that many larger cities might envy for the variety of its exhibits, classes, and workshops.

Stanley was proud of his hometown, and at times he eagerly showed visitors around the city. He often told friends, as mentioned earlier, "The world is made up of thousands of Muscatines." In July 1978, when the Stanley Foundation's Conference on the United Nations of the Next Decade met on the University of Iowa campus at Iowa City, Stanley arranged to bring the participants to Muscatine, forty miles east of the conference site. The visitors — about fifty of them from such countries as Egypt, Austria, Sweden, Argentina, India, and Japan — were brought to the Stanley home for coffee and then taken on a sightseeing tour of the city. Then they boarded the Kent Feeds excursion boat for a trip on the Mississippi River. Jack Smith, of the foundation, recalled how enthused many of them were to see what they presumed was a typical Midwestern city, to sail on the Father of Waters, and to get a glimpse of what one of them called "Mark Twain country."[12]

On the return trip to Iowa City the bus carrying the visitors headed into a Muscatine sunset made famous by Twain in a passage in *Life on the Mississippi*.[13] Mary Jo Stanley recited the words:

> And I remember Muscatine — still more pleasantly — for its summer sunsets. I have never seen any, on either side of the ocean, that equaled them. They used the broad, smooth river as a canvas, and painted on it every imaginable dream of color, from the mottled daintinesses and delicacies of the opal, all the way up, through cumulative intensities, to blinding purple and crimson conflagrations, which were enchanting to the eye, but sharply tried it at the same time.[14]

President William Tubman of Liberia was to have been the recipient of Muscatine's hospitality on a trip to the United States in the spring of

1968. Stanley arranged a banquet to honor the African leader with whom he had friendly relations stemming from the engineering firm's Liberian work, including the contest award for the Executive Mansion in Monrovia. First though, the Stanleys, Betty and Max, went to Washington to attend a White House dinner honoring Tubman and to take part in other affairs scheduled for the state visit. Then Tubman decided abruptly that he did not want to take a trip to Muscatine and then back to the East Coast. When they returned home, the Stanleys, disappointed but undeterred, went ahead with the black-tie dinner although the guest of honor and his entourage were not there. Unusual as the event was, it served Stanley's aim of dramatizing for his townspeople the economic benefits they derived from good relations with an African nation.[15]

Stanley's work with the Boy Scouts — fifteen years as scoutmaster of Troop 127 — took on a legendary quality in Muscatine. To get ahead at Stanley Engineering or at Home-O-Nize, community banter had it, an ambitious young man would do well to have a Boy Scout connection. Stanley picked up on the jest for his column in a 1961 issue of *Compass,* the employee publication of Stanley Engineering. He pointed out proudly that more than fifty employees and spouses had taken on scouting responsibilities. He credited those members with a "significant contribution to a worthwhile community activity."[16]

Hundreds of boys came under Stanley's influence through Troop 127, and many of them became business and professional leaders in Muscatine and elsewhere. His two sons, Dave and Dick, were among those attaining the Eagle rank. Alfred Balk, editor of *World Press Review,* was another Eagle Scout from the troop, and Stanley Howe, the top man at HON, would have obtained the honor if it had not been for a physical handicap caused by polio. Howe went on to be the adult adviser of the Explorer unit.

Scouting, of course, was only one avenue for Stanley and many of his associates to enhance community life. Stanley insisted that the organizations he headed were to be good citizens in a corporate sense, and that meant doing things for community betterment. Providing jobs was part of it, and from that flowed an array of economic benefits to retail merchants, service and professional people, and to government agencies. Another part was providing support to civic and cultural endeavors through financial gifts and voluntary help. As a result, men and women from HON, SCI, and the foundation were involved in most major undertakings in the city, from the sheltered workshop for the handicapped to local political affairs to a nine-hole expansion of the country club golf course.

Stanley reacted in a *Compass* column to criticism in the community that SCI was living on the largess of local governments. In the 1967 fiscal year, he wrote, the company had revenues totaling nearly $170,000 from the city, the water and light service, the school system, and the park commission. That accounted for 3 percent of the company's business. At the same time, the company produced a payroll of nearly $2,750,000 for members working in Muscatine. Stanley said that SCI was "deeply appreciative" of its public projects, but he added that "we return fifteen to twenty-fold" to the community for every dollar earned from such work.[17]

Relations between the city government and SCI were strained in the late seventies because of a dispute over faulty equipment used in a new wastewater treatment plant. The plant was smelly, and the wastewater treated for return to the Mississippi River failed to meet the antipollution standards of the Iowa Department of Environmental Quality. The city and Grain Processing Corporation, the main source of waste in the system, filed an $11 million lawsuit in 1978 against SCI, which designed the $16 million plant, and the general contractor and the equipment manufacturer. After protracted legal negotiations, SCI agreed in 1982 to pay the city $2.2 million as its part of a settlement. In turn the city assumed responsibility for pursuing legal action SCI had started against the contractor and the equipment manufacturer.[18]

A more rancorous public controversy broke out in the midseventies over an urban renewal plan centering on the construction of a new SCI headquarters building in downtown Muscatine. The company management at the time was considering the possibility of consolidating its Muscatine operations in a new building on land the firm owned near the city's western outskirts. But many city officials, civic leaders, and downtown merchants wanted the company to stay put, fearing that the loss of several hundred workers might imperil a number of downtown stores and eating places. The proposed solution was a city-sponsored redevelopment plan contemplating SCI's acquisition of about a quarter of a block at Iowa Avenue and Third Street for a $3 million headquarters building that would furnish a link to company functions in the Hershey and Laurel buildings, which stood at diagonal corners of the block.

The city condemned two buildings on the corner and ordered them razed. SCI submitted the only bid for the land. But Robert E. Shoemaker went to court to try stopping the project, arguing that he should have received more than the $82,500 he was awarded by condemnation for his buildings. Judge Max Werling granted a temporary injunction, but four days later he allowed the city and SCI to proceed.[19]

The judge's decision riled Dorothy Pape, and she began a personal protest against the Stanleys that lasted for several years. She and her husband ran a stationery store in one of the condemned buildings. In the spring of 1980 the Iowa Engineering Society, which was meeting in Muscatine, was invited to tour the new SCI building. Max Stanley noted in his journal the presence of "an uninvited guest"—Dorothy Pape who walked with a placard in front of the building. About a week later she appeared for the HON annual meeting carrying a sign that read, "HON STINKS—HON Unfair to Muscatine." Two and a half years later she was still angry and, as Dan Clark of the foundation recalled, when Stanley was about to lead a discussion on disarmament at a United Methodist conference at Wesley Church, she stood up to ask sarcastically how he could talk about peace after causing community discord. Stanley said nothing to her and, when none of the others responded to her, he proceeded with the topic assigned for discussion.[20]

Dorothy Pape was the most visible of the Muscatine residents who were upset about what they perceived as a slick deal between SCI and the city. Susan Koehrsen, former associate director at the foundation and a former member of the Muscatine City Council, sensed that Stanley felt hurt by the public controversies, along with the persistent sniping at his internationalist views and his older son's political activities. She saw him gradually withdrawing from leadership roles in community affairs, although he continued to exert influence behind the scenes.[21]

Harold Ogilvie and Ib Petersen, a merchant who joined the Chamber of Commerce to head its retail division, agreed that the new SCI building helped rejuvenate the downtown business district, whatever critics may have thought about the redevelopment plan. They saw it as another example of the Stanleys aiding the community, although a new building on the city's outskirts might have been easier to justify from a corporate viewpoint.[22]

So strong was Stanley's loyalty to Muscatine that he shunned suggestions to move his enterprises. Apparently the only time he seriously considered moving was shortly after the end of World War II when he and his brother talked about shifting the engineering firm to Davenport, Cedar Rapids, or possibly Newton. Newton was a way of avoiding Des Moines because they did not want to get into head-to-head competition with their friend Ken Brown and his associates. After the firm achieved national and international repute, Roy Vanek, a vice-president, and a number of key engineers tried unsuccessfully to persuade Stanley to consider putting the company headquarters in Chicago or St. Louis. A branch had been set up in Chicago and another was started in Atlanta, Georgia. Likewise, Stanley was urged to move the Stanley Foundation offices, or a branch office, to Washington, to be near the State Department and the foreign embassies, or to the United Nations neighborhood in New York. He said no, insisting that the foundation would make a greater impression, especially on foreign diplomats, by being a solo voice from the American Midlands rather than part of a chorus of advocates and pleaders from Washington or New York.[23]

Betty Stanley suggested moving to Iowa City after her husband relinquished direct management of Stanley Consultants and HON Industries. She reasoned that they spent a great deal of time there attending concerts and other performances at Hancher Auditorium, seeing exhibits at the art museum, and going to football and basketball games. But he dismissed the idea, saying he did not care to live in a college town.[24]

Stanley nourished his boyhood roots by returning periodically to Corning for family doings and high school class reunions. It was a day or two after one of those reunions that Stanley met Roger Lande, his lawyer, for lunch. "All he could talk about," said Lande, "was how much fun he had because all four members of the mile relay team were there."[25] There must have been momentary solace in that, moving from global tensions and business problems to the nostalgic scenes when he and three buddies outran four fellows from Red Oak or Creston.

In 1958 Stanley honored his father, Claude M. Stanley, by providing a $500 college scholarship to a graduating senior at Corning High School. The elder Stanley, before he was elected to the Iowa Senate and appointed to the Iowa Employment Security Commission, had been a member of the Corning School Board, serving when the present high school was built in 1927. Father and mother were there on May 28 when their son presented the first scholarship to Robert Miller, who pursued a legal career and became a U.S. district attorney in Colorado.[26] A trust fund established by Stanley continues financing of the scholarships.

A visible token of Stanley's affection for Corning is an addition to the public library, which was completed in 1981. The addition contains the Stanley Reading Room where a dedication wall plaque remembers the ". . . generations of Stanleys who have contributed to the Quality of Life in Corning."

Stanley was approached early in 1980 about contributing to the proposed project to enlarge and remodel the library. At the time a fund-raising appeal had yielded half of a $200,000 goal. The Library Board was discouraged about reaching the goal. Hearing of the board's plight, Willard Archie, a Corning native who was editor of the *Shenandoah Sentinel,* suggested to JoAnn Turner, the Library Board chairwoman, that she get in touch with Stanley.

When Max and Betty Stanley were in Corning late in May for the high school commencement and the awarding of the Stanley scholarship, they met on a Saturday morning with the Library Board. After a break for lunch they gathered in the livingroom of the Austin Turner home. JoAnn Turner remembered that the Stanleys sat on a Victorian loveseat while she and Joseph Kobes, the architect, sat on chairs on either side. The other board members sat about the room.

"Then Max announced in a quiet, austere way that he and Betty had decided to give $100,000," Mrs. Turner said. "The board members looked around at one another, not sure how to react, and then I said an appreciative thank you. Then Beth Harris said, 'Well, I'd just like to shout hallelujah!' and then everyone started laughing."[27]

11

Family Bonds

When Max Stanley needed a date in his senior year for the Mecca Ball, the annual dance of the engineering students at the University of Iowa, he called his cousin Marian Stephenson to see if she could find a companion for him among her sorority sisters at the Kappa Delta house. She did. Her roommate, Elizabeth M. Holthues, known as Betty, was willing to go with him.[1]

"So I had this date with him," she said many years later, "and I was not terribly impressed. He seemed like a nice person, but rather quiet."

He was persistent though, and even impulsive at times, as she learned later. He invited her to go with him to the Junior Prom, and she accepted. With other couples they took drives in the country, went to movies, and floated down the Iowa River in a canoe. Betty, however, continued going out with other men.

After he was graduated in late spring, Max stayed in Iowa City to work on the design and construction of the university's Hydraulics Laboratory. With his first earnings he bought a Model T Ford, which he drove to Clay County, in northwest Iowa, where Betty was spending the summer on the family farm. They joined some of her friends for a picnic at Storm Lake. As they drove back to the farm that night, Max asked Betty to wear his Theta Tau fraternity pin, which she agreed to do. That was tantamount to engagement.

Betty received her degree the next spring, in 1927, having majored in philosophy and psychology. She was promised a scholarship to study law, but decided against that, temporarily at least, when she was offered a job as an inspector for her sorority. She was to visit the Kappa Delta chapter houses in several southern states, offering advice to the sisters and assessing their activities and conduct. Max, meanwhile, remained in Iowa City working on the Hydraulics Laboratory project.

They talked about setting a wedding date for June of 1928, but her absence made him think of shortening the interval. He took time off in November to travel to Memphis, Tennessee, where she was visiting a chapter house. He immediately broached the idea of a Christmas wedding. Then suddenly he asked her to marry him there, in Memphis, before he returned to Iowa City. She showed him she could be impulsive, too, and said yes. They were married on November 11, 1927, by a Methodist minister in the home where she was staying with a Kappa Delta alumna. Several sorority sisters provided appropriate music. The families greeted the news with surprise and even consternation when they were told by the bridal couple, for such hasty action was out of character for either Max or Betty. When the Kappa Delta national president heard about it, she suggested that Betty join her husband in Iowa, thus ending a brief career as a sorority inspector.

Only Max's death, nearly fifty-seven years later, ended a partnership that withstood many trials — the late-night vigils with sick children, business uncertainties, family disappointments, cancer — and led to the contentment that time's passing brought them. Although he seldom showed it in business dealings, Max had a soft side, which became more pronounced after Betty had surgery for breast cancer in 1972. "How unexpectedly and how quickly things happen!" he wrote at the end of a somber journal entry.[2] Jane Buckles, their daughter, said that "for the first time Dad felt the fragility of Mom's life. . . . I saw a real, greater, outward expression of tenderness after that." In the years that followed he showed his affection for her in many ways, from quiet walks to the Muscatine Art Center or along the shell-strewn beach on Sanibel Island to helping with a few kitchen chores, such as fixing lunch or loading the dishwasher.

Typical of a woman of her generation, Betty Stanley fitted her life to that of her husband. Yet the two of them devised their own working partnership, from which grew mutual encouragement and emotional support as well as tending to the day-to-day family responsibilities. Betty was in charge of running the household, which to her meant not only the usual domestic duties but trying to create a pleasant environment for family growth. Only once did Jane hear her mother wonder aloud what she might have done if she had pursued her own interests. As Jane prepared to leave for college, Betty talked about working toward a master's degree and preparing to become a school counselor. But that was at a time when the Stanley Foundation activities were beginning to take form, and Max wanted her to go with him to the conferences, at which she often acted as hostess. It became a custom at the United Nations of the Next Decade conferences for her to give a welcoming address and to say a word of farewell to the departing participants and their spouses. She often joined Max at the social events connected with the business and educational meetings he attended. Their collaboration was evident in altruism, too, for large financial gifts for the Stanley Gallery of the Muscatine Art Center, the Corning library addition, and various projects at Iowa Wesleyan College and the University of Iowa were given in both their names. In private moments the two of them frequently discussed some of the problems he had to deal with; she was his private sounding board, especially for human relations matters. She was a vital part of his success, and he was proud of her.

Through the years Max left traces of his feelings for her among the notes in his journals. Here are samples:

> Dinner (anniversary) — at Empire Room — Waldorf-Astoria — Benny Goodman Orchestra. [Nov. 11, 1966, New York City, the night before a trip to Nassau where Max had conferences on an engineering project]

> Betty in car crash — broken collarbone — bruises — 1965 gray Buick totaled. Betty in amazingly good spirits — What a gal! [May 8, 1973]

> Full moon — walked with Betty about 10 P.M. [Feb. 6, 1974, Sanibel]

> To airport for Betty. Ate at Harbor House. Good to have Betty back. Lonesome alone. [Jan. 21, 1976, Sanibel]

> All-Alumni luncheon — Betty honored with Distinguished Alumni Service Award — She made a fine, brief response — A deserved honor. . . . [June 5, 1982, Iowa City]

Symbolic of his attachment to her, he accepted from her a wedding band (white gold with a small diamond) to mark their golden anniversary in 1977. He had not worn one previously. They were still a devoted couple, attracting the admiration of friends who saw them walking hand-in-hand like young lovers when they went to a dinner, a concert, or an art exhibit.

The Stanley children — Dave, Dick, and Jane — were brought up to be "achievers." And so they were — superachievers actually. Dave was the valedictorian of his high school class, Dick tied for second in his, and Jane was fourth in hers. All excelled in debate, winning top honors in state competition. Dave played football and Dick and Jane were in the band, as well as in other activities. All were in scouting, with the two boys earning the Eagle rank in the troop guided by their father.

"My parents are the kind of people who set very high standards for themselves and kind of make children feel that they want to live by equally high standards," Dave once said in a newspaper interview. "The biggest thing my parents have ever given me is example."[3]

Respect for the work ethic was one example, and living by it was fundamental in the Stanley family. Even at family gatherings, Dick remembered, his father often slipped away for an hour or two of work in the office he kept at home. By junior high the children had part-time jobs, both to learn the value of work and to earn spending money. The family fortune had not materialized then. The boys usually worked at the family enterprises. Dave spent time with a surveying crew, and Dick processed blueprints on Saturdays at Stanley Engineering for 20 cents an hour, and he spent a summer on the Home-O-Nize loading dock wrestling with the corn pickers of an ill-fated episode. Dick set his sights on going to the National Scout Jamboree in 1947, and he was told that he would have to find a job to pay his way. But not being sixteen, he was unable to get work that paid enough for his expenses, so he stayed home. Jane got extra money one summer working on the ketchup line at the Heinz plant during the peak canning season. She also was a sales clerk at Woolworth's, then moved to Barton's, a woman's apparel shop, where she spent most of her earnings on new clothes.

Coupled with the work ethic was prudence, which extended from the use of money to proper behavior. Money earned was not solely for personal gain and certainly not for frivolous extravagances; wealth was to be shared with others or invested in worthy causes. Frugality was the rule, Jane recalled, even in the fifties when the family's financial circumstances were improving; her weekly allowance was one dollar while several of her girlfriends got five or ten dollars. When the children went away to college, they were expected to send their father a monthly ac-

A picture for Dad: Betty Stanley with her children, Dave, Jane, and Dick. (Chamberlain Studio)

Lincoln Stanley (1953) drew admiring attention from father Dave, great-grandfather Claude, and grandfather Max.

Betty and Max in front of their Muscatine home, which he designed and had built in 1940. (Joan Liffring-Zug)

At family get-togethers, Max often presided at the grill.

An Eagle quintet: Max, longtime scoutmaster of Troop 127, joined his sons Dave and Dick when grandsons Joe and Nathan became third-generation Eagle scouts in the troop.
(Muscatine Journal)

counting of how they used the money he provided. Betty canned and pickled vegetables from the family garden (the children sometimes were recruited to shred cabbage for sauerkraut), and she sewed clothes (in her early teens, Jane recalled, they drove to the Amana Colonies woolen mill to buy material for skirts). During World War II, when meat was scarce, the Stanleys kept chickens, and some of Max's spare time was assigned to planting and hoeing in the Victory garden (in a rare journal note on domestic chores, possibly inspired by the aftereffects of stoop labor, he reported setting one hundred asparagus plants).[4]

Prudent conduct was supported by the Christian teachings that formed a substantial part of the core of family life. Supplementing the religious admonitions were "the Gothic oughts," as Jane called the assorted rules, warnings, and not-so-subtle hints that defined what was appropriate behavior, whether that had to do with keeping a clean room or how to act with a date on Friday night. In this atmosphere, Dick said, he grew up to be a "straight-arrow kid," trying to do what was expected of him at home, at school, in scouting, and on his part-time jobs. When misbehavior required punishment, some form of deprival usually was ordered. A common penalty was sitting on a chair and staring at a corner for half an hour, a loss of playing time outside. Any form of physical punishment, even a slap, was rare. Dave, however, recalled the day his mouth was washed with soap because he had said "shit" within earshot of his mother.

Although the young Stanleys were given considerable freedom to pursue their interests, conventional Protestant morality and provincial attitudes were constraining forces. Of the three children, Jane felt those constraints most acutely when she let it be known that she wanted to move to New York to try becoming an actress; instead she became a college theater instructor. Years later, when Betty and Max took frequent trips to New York, they enjoyed a night or two at the theater—evidence of flowering sophistication as provincialism receded.

Max and Betty had sustaining attachments to their families and hoped to imbue similar familial loyalty in their children. The building of sturdy bonds began with the family's daily routines. Breakfast and dinner were family meals, eaten together. Busy as his days were, Max tried to avoid dinners and evening meetings with business associates and clients; he preferred to go home. After dinner, he often worked in his home office for a while, emerging to listen to a favorite radio program (Fred Allen and Bob Hope made him laugh) or to propose a game of hecksapoppin (also known as O hell), hearts, pitch, or Chinese checkers. The children learned early that their father did not like to lose even at games, and that sharpened the fun of their competition. The children's school activities — and later the grandchildren's — always drew the Stanleys, even if that meant shivering on a wooden plank on a chilly fall night to watch Dave try to impede the progress of a charging fullback. School plays, concerts, debates, and, of course, commencement ceremonies provided many diversions for Betty and Max as their children grew up. Summer days brought frequent picnics in a city park, occasional outings at Wild Cat Den State Park, and vacation trips to the George Williams College Camp at Lake Geneva, Wisconsin. Such doting attention to the offsprings' doings forged devoted, secure relationships that withstood severe stresses in the decades that followed. The Stanleys were not hugging-and-kissing types, but they realized from their experiences that *presence* — being available in good times and bad — was reassuring proof of family solidarity.

Many of Jane's memories of her father are reminders of the emotional and financial support he gave her as she weathered personal crises stemming from two divorces and recurring business problems. He was there to help her in good times, too. When she and her second husband, actor Donald G. Buckles, wanted to start a summer theater in Springfield, Illinois, in 1960, Max put up the money to get them started, and he and Betty and other family members made periodic trips to the Tent at the Lake to see the plays. Max also backed Jane and her husband in other ventures when they decided to move west, first to New Mexico and then to Denver, Colorado.

"Anytime I had a problem or needed advice, it was Dad that I would go to," she said. "He was a problem solver. He would look at a problem and, emotions aside, he would say this is what ought to be done and proceed. . . . When I went through the hard times, I knew that he was always there."

The family bonds were extended as the children were married and had children of their own. Since the two sons chose to live in Muscatine, their wives — Dave's Jean and Dick's Mary Jo — had to try accommodating to the habits and rituals of a close-knit family. It was not always easy, for Max did not like his sense of order disturbed. But both he and his daughters-in-law adjusted to changing circumstances as a new generation began.

Dave and Jean had four children: Lincoln, Rebecca, Nathan, and Elizabeth. Dick and Mary Jo had three: Lynne, Sarah, and Joseph. Jane and D. G. Buckles had three: Donna, Guy, and Laura.

"Lincoln is quite a guy," Max wrote in his journal after seeing his first grandchild on a visit to Iowa City, where Dave was in law school.[5] About six months later the proud grandfather was spooning ice cream into the baby's mouth. When Linc was in his late teens and early adulthood, he could count on his grandfather listening to him as he, not unlike many of his generation, talked about trying to find his way, more out of anxiety than with confidence, through national upheaval.

Once again, school activities, this time of their grandchildren in Muscatine, figured importantly in Betty's and Max's activities. Periodically they traveled to Colorado to see Jane's children, and in 1978 they flew to Pakistan for granddaughter Donna's graduation from the American School in Karachi, where Jane and her children were living at the time.

Boy Scout Troop 127 was virtually a family institution. Max was the scoutmaster for many years, including the time that David and Dick moved through the classes to attain Eagle rank. When Max was in his forties, he decided he wanted to complete the requirements for the Eagle rank, which he did while the troop was at Camp Minneyata, near Dixon, Iowa, in the summer of 1946. Dick recalled how his father sprinted up and down the gravel road leading to the camp so he could be in shape to earn his athletic merit badge. But passing the swimming and lifesaving requirements was his most difficult test. The summer encampments in northern Wisconsin—Red Arrow for the boys and Osoha for Jane— gave Betty and Max enough reason to head northward for a few days at some nearby resort. The three grandsons in Muscatine—Linc, Nate, and Joe—also were members of Troop 127, with the latter two becoming Eagle scouts. Dick was the troop's scoutmaster in the late fifties and early sixties, and Nate became the leader in the mideighties.

As individual interests tended to draw the children and grandchildren away, Betty and Max arranged family get-togethers to help sustain family ties. There were winter trips to a resort in Scottsdale, Arizona, or to Sanibel and summer gatherings at Vail, Colorado. From time to time, family reunions brought the Muscatine Stanleys together with the branches in Corning, Peterson (Betty's home), and other parts of the Midwest. Max never hesitated about adjusting his tasks and appointments to fit family occasions—a niece's wedding, a cousin's anniversary, an aunt's funeral. Betty's family, the Holthueses, gathered in Muscatine a few months before Max died. In his journal he wrote that he had a great time and was happy that so many from the third generation had come and showed so much interest in family doings.[6]

Max's mellowing was a gradual modifying of the inner forces that drove him: The restless energy gave way at times to periods of leisure; the demanding manner took on a tolerant tone; the work ethic was tempered by golf. He accepted life with a more serene outlook, which was reflected in warmer relations with the family. He was less intimidating to his daughters-in-law, not so awesome to his grandchildren, and more willing to get on good terms again with his brother.

Jane recalled an incident that demonstrated her father's changing outlook. Late one afternoon in June 1964 (he had just turned sixty) he drove home in a new, yellow Ford Thunderbird. "And he said something like, 'Well, I couldn't buy it any younger.'" When he was younger, he had bought less expensive, workaday models, which satisfied him if they provided adequate transportation. Many of his business associates owned Cadillacs; he never had desired one. A car was not a status symbol for him. But with the elegant, jaunty Thunderbird, he intended to enjoy a car, not just drive it. Such extravagance would have been unthinkable to him twenty or even ten years earlier.

A growing fortune allowed both Betty and Max to do things they had denied themselves in their early years together or had given no thought to doing. There was, of course, the beach house on Sanibel Island. There was more traveling, especially in foreign lands. Betty had the chance to cultivate a latent interest in art, and she acquired a diverse collection of paintings and prints for the house on Sunset Drive. Her collecting must have awakened a dormant urge in Max, for in his later years he accumulated a collection of African art that ranks among the finest in the country.

As the years passed, Max became more conscious of the shortening time ahead of him. Brief, reflective comments appear in his year-end summaries in the journal: 1975, "Another year gone by—how fast they go!" 1977, "What a busy, enjoyable year. . . . Sad though that we grow older and can, and must, see the end of life on this earth. . . . Glory be for life & health." 1980, ". . . But life is good. Enjoy it. It is later than we think and admit."

He revealed some of his inner thoughts for the family in a poem he wrote at Christmastide in the late sixties or early seventies. Before the holiday, Betty asked the adults and older children in the family to write poems that would admit them to the table for Christmas dinner. Here is Max's offering, in which he disregarded the normal rules of punctuation:

> Poor are the gifts I give you
>   On this bright holiday
> Rich are the gifts around you
>   Oh grasp them while you may
>
> Grand beauty of God's great earth
>   Bright colors of the sky
> Fond embrace of a loved one
>   Warm words from passers by
>
> Memories of days gone by
>   Some with touch of sorrow
> The joys of work, play and life
>   And hopes for tomorrow
>
> Use of heart and soul and mind
>   In every way one can
> Building a better world with love
>   Peace and goodwill to man
>
> Would that I could give you these
>   On this bright holiday
> Not mine to give but yours to take
>   Oh grasp them while you may

12

Political Interludes

The depth and fervor of Max Stanley's devotion to his family was conspicuously evident in his efforts to help his son Dave win election to the U.S. Senate. Serving in the Senate was the son's long-cherished dream, and twice, in 1968 and in 1974, he tried to bring the dream to reality. In both contests Stanley was at his son's side, as finance director, a member of the executive committee, and an adviser on campaign issues. They were spirited campaigns, the first against Harold Hughes, the most popular Democratic governor of Iowa in modern times, and the second against John Culver, a five-term representative from the Second District in northeast Iowa. Stanley's journal notes from the campaigns, from early planning to election days, convey the excitement he felt, both by being an insider in the political bustle and by the prospect of seeing Dave in the Senate.

Until then Stanley had approached political affairs as many responsible citizens did: He studied the principal issues and discussed them with friends, wrote occasional advice to congressmen on legislation that interested him, contributed money to his favorite candidates and party, and voted. Although he once thought of pursuing a political career, he decided it was not the life for him: The demands of campaigning, fundraising, and political fence-mending outweighed the potential satisfactions he might get from helping shape public policies.

The younger Stanley, who had been serving in the Iowa General Assembly since 1959, often advocating legislative reforms with the zeal of a Young Turk, was ready to make his move for national office in the spring of 1967—a daring move since longtime Senator Bourke B. Hickenlooper, a fellow Republican, had yet to say whether he wanted to run again. Dave recalled that his father encouraged him two years earlier to seek a seat in Congress.

"He had not encouraged me to run for the Iowa Legislature, but he often expressed agreement with my legislative work and my stands on most state government issues," Dave said. "He and I agreed on most national and international issues."[1]

When Hickenlooper decided to retire, three other Republicans — former Congressman James Bromwell (carrying Hickenlooper's endorsement), former state Attorney General Dayton Countryman, and Des Moines insurance executive William Plymat — joined Dave in some lively skirmishing for the Republican nomination. Dave won with surprising ease. Ed Failor, who had known Dave in law school, headed the campaign staff and organized more than 50,000 volunteers to get out the vote for the Muscatine legislator.

Matched against Hughes, who was in his sixth year as governor, Dave proved to be a relentless campaigner as he crisscrossed the state giving speeches, shaking hands with workers outside factory gates, and attending neighborhood coffees, service club luncheons, fund-raising dinners, picnics, and barbecues. Jean, his wife, was on the campaign trail, too, and Betty made occasional appearances on behalf of her son. Max, however, preferred a behind-the-scenes role soliciting money to finance an expensive campaign.[2]

Dave had modified his progressive views by the time he ran for national office. Dick recalled that his brother was not such an outspoken internationalist as when he worked for the United World Federalists. Dave acknowledged that some Stanley Foundation activities, along with the continuing involvement of other family members in the world federalists, were a political liability. (He had been attacked by some Republicans during the primary campaign for his old UWF connections.) Distressed by violent demonstrations against the Vietnam War and repelled by the "flower children" and the "hippies" who represented changing social and sexual standards, Dave stressed a "law-and-order" attitude.[3]

Press coverage of the Senate campaign focused public attention mainly on the running debate between the candidates on the Vietnam War and how it muddled American behavior at home. Consequently, discussions of such domestic matters as taxes, government spending, and inflation, as well as Dave's attempts to attack Hughes's record, were a blur to many voters. The governor had broken with President Lyndon Johnson on the U.S. intervention in Vietnam, and he urged the withdrawal of U.S. military forces, beginning with a halt in the bombing of North Vietnam. Dave disagreed, contending that stopping the bombing "would allow the enemy to kill more American soldiers." He called for negotiations that would lead to free elections in Vietnam, including Communist candidates. Hughes tried to cultivate antiwar sentiment and labeled the conflict the "Johnson-Stanley War." Dave appealed openly to Iowans who wanted "law-and-order" solutions for rising crime and violence. Here is how he summarized the stakes for one reporter: "Vietnam and violence—peace abroad and peace at home."[4]

The campaign took a dramatic turn in mid-October after the *Des Moines Tribune* gave prominence to Dave's suggestion in a Fort Dodge speech that the United States consider seizing North Korean ships on the high seas to hold as ransom for the release of the USS *Pueblo* and its crew, captured by the North Koreans in January. He had mentioned the idea in earlier talks, but without gaining the media attention that followed the *Tribune* story. In his comments he also said that seizure should be a "last resort," but the qualification was lost in the furor over his call for retaliatory action. "Dave goofed," wrote his father in a journal note. The Hughes organization quickly produced television commercials attacking Dave's "gunboat diplomacy." After showing steady gains in public opinion polls, Dave's support stalled "on a plateau" for two weeks, Failor recalled.[5]

As election day neared, Max Stanley rejuvenated his normally optimistic spirit. The last preelection Iowa Poll published in the *Des Moines Sunday Register* showed Hughes favored by 52 percent of the likely voters and Dave by 48 percent (the campaign began with Hughes holding a 3-to-1 advantage). Two days later on election day, November 5, Stanley wrote in his journal, "Confident but jittery! Only hope organization can close gap. Don't know what more we could have done." He left his office early to get ready for a long night. Daughter Jane made a surprise appearance, flying from Colorado, and he was "very pleased" by the family solidarity that night. Later he wrote, "A night of suspense! A night of sorrow! Dave close, but by 3:00 A.M. it was obvious Hughes was the winner." But it was hardly a resounding victory; the man who four years earlier had won reelection as governor by more than 400,000 votes was sent to the U.S. Senate by fewer than 6,500 votes.[6]

Dave's defeat lingered in his father's consciousness. Two weeks later he noted in his journal, "Not yet back on even keel after election — anger follows sorrow."[7]

Nine months after losing to Hughes, Dave began charting a campaign to unseat First District Congressman Fred Schwengel, a Davenport Republican with a moderate-to-progressive voting record. But the incumbent defeated the challenger in the 1970 June primary. "A heartbreaker," wrote Stanley, "as we all thought David was in. Can't beat the establishment, I guess."[8]

Four years later Dave had a second chance to win a Senate seat after Hughes decided to lay aside his political career and to concentrate on religious activities. That set up the Culver-Stanley race, which was overshadowed by the Watergate scandal. Once again Max Stanley was his son's finance director, and he soon sensed that what he referred to as the "sordid mess" in the Nixon administration would have an adverse effect on his fund-raising efforts. Throughout the summer he fretted about "tight" and "disappointing" contributions from Iowans and the lack of sustaining support from the Republican Senatorial Campaign Committee, which was financially strapped, too. Hopes to raise about $400,000 for Dave's run fell short by about $100,000.[9]

Then on August 8 a journal note exults: "Momentous day! Nixon resigns. Now we can get on with our U.S. and foreign problems. Resignation can only help Dave's campaign." A month later the mood was subdued: "Ford pardons Nixon! Blow to Dave's campaign." A week later a capsule analysis: "Campaign outlook — pessimistic from my view — bad week — pardon — bad press." An Iowa Poll early in October showed Culver leading, 46 to 33 percent. "Bad," wrote Stanley.[10]

In the last month of the campaign his spirits lifted as Dave began gaining on Culver. Ten days before the election Stanley was thinking "upset," and two days before the voting he was "confident of narrow victory." But Dave was caught in a sweeping Democratic tide, along with fellow Iowa Republicans seeking national offices, other than Charles Grassley, who was chosen to succeed retiring Representative H. R. Gross. "Tragedy," wrote the disappointed father. "Best man didn't win. What a loss to Iowa and the nation."[11]

Ironic, indeed, was a prevalent characterization of Max Stanley as a "kingmaker" who used wealth and influence to advance the political careers not only of his older son but of other chosen candidates. That, unfortunately, is how Stanley was perceived by many Iowans who apparently were unaware of his more significant, nonpolitical accomplishments. In 1968 particularly, he was seen by some as the rich daddy trying to buy a Senate seat for his son. Understandably, the Muscatine entrepreneur attracted attention among Iowa Republicans. He was a successful engineer, businessman, and community leader, the son of a respected state official, a generous contributor to the party and its major candidates, and the father of a son with political promise of a high order. Even by the time Dave first ran for the Senate, the elder Stanley was something of a phantom figure in party circles. Rumors circulated periodically about how he was bankrolling a favored candidate or maneuvering quietly for favored policies. Such stories owed more to the imagination of political enthusiasts than to any scheming by Stanley, who seldom appeared at party functions or conferred with party leaders. Although he had a lively interest in how Iowa was governed, he was no more active in state and county political affairs than many of his Muscatine neighbors — except when Dave was running for the U.S. Senate. He bought tickets to party fund-raising dinners in Des Moines, but he rarely went, usually giving his tickets to friends who were more enthused than he by mingling in large crowds. He abhorred conventions, which were not his way of getting things done. In 1960 he was appointed to a state commission to study legislative reapportionment, but he saw the panel's proposals torn to shreds when the General Assembly began a series of acrimonious clashes on that vexing issue.[12]

That Stanley put a great deal of money behind Dave's desire for a legislative career in Washington is undeniable. The two Senate campaigns and the primary challenge of Congressman Schwengel cost more than a half million dollars of family money. The abundance of Stanley money was a recurring complaint of some of Dave's opponents and a source of fascination for many voters. In 1968 father and son kept silent amid growing speculation that the spending for Dave's race against Hughes would reach the million-dollar range — an exorbitant amount for an Iowa political race of that time. Early in 1970 rumors circulated that tax-exempt funds from the Stanley Foundation had been used in the 1968 campaign and, by implication, might be used in the primary contest with Schwengel. Stanley opened the foundation's books to inquisitive reporters and produced an Internal Revenue Service audit verifying the foundation's credibility.[13]

When the spending issue resurfaced in 1974, the Stanleys decided to give a public accounting of the 1968 campaign, mainly because Dave wanted to show the difference between the actual expenditures and the rumored amounts. In a sworn and notarized report made public September 2, Stanley showed that he and Betty contributed $105,350 to their son's 1968 campaign and that he later put up $206,179 to cover leftover debts. Dave and Jean spent $17,282. As for a million-dollar campaign, Stanley insisted that the combined spending of the different campaign committees for the primary and general elections did not exceed $560,000. Two years later, when Dave challenged Schwengel, Max and Betty contributed $48,000 and Dave and Jean $5,422. The father took care of about $96,562 in unpaid loans and bills after the primary. In 1974 federal law limited a family's political contributions to $35,000. That year Dave and Jean put up $28,000, Max and Betty $3,000 each, and Dick $1,000.[14]

Journal entries indicate that Stanley agonized for a month or more over the public accounting. He discussed the matter several times with his son, with his lawyer Roger Lande, and with campaign advisers in Des Moines. On August 31 he completed work on the statement that was supplied to the news media. "Die is cast," he noted in his journal. "I'm doubtful it is right decision—time will tell. But relieved that decision is made." Recalling the episode, Lande said Stanley had two concerns: Since he was self-conscious about his wealth, he resented any suggestion that the public had a right to know how he used his money, whether for politics, loans to friends, or church donations; he was afraid that the disclosure would hurt rather than help Dave's campaign as it reached a climax. The spending report cleared the air and apparently caused little appreciable damage to Dave's efforts, far less certainly than voter reaction to the Watergate scandal.[15]

National politics had far more appeal for Stanley than state affairs. What happened in Washington—in the White House, Congress, and the State Department—touched several of Stanley's interests: the intellectual curiosity of a global citizen concerned about the fate of this planet; the place of the United Nations in U.S. foreign policy; the direction of Stanley Foundation programs; the future of development projects in the Third World, many of which were dependent on foreign aid. His correspondence file includes numerous exchanges with Iowa's senators, First District congressmen, and chairmen of committees and subcommittees dealing with foreign policy and foreign aid; few are the letters written to Iowa governors or legislators.

Stanley usually was identified with the progressive, or moderate, wing of the Republican Party. That was understandable in view of his internationalist attitude, although on some foreign policy issues he held opinions that went beyond the conventional progressive, and even liberal, positions. Much of his thinking was generated by his association with U.N. diplomats, and he continued to believe in the potential of the international organization after many U.S. political leaders had lost faith in it. Stanley was not easy to classify on domestic issues, but he tended to favor conservative policies on economic matters. He was concerned, for instance, that excessive taxing and spending by governments, especially at the federal level, would inhibit the private incentives that motivate capital investment for the goods and services that provide jobs in American cities and towns.[16]

In 1980 Stanley joined in a campaign to call a state constitutional convention to propose an amendment to limit taxing and spending (Iowans for Tax Relief, an organization led by his son Dave, was the main proponent). That same year Stanley helped advance efforts by some United Nations representatives who favored Global Negotiations, a proposal to improve the economic balance between the industrialized nations and the developing ones through greater financial and technological assistance and changes in trade policies, monetary practices, and energy supplies. The state proposition was termed conservative; the proposal before the United Nations generally was seen as liberal by American commentators. The labels did not matter to Stanley.

Dave's campaigns offered the father hopeful possibilities of extending his influence, albeit vicariously, to the center of national power. Stanley was confident that Dave would be a good senator, probably even a great one. So he approached the campaigns with an intensity roused by a mixture of primitive loyalties and time-honed convictions about national imperatives, especially in international affairs.

"I don't think there was a thing Max wouldn't have done to get Dave elected to the Senate," Walter Shotwell said during a recollection of the 1968 campaign, in which he handled advertising and publicity for the Republican candidate. Shotwell, now a writer with the *Des Moines Register,* came away from the experience with a dislike for both Stanleys, who, as he put it, "thought they had the answers to all the world's problems." Ed Failor, on the other hand, grew fond of the elder Stanley and was impressed with the enthusiasm and intelligence he brought to the campaign.[17]

The two Senate elections left a few unpleasant memories with Stanley. For a long time he carried resentful feelings toward Hughes, disregarding the similarity of views they held on foreign relations, including the war in Vietnam, after the governor went to Washington. Three years after the election, Stanley attended a Methodist dinner in Des Moines at which Hughes, a Methodist lay preacher, was the speaker. The journal has this comment on the affair: "Oh, if Dave could have had +6,000 votes."[18]

Stanley's feelings cooled toward Governor Robert Ray, a Republican, after he gave only a lukewarm endorsement to Dave in the 1974 contest against Culver. However, when Ray was appointed to the U.S. delegation to the United Nations in 1984, Stanley forgot the old hurt and met with the former governor to discuss U.N. matters and how the Stanley Foundation might help ease the adjustment to the global forum.[19]

Dave's political defeats wounded Stanley as much as if they had been his own. In retrospect, the political arena was not the most suitable forum for Max Stanley. He never liked to lose, and he had difficulty coming to terms with the sweeping effect of an election day loss. It was not merely a momentary setback that might be corrected or overcome in a few weeks or a few months, as Stanley knew could happen in business. In Dave's case, the 1968 and 1974 defeats meant that a dream was slipping away.

Stanley worked enthusiastically in one other election contest. That was in 1980 when he joined the campaign of Republican Congressman John Anderson of Illinois, who ran as an independent presidential candidate. Stanley feared that the probable defeat of President Jimmy Carter by Ronald Reagan would lead to a radical disruption of U.S. foreign policy. More about that later.

13

Welcoming Change

Learning never stopped for Max Stanley. He had a restless curiosity about the contemporary world. Ron Barrett, of Stanley Consultants, once said of him, "He was the youngest eighty-year-old I ever met. Even as he aged, he had a nimble mind."[1] Education was a vital interest to Stanley, both in institutional terms and as a route to his own intellectual fulfillment or vocational betterment. Education—the exchanging of ideas to stimulate thought and imagination—helped him welcome change in his own life and in the world he had come to understand.

Dick Stanley, in an insightful comment about his father, said he "approached things with a view to the future; he was not much interested in rehashing the past."[2] The annual lists Stanley kept of the books he read show few historical works, and virtually all the biographies, memoirs, and books on foreign affairs listed are about people and events of the times he lived through. Even about his own ancestors Stanley had only an elementary inquisitiveness.

Obviously, Stanley could have no effect on the past, but he could influence the future, and education was the best avenue for doing so. From its beginning the Stanley Foundation was committed to educational purposes in all its activities—the various conferences, the school programs, the Policy Papers, the radio series "Common Ground," and *World Press Review*. Many of the articles Stanley submitted to professional engineering journals had an educational dimension when raising an ethical question or inviting concern about environmental problems engineers needed to consider. Rarely did he speak before a group without intending to pass on some knowledge or to exchange ideas.

Max and Betty Stanley contributed thousands of dollars a year to educational institutions and foundations — as much as $100,000 in a 1970 pledge for capital improvements at Iowa Wesleyan College, which also received a $400,000 bequest after Stanley's death in 1984. The couple supported various music and dance programs at the University of Iowa, and Stanley's will left $100,000 to the University of Iowa Foundation, on whose board he sat nine years. Through their own foundation the Stanleys provided more than $200,000 in 1972 to start the Center for World Order Studies at the university. The center, under the direction of Law Professor Burns Weston, was set up to broaden and improve classroom teaching and adult education on subjects related to international affairs, reaching beyond Iowa City to other colleges and universities and to high schools and grade schools in the Midwest. However, the foundation discontinued financing in 1975 when the university had not integrated the project into its academic program.[3]

Kosta Tsipis, a physicist at the Massachusetts Institute of Technology, once referred to Stanley as the founder of MIT's Program in Science and Technology for International Security, which deals with the technical and scientific aspects of arms control. In the late seventies Stanley agreed to give Tsipis $25,000 a year for five years as "seed money" for his project, which then gained a grant from the Ford Foundation. "So I count the program here at MIT as one of Max's accomplishments," Tsipis said.[4]

Stanley's collection of African art was a significant gift to the University of Iowa in 1978. Willard Boyd, then the university's president, recalled Stanley's insistence that the collection should be used for more than show and that the university should commit funds to the study of African art. That was done, and Christopher Roy, an authority on the arts of African peoples, was added to the faculty as an art historian. The Stanleys then augmented Roy's university salary by providing him with funds for research trips to Africa.[5]

Long years of service to institutional boards and organizations formed a large part of Stanley's contributions to education. For thirty-three years he sat on the board of trustees of Iowa Wesleyan College and was the board's chairman in the early sixties. He headed a successful $1,250,000 fund-raising drive that led to construction of a science hall on the campus at Mount Pleasant in 1961. He also was on the board of Garrett Theological Seminary at Evanston, Illinois, in the seventies.

He spent nine years on the board of the University of Iowa Foundation, serving as chairman from 1971 to 1975. Darrell D. Wyrick, the foundation's executive director at the time, particularized Stanley's term as chairman as one of financial growth, with gifts, other income, and pledges rising from about $2 million to more than $8 million. In that period Roy J. Carver, another Muscatine resident and the head of Bandag Incorporated, gave more than $7 million to the university, much of it for health-related projects, endowed professorships, and intercollegiate sports. Stanley was the first chairman of the President's Club, the university's major donor group, and he saw it grow from eighty-three members to about three hundred by 1975.[6]

In 1979 he set up the Stanley-University of Iowa Foundation Support Organization to receive funds for favored causes, such as continuing support for the African art collection and its educational offshoots. HON Industries financed a professorship in the College of Business Administration in Stanley's honor.

Stanley was awarded three honorary degrees: from Iowa Wesleyan College in 1961, from the University of Manila in the Philippines in 1970, and from Augustana College at Rock Island, Illinois, in 1978. He was named an honorary rector of the University of Dubuque in 1983 and was honored in different ways by the University of Iowa, including the Distinguished Service Award in 1967, the Hancher-Finkbine Medallion in 1971, and the Oscar Schmidt Iowa Business Leadership Award in 1980.

As devoted as Stanley was to institutional education, he carried with him concerns about academic practices, many of which he felt should be tested against business practices. He was keenly disappointed when the university did not follow through on the foundation plan for the world order studies program, sensing that the institution "seemed to be protective of its territory, not being inclined to allow an outside organization to meddle in its internal affairs." Weston surmised that Stanley "did not understand university politics" and persisted in believing that managerial methods could be applied successfully to teaching and research, regardless of accepted scholarly methods, academic freedom, tenure policies, internal budgets, and state appropriations. Wyrick credited Stanley with improving the foundation's business methods and investment practices, but acknowledged that he "was impatient sometimes with the pace of academia. He had this mind that said let's make a list of our objectives and then decide when we can get these things done."[7]

John Redick, former research associate at the Stanley Foundation, said Stanley had an "ingrained disdain for the ivory-tower types." Redick left for the University of Virginia in the summer of 1983 after a prolonged disagreement with Stanley over the foundation's research objectives. Redick had moved from Muscatine to Iowa City to pursue foundation research while teaching in the university's global studies program. When Stanley decided to consolidate all foundation activities in Muscatine, he asked Redick to return. Redick refused, arguing that the foundation should retain ties to the academic community and its resources. The dispute lasted off and on for more than a year and a half as the two men failed repeatedly to find a compatible solution, except finally to part with mutual respect.[8]

Jack Smith said Stanley respected academic "doers"—the scholars who taught and wrote and did research with a view to "taking it to the people" instead of simply passing knowledge among other scholars. One consequence of Stanley's attitude was a sparsity of professors at foundation conferences, and those who were invited usually were friends of Stanley or had earned recognition in political or diplomatic circles for their writings, research, or previous government activity.[9]

When he chose Redick's successor, Stanley picked David Doerge, who along with academic credentials drew on varied experience with several congressional staffs and a Washington organization interested in military affairs. Doerge was accustomed to working up the "quick studies" that legislators wanted, and that Stanley wanted as well, rather than extended, often time-consuming academic research.[10]

The shortcomings Stanley saw in American leadership were traced partly to educational failings. This view emerged in his opening remarks at a forum on "Education for Peace and World Order" at Iowa's Center for World Order Studies in the fall of 1974. Of the nation's leaders, he observed:

> They are the products of the last four decades of our educational systems. Their attitudes are shaped, for the most part, by domestic events and moods since World War II. From years of contact with many of these people, I conclude they have been poorly prepared by education and environment to think positively on the global problems created by growing interdependence. Rather, their attitudes continue to emphasize, with but occasional doubt, the independence, power, and manifest destiny of this country and its commit-

ment to exponential growth. Too few realize that the complexity and magnitude of global issues have outstripped the capacity of national governments to deal with them.[11]

In that talk he urged educators to devote more time to developing "a specialized type of adult education that can have influence, namely, conferences and seminars bringing decision-makers and opinion-shapers together with academicians." In other words, get the professors to mingle with the power structure and to participate actively in the decision-making process. He reminded them—administrators and faculty members from Iowa schools were in the audience—that the "ivory towers and campuses" had been influential in the civil rights movement and the protests against the Vietnam War. Then he told them to be "participants, not bystanders" as the United States joined other nations in preparing for "major changes in the international political system" to solve a broad range of global problems.

Stanley showed them a glimpse of the future to which they should lead their students: a disarmed world with an "alternate security system" that would allow nations to dismantle their own military forces; permanent U.N. peace forces to prevent international conflicts; a world judicial system to resolve disputes between nations; equitable systems for managing the distribution of natural and economic resources; monetary systems assuring fair trade and commerce in an interdependent world; stabilized population growth; protection for the global environment.

"While it is beyond my competence to design educational processes," Stanley said in conclusion, "I am utterly convinced that, with few exceptions, present approaches are failing: graduates are not prepared for responsible citizenship and leadership in the world of tomorrow."

The talk revealed Stanley's ambivalence toward higher education. Harsh as he was—or thought he was—on academicians, he did not want to shatter their world. He still had faith in the educational system and believed it was capable of serving the nation's needs in the global community he envisioned. But he challenged the educators to reform their system so that it would produce more participants and fewer bystanders.

Over the years Stanley's contributions to educational endeavors were balanced beneficially by educational contributions to his life. Friendships grew from his associations on the institutional boards and from those with administrators and some faculty members. Although he met infrequently with many students, his exposure to their environment made him sensitive to much of the dissent and discontent of the late sixties and early seventies. As his grandchildren matured, he was aware, too, of the changing attitudes motivating their thoughts and actions.

Change was a favorite theme of Stanley's, and he found it especially pertinent as the campus unrest evolved into a broader public consciousness of misplaced national values and neglected social, economic, and environmental problems. His pleas to welcome change often were coupled with an assertion of his belief in the power of a single person to cause change. He first struck on change when he spoke at the Finkbine Dinner at the University of Iowa in the spring of 1963. Student leaders were invited to the dinner, along with selected faculty members, administrators, and alumni.

"My class of 1926 marched from this campus into an apparently settled, prosperous and peaceful world," he said. Then he clicked off a series of events that led to economic depression, World War II, and the threat of nuclear holocaust.

> We were upon the very shore of a violent sea of change which would shake the world and we didn't know it. But we students were not alone in our simple dream of stability, peace and prosperity. With few exceptions, the leaders of that day were equally blind. Might the world be different today if its leaders of the past half-century had understood that change is inevitable—a challenge to be met and an opportunity to be grasped, not a specter to be resisted and avoided? . . . We thought of change in the past tense or perhaps the present: certainly not as a future event confronting us at every turn of the road. You, too, will encounter change, change and more change. You start your careers in the most dynamic period of history. You are about to step into a world which is undergoing and will continue to undergo rapid, significant and even violent change. . . .
>
> If you are to lead, you must cope with change in a positive fashion. You cannot hang back or seek to avoid it. You cannot ridicule or resist it as the work of radicals, crackpots or starry-eyed idealists. You must meet change head on, taking it as a normal and expected fact of life.[12]

Six years later Stanley focused his concept of change on campus unrest. Speaking at the dedication of the Iowa Wesleyan College library, he said students "are not wrong" when they demonstrate against war, racial prejudice, and social and economic discrimination. While he did not condone violence or lawlessness, Stanley was tolerant of other forms of protest. "We should thank our awakened students for pressing for action now," he said.[13]

Likewise, when he was awarded a doctor of humanities degree from the University of Manila in 1970, he cautioned: "We might listen to the student protest. In my country one of its root causes is the hesitation of universities — as well as government — to face squarely the problems of peace. . . . They [students] sense, though they do not always articulate, the impact of modern weapons upon civilization. They know war is no longer a tolerable or sensible exercise. They feel human values transcending national interests."[14]

So it should not have been a surprise that Stanley backed his friend Willard Boyd, the University of Iowa president, when he ordered an early closing of classes in the spring of 1970 as a response to student demonstrations after the shooting of four students at Kent State University by Ohio National Guardsmen. Stanley's defense of student protests may well have given him vicarious satisfaction since he was not a demonstrative person. Three years earlier, Stanley justified dissent as he spoke to the Wesleyan Associates, a group of business and professional men who met periodically at Iowa Wesleyan College. He said:

> My question is whether America can close the gap between her capacity and performance. My hope and my belief are that she can, that she has the human resources to conduct her affairs with maturity which few if any great nations have ever achieved: to be confident but also tolerant, to be rich but also generous, to be willing to teach but also willing to learn, to be powerful but also wise.
>
> I believe that America is capable of all these things; I also believe she is falling short of them. If one honestly thought that America was doing the best she is capable of doing at home and abroad, then there would be no reason for criticism. But if one feels certain that she has the capacity to be doing very much better, that she is falling short of her promise for reasons that can and should be overcome, then approbation is a disservice and dissent the higher patriotism.[15]

When Vice-President Spiro Agnew heaped caustic comments on the report of the President's Commission on Campus Unrest in 1970, Stanley reacted angrily. By letter he advised Jeremiah Milbank, Jr., of the Republican National Finance Committee that he was "making no further contributions to this year's campaign." He wrote that Agnew's rhetoric "is more than I can take." From his experience as a college trustee and a university foundation board member, Stanley said he found the commission report "balanced and sensible." This brought a reply from Rogers C. B. Morton, the party chairman, suggesting that Stanley had gotten a "wrong impression" of Agnew's remarks and asking that he "extend additional time before making a final evaluation and judgment of our distinguished Vice President." There is no correspondence to indicate that Stanley changed his mind.[16]

Pragmatic man that he was, Stanley was not the sort to bind himself to a definable and affirmable philosophy of education. The closest he came was a four-paragraph comment printed in 1970 in the Sunday magazine section of the *Des Moines Register* under the heading, "The Best Advice I Ever Received." He began by saying it was impossible for him to choose the "best" advice. What he hit upon was advice that was "both unique and excellent." It had come many years earlier from one of his engineering professors, Byron J. Lambert, whom he referred to as B.J. Of him Stanley wrote:

> I remember his prancing back and forth before the blackboard, demonstrating the effect on a bridge truss of loads added at various points. But the wisdom he imparted to his students went far beyond his chosen field of structural and civil engineering.
>
> His unique advice was that agreement seldom, if ever, advances our knowledge or understanding. "When you are in a group discussing any topic," B.J. told us, "and everyone seems to agree, take the other side whether you believe it or not. The resulting debate will stimulate thought, bring out new points, and reinforce old ones, while placid agreement will only stifle thinking and imagination."
>
> This advice has served me well over the years. I have used it repeatedly, both to develop new ideas and to strengthen previously held ones. I have found, too, that the process often leads one to change his mind, and discard previous convictions unworthy of challenge.[17]

Such advice suited Stanley because it appealed to his analytical, problem-solving nature—in this case the consideration of alternate ideas. This certainly was what he saw the student dissenters doing: stimulating the exchange of ideas; compelling the older generation to test its beliefs, values, and conventional wisdom; bringing change that would be good for the country's future.

14

A Widening Faith

In the story of Christ's birth in the Gospel of Luke, an angel announces the event to shepherds watching over their flocks on the Judean hillsides, and then an angelic choir sings, "Glory to God in the highest, and on earth peace, goodwill toward men." That promise, peace and goodwill on earth, became a recurring theme for Max Stanley as he tried to enlist various groups, especially religious groups, in his efforts, personal and collective, to fulfill the angels' song. This was a realizable dream for Stanley, not merely a vision of a far-off millennium.

Stanley's religious faith was never far removed from the day-to-day activities of his life, especially those connected with "the quest for a secure peace with freedom and justice," as he liked to phrase it. He also liked to quote a passage from Isaiah: " . . . they shall beat their swords into plowshares and their spears into pruning hooks; nations shall not lift up sword against nation, neither shall they learn war anymore."

It is not an exaggeration to suggest that Stanley felt a mission, as that term is understood among religious people, to work for the eradication of war. This goal was augmented over the years by his support of proposals, from both religious and political quarters to improve the lot of the world's poor peoples. He never claimed a divine calling for his mission or surrounded it with sacred words of investiture. It was simply something he had to do, and he had to do it because of what he believed about God, the Creator's universe, and his will for the betterment of humanity.[1] He touched on this in his book *Waging Peace:*

> The most fundamental truth is that all rights man enjoys are
> God-given. No act or policy of nations should be allowed to hinder

the development of these rights—neither communism, colonial imperialism, nor blind nationalism.

The rights with which man is endowed by his Creator are the foundation of individual sovereignty. The people may delegate some of their powers to various governments in order to safeguard their rights and to achieve peace.[2]

He then referred to the Declaration of Independence and its words about men being created equal and endowed by their Creator with certain rights—"life, liberty, and the pursuit of happiness." To him, then, religion, or a person's faith, could not be separated from the conditions that determine personal well-being.

Yet he once said of his religious beliefs, "I don't wear them out on my sleeve." That would not do, he added, "as we're working with people in the international arena. After all, if you're going to solve some of these problems on a world basis, you've got to work with Hindus and Arabs and people from a wide range of other religions as well as many people who do not profess any religious belief. They're all human beings, and they must all work together if we're going to accomplish the kind of goals that I hope we can."[3] This was recognition of the global dimensions of religious pluralism, born of a nonsectarian spirit.

Going to church had been an indispensable part of Max Stanley's life since his boyhood in Corning. His mother and father were active in the Methodist Church, and Stanley was content to follow their example. Biblical teachings shaped much of his thinking and motivated many of his actions. The quiet but steady confidence, the optimistic outlook, even the bold risk-taking in business bore testimony to his belief in a provident God. Religious convictions stood behind many of the principles and policies advanced by the Stanley Foundation. Keeping Home-O-Nize going so there would be jobs and stability in the community fit Stanley's understanding of what a good steward did. A missionary impulse may have buoyed Stanley's urge to start engineering work in Liberia (he was aware, as he mentioned in a talk to the United Methodist bishops, that the first foreign mission of the Methodist Church was started there in 1834).[4]

Stanley's beliefs grew from conventional American Protestant teachings, which then were nourished by the moral imperatives evolving from the Social Gospel movement. The result was a resolute determination to serve humankind. As his son Dave explained, "Faith is not just a matter of believing, but it is carrying that belief into practice." Stanley tended to be skeptical of those who professed a Christian belief without showing it in the ways they lived. The demonstration of faith, in fact, was more important to him personally than the public expression of it. Dave added: "He certainly saw his faith as affecting life, affecting decisions, affecting what you do and how you do it, how you use your time and your money. . . . He would not be one to grab you by both lapels and ask, 'Brother, are you saved?' He felt more comfortable trying to show his faith by how he lived and by what he did."[5]

Nor was outward piety the way Stanley showed his faith. He subscribed, of course, to most teachings of the Methodist Church and followed much of its discipline. Publicly, he was more likely to speak of himself as a Christian, without attaching a denominational label. He did not see great differences in teachings among most of the major Protestant bodies, and his international activities made him conscious of the beneficial influences of other faiths. At home the family commonly asked a blessing on the evening meal, but otherwise there were no regular devotional practices. Daily Bible reading was not a habit Stanley cultivated, and neither religious literature nor theology appealed to him. Yet going to church was an every-Sunday pattern (usually the fifth pew from the front), and church activities on two or more evenings often were part of a month's schedule.[6]

Busy as he was with his various interests, Stanley seldom turned down a church request for some of his time. For several years in the early sixties he was a member of the Board for Christian Social Concerns of the Methodist Church, serving on the Executive Committee and the Division of Peace and World Order. As a representative of that board, he appeared before the Senate Foreign Relations Committee in 1961 to urge passage of a bill to establish a U.S. disarmament agency. He was a leading supporter of plans for the Church Center of the United Nations, which the Methodist Church undertook in 1961. The twelve-story building, erected on the U.N. Plaza, provides offices, conference rooms, and meeting space for many denominations.

Stanley was a trustee of two Methodist educational institutions, Iowa Wesleyan College, at Mount Pleasant, and Garrett Theological Seminary, at Evanston, Illinois. He performed a number of tasks for the Methodist Church in Iowa and for his local congregation in Muscatine, originally the First Methodist Episcopal Church but later renamed the Wesley United Methodist Church. Although he sat on several boards and committees of the congregation over the years, he devoted much of his time to the youth as a Sunday school teacher and as the leader of the Boy Scout troop sponsored by the congregation.

John Schenkel, who became a carpenter in Muscatine, took away from Stanley's Sunday school class this application of the Golden Rule: "If you build a house for someone, build it as though you might have to live in it yourself someday."[7] From his Boy Scout experiences, Dave Stanley remembered the time his father took the troop to Springfield, Illinois, to visit the Lincoln historic sites in the area. The boys camped overnight near a lake. The next morning, as the scouts packed for the trip home, the scoutmaster ordered them to pick up all the litter, including refuse thrown away by other campers. That caused some grumbling, to which Stanley replied, "Wherever you go, you leave it better than it was when you found it." To Dave Stanley, his father's words conveyed as much about his religious thinking as they did about his desire for a clean campground.[8]

Pursuing this thought, Dave said he learned two important ideas about Christian living from his father: "There's an obligation to put a lot of your time into something that helps other people, or leaves the world, or maybe a small corner of the world, a better place. And then there's also the idea that this is really where the fun is in life. Much as my father enjoyed making money, I think he saw it much more as a tool you use to accomplish something worthwhile than as something you pile up for self-satisfaction, or to pass on to your heirs, or to impress people with your status."[9]

Stanley knew the biblical injunction from Luke, "Every one to whom much is given, of him will much be required; and of him to whom men commit much they will demand the more." Christian stewardship — the wise use of "time, talent, and treasure" — had a fundamental claim on Stanley's life, and this meant that his growing wealth often was as much a burden as a blessing. How to use his money to the best advantage, not merely for personal satisfactions, was a persistent question for him. Tithing, giving to the church a tenth of one's income, was customary for Betty and Max, and their sons and their wives adopted the practice.[10]

This attitude was cast in organizational form when Betty and Max established their second foundation, E & M Charities, in 1979. Disbursing grants to religious, educational, and charitable organizations is the sole function of E & M Charities (the Stanley Foundation does not give grants). E & M was financed at its inception with 94,000 shares of HON common stock valued at about $1,500,000. Stanley's will left half his estate, about $11 million, to the foundation. Growth in stock values and gifts by Betty increased estimated assets to about $26 million in 1986.

Iowa Wesleyan College and Wesley Church in Muscatine are among several Methodist beneficiaries of E & M grants, most of which were made after Stanley's death. Other educational recipients have included the University of Iowa Foundation, Iowa College Foundation, United Negro College Fund, University of Dubuque, Central College, and the schools and community college in Muscatine. Grants have been given to such diverse causes as the Christian Children's Fund, Church World Service, Amnesty International, International Peace Academy, World Neighbors, Heifer Project International, Nature Conservancy, the Salvation Army center in Muscatine, the Center for Asian and Pacific Studies at the University of Iowa, Marriage Encounter groups, and three tax education foundations.[11]

The Stanleys showed their generosity in another way in 1971 when they brought a Liberian youth, Thomas Ross-Barnett, to Muscatine and helped him through Iowa Wesleyan College and opened their home to him for holidays and summer vacations. As a child, Ross-Barnett was crippled so badly by disease that his playmates called him "the grasshopper boy." The term became the title of a book written about him by June Johns and published in England in 1967. Operations enabled Ross-Barnett to walk with a cane by the time he flew to the United States. When he was unable to enroll in an American medical school, he returned to England, where his adoptive mother lived.[12]

Stanley felt no hesitancy about linking his faith to world peace as he talked to fellow Christians about the kind of world he hoped for. He spoke to bishops and denominational executives, to seminary professors and educators, to pastors, and to lay men and women. He told them that "Christianity has a greater chance in a world of peace, freedom, and justice," and he added that an effective world government could "advance us toward the brotherhood of all men." But he also told them that they would have to work hard and give up much to fashion such a world. He did not anticipate miracles.[13]

In 1971 Stanley appealed to the United Methodist bishops to help improve the environment in America for world government with "a greater commitment of resources—human and financial." He suggested information and educational programs to offset growing criticism and dwindling support of the United Nations by the U.S. government. Methodists, he added, "have a sound background for this endeavor founded upon our social gospel and our long concern for peace and world order."[14]

In 1974 Stanley spoke at a Conference on Peace and Theological Education at Garrett Seminary. His thrust there was "grass roots involvement" by the laity in peace efforts. He commended the bishops for issuing a "call for peace and self development of peoples," but he added that "our efforts and programs are pitifully meager when measured against the urgencies of the day." He recommended the formation of a lay commission on peace in each congregation to provide leadership to "stimulate and encourage the pastor and congregation to give more attention to the quest for peace."[15]

By the early eighties Stanley could say that "one of the most encouraging things today is the reawakening of the leadership in a number of our churches." Not only were religious groups supporting various peace efforts, including nuclear-freeze legislation, they were backing proposals for Third World development, opposing the Reagan administration's withdrawal from UNESCO, decrying the administration's refusal to exert pressure against South Africa's apartheid policy, and protesting U.S. military intervention in Central America. Surmising that many church leaders in the past had put peace in the category with "motherhood and apple pie," Stanley said they finally had begun to realize that "it isn't something you can sit back and wish for and pray for and have it come about."[16]

An example of what was heartening to Stanley happened a few days before Christmas in 1983 at Iowa City. The Iowa Inter-Church Forum brought together eighteen religious leaders from the state to prepare a joint pastoral message on peace. Stanley was invited to be a technical consultant. The meeting began with a worship service at which each participant was given a plowshare pin made from the metal of a scrapped F-84 Thunderjet fighter from the Korean War. Then the churchmen from nine Protestant denominations and the Roman Catholic Church began working on their statement.

The message, entitled "Our Faith Compels Us to Speak," contained a series of affirmations intended to stimulate discussions in congregations and parishes. The conferees agreed that keeping the peace was a moral as well as a political "imperative," that nuclear war cannot be justified "under any circumstances," that the idea of nuclear deterrence is "morally unacceptable," and that a nuclear weapons freeze merited immediate support. The message then moved to economic and social matters. One affirmation stated that for "many millions in the world the most immediate threat to human survival is starvation, homelessness, lack of jobs, and alienation from hope and love." Another said that "life for all people is increasingly interrelated. . . . "[17]

Stanley surely was pleased with the message, which eventually was signed by twenty-four church leaders. They passed beyond simple slogans about peace and war, and left behind them a few theological positions—the Just War theory, for instance—that they believed had been made obsolete by nuclear warfare. They acknowledged the global dimensions of poverty, hunger, and disease, and even hinted, if not in so many words, that the religious tribalism of western society might be irrelevant in a world threatened by nuclear extinction.

The Iowa churchmen had begun to see what Stanley had seen. If peace was to have meaning for the world's people, it had to be more than the promise in a treaty or a "mutually verifiable agreement" on the testing, production, and deployment of nuclear weapons. Peace had to bring hope to the poor, the hungry, and the diseased. Beginning in the seventies, Stanley put increasing emphasis on global problems that no longer were peripheral to peace and disarmament. When he appeared before the Methodist bishops in 1971, he followed warnings about nuclear war with concerns about the dangers of various forms of pollution, unchecked population growth, diminishing natural resources, and the serious imbalance of financial resources between the haves and have-nots.[18]

Stanley stood in the pulpit of Wesley Church in Muscatine one Sunday in June 1980 and invited his fellow members to join him "on an imaginary flight to a few of the many countries striving desperately to improve their economic and social lot."

> In India, Bangladesh, and Ethiopia we encounter villages filled with some of the one and a half billion inadequately fed people of whom half a billion are severely malnourished. In Niger, Chad, and countries of the African Sahel, we see the ravages and starvation resulting from recent drought and the constant southward encroachment of the Sahara Desert. In capital cities we are shocked by the crowded shacks, the abject poverty, and unemployment rates of 60 to 80 percent. We visit with intelligent, concerned citizens striving to cope with such problems. We talk with dedicated public officials and

learn of their frustrating struggle to create employment and better
the life of their people. As our trip ends, we better understand the
human needs for economic and social development.

By contrast, Stanley said, the United States "has been given much," with
an average per capita income then of $9,650, or ten times that of the top
scale in developing countries. "Unfortunately, we are giving too little," he
continued. "The proposed 1981 U.S. budget allots to nonmilitary development assistance a mere 2½ cents for every dollar to the Pentagon:
pennies to aid our fellowman; dollars to build our military might."[19]

It is no wonder that Stanley, before the year was over, joined several
U.N. leaders in attempts to speed up deliberations on "Global Negotiations" before the Reagan administration came to power.[20] Global Negotiations was a proposal to improve the economic balance between rich
and poor nations through financial and technological assistance and
changes in trade policies, monetary practices, and energy supplies. Stanley's support of the proposal provides a clue to how he had resolved his
own private ponderings about the uses of wealth: It was to be shared
with those in need. His experiences in Africa reinforced his understanding of the humanitarian imperative and the results it could achieve. In
Global Negotiations he saw a chance to reach out to all of the Third
World.

After Stanley's death, at the memorial service in Wesley Church, the
Rev. Paul Williamson suggested that the Hebrew word *shalom* best fit
Stanley's idea of peace. "This word, translated 'peace' in the Old Testa-
ment, means something more than the cessation of conflict," said the
congregation's pastor. "It means wholeness. A peace which only tolerates
opposing systems is not *shalom*. To have *shalom,* there must be understanding, cooperation, and genuine respect for the freedom and dignity
of opposing ideologies. Wholeness for the human race is a dream, an
enormous vision, but Max Stanley made it believable."[21]

It was a minister's tribute to a layman whose faith saw the possibility of making real the biblical promises of peace on this planet in this
time.

15

Joys of Life

———

Golf was one of Max Stanley's passions. It was a late-blooming diversion, a game he did not begin to fully appreciate until midlife. Even then the game often baffled him. His old friend Harold Ogilvie told of a day when too many wayward shots had Stanley shaking his head and saying, "I can't think worth a hoot over a golf ball. I know I'm supposed to keep my left arm stiff and keep my head down, and then I jerk my head up or do something else."[1]

At times the game was exhilarating to him, at other times humbling. Once, after shooting 39 for nine holes, Stanley was almost rapturous (for him) in his journal, "A long pursued target achieved," presumably meaning a score under 40. A poorly played round was dismissed tersely as "horrible" or "lousy." The day he played the storied Pebble Beach course on California's Monterey Peninsula, Stanley noted that "all as touted — beautiful — tough — played badly."[2]

What should have been one of his memorable achievements was a hole-in-one, carded on the old second hole at the Geneva Golf and Country Club. He was two over on the par-five first hole. The second was a par three, about 115 to 120 yards, down and then over a gully, a relatively easy drop shot with an eight or nine iron. Stanley topped his stroke, but the ball leaped away, negotiated the gully, and rolled into the cup. Ogilvie, who was there, recalled, "Without any shouting or any show of emotion, he said simply, 'That makes me even par.'" In his journal for that day, August 2, 1961, Stanley wrote nothing more than "Hole in one on Geneva #2."[3]

Trodding the fairways was a way for him to escape the problems and tensions spinning off his different endeavors. Whether in Muscatine or on Florida's Sanibel Island for the winter, he tried to play two or three times a week. If he was intent on solitude, he played alone, hitting two balls for nine holes. For a number of years he played on weekends in a foursome known as the Duffers. Others in the group were neighbor Bob Roach, high school principal Fred Messenger, and physician Robley Goad. Ogilvie, who worked with Stanley on industrial development in Muscatine, joined him at the country club at times, as did Douglas Coder, a real estate agent; William Catalona, an orthopedic surgeon; and several HON executives, including John Axel, Harold Bragg, and Edward E. Jones.

Bragg, a two-handicap golfer, diagnosed Stanley's weakness: "His hands were always ahead of his swing." A Florida professional put it differently, telling Stanley he had a faulty pivot. In his eightieth year, he was convinced a new set of clubs would remedy some faults, so that is what he bought, including woods with metal heads. Then he finished up the winter season in Florida with a 46, which merited two exclamation points in his journal.[4]

On a golf course, Stanley not only relaxed but, according to his companions, freed a dry sense of humor that was not always evident in his offices. Bragg told how his boss loudly oohed and aahed over another player's good shot and then suggested that such skill was surely proof of a misspent youth. Stanley once sent a note to a Chicago businessman with whom he had played in Florida, expressing hope that they would meet again "some place where we can hook and slice, and occasionally par." The first time they played, Ed Jones, knowing of Stanley's dislike of gambling, suggested, "If we're not going to bet anything, I don't want to play." Without missing a beat, Stanley replied, "How about your job?" In good spirits they then agreed to play for a quarter.[5]

As a teenager in Corning, Stanley learned to play tennis on a court a doctor had built for his two daughters. It was the only place in town to play tennis.[6] In the 1936–1937 edition of *America's Young Men,* Stanley listed tennis as his favorite recreation; but he took little time for it, or any other physical games, as business and family demands increased. Later, tennis was not the game he wanted or needed.

After golf became serious play for him, he marked most of his scores in his journals. Rarely did he put down the scores of his playing companions, or indicate whether his score was better than an opponent's. What mattered was *his* score and how *he* performed. The journal entries, brief as most of them are, show how self-critical Stanley was of the way he played. Golf can be competitive, but that does not seem to have been Stanley's reason for playing. Much as he thrived on business competition, he did not care much for it on a golf course. He often played poorly in club tournaments, and he admitted, at least in the privacy of his journals, that he had a tendency to "clutch" under pressure. While wintering on Sanibel Island in 1976, he went to the eighteenth hole of a match-play event before losing by a stroke. Afterward he wrote, "For first time I didn't panic on tournament play."[7]

A good golfer needs a high level of concentration and self-discipline. Tennis requires improvisation. Playing golf, Stanley could control his game, or try to, matching his performance against the standard set for the course. For him it was immensely satisfying to put together a string of pars after a run of bogeys and double bogeys, or to lower his handicap from 27 to 24, as he did in 1982 after working on his pivot. Had he played tennis, his performance would have been affected by the returns of an opponent and in doubles by the good or bad play of a partner. Golf provided him with camaraderie, as often as he desired, and still permitted him his private autonomy.

The beach house on Sanibel Island, off Florida's Gulf coast near Fort Myers, was a continuing source of pleasure for the Stanleys, for Betty and Max particularly, but also for their children and their families, after it was completed in the spring of 1971. The frame building, elevated on pilings, is fronted by a screened porch that looks toward the Gulf, about one hundred feet away. Inside are the main living area, under a pyramid roof, two bedrooms, a guest area that sleeps four, and two small work rooms for Max and Betty. In his, he set up his office away from home, and from there he kept in touch by telephone with SCI, HON, the foundation, *World Press Review,* and other interests.

For his associates at SCI, he once wrote, almost lyrically, about life on the island:

> . . . Looking south from our porch through sea grape, Australian pine, and coconut palm, we saw a white beach and, beyond that, the Gulf of Mexico—a view that was unique to each new day. The colors varied from blue to green to gray. The surf changed from a dead calm to raging storm—sending salt spray a hundred yards on shore. Frequently we watched playful dolphins while flocks of ducks floated on the water and sandpipers scurried on the beach. Pelicans

and gulls were ever present, often diving boldly into the sea in quest of fingerling fish. Now and then a lone heron from nearby Ding Darling Bird Refuge stalked haughtily along the beach as if he owned it. Along the shore familiar two-legged creatures could be seen, even carrying flashlights before the break of dawn, hunting the shells that make Sanibel famous: welks, olives, conches, turkey wings, and what have you. Betty's best shell finds were an eight-inch tulip and a pair of angel wings.

In this atmosphere, he added, the two of them "experienced a remarkable change of pace: a most relaxed way of life." They were on the beach every day, and he played golf two or three times a week. He had found the pattern he wanted: "a few hours of work and writing each day to comfortably blend with the beach and golf."[8]

A quiet evening at home suited Stanley just fine. He was uncomfortable in large gatherings, impatient with the small talk common at cocktail parties. He was comfortable alone or, preferably, with Betty sitting in a chair near his. In their Muscatine home or at the Sanibel beach house, they paused from their steady rounds of activities to watch "M*A*S*H" on television, to listen to Rodgers and Hammerstein tunes on the stereo, or to read. For a time, they were "caught," to use his word, by the crossword puzzle fad.

The term voracious reader fit Stanley. It was not unusual for him to read forty to fifty books a year, in addition to the reading he did in connection with his work at SCI, HON, and the foundation. On an airplane he had a book open as soon as his seatbelt was fastened. He once told Betty that he would not mind going fishing with friends on the Mississippi if he could hold a book instead of a rod and reel.[9] Meticulously, he kept year-by-year lists of the books he read, dutifully marking a (C) behind those he had read in a condensed version. The lists, unfortunately, do not contain comments on his opinion of an author's work, especially on subjects in which he was knowledgeable. To satisfy particular interests he read, in his last years, *The Nuclear Delusion,* by George Kennan, *The Fate of the Earth,* by Jonathan Schell, *High Output Management,* by Andrew S. Grove, *Building a Sustainable Society,* by Lester R. Brown, and *Collecting African Art,* by Werner Gillon.

To Don Wooten, at Augustana College in Rock Island, he wrote a letter recommending Barbara Tuchman's *March of Folly,* observing that "much of U. S. foreign policy fully conforms to Tuchman's definition of

Max began his first stint as president of the United World Federalists in 1954, succeeding author-editor Norman Cousins. (Gansler Studios)

General Carlos Romulo, foreign affairs secretary of the Philippines, greets Betty and Max at his home in Manila.

Conferences on the United Nations of the Next Decade became an annual event of the Stanley Foundation. At the fourth conference, in Quebec in 1969, Max, second from left, visits with Muhammad Zafrulla Khan of Pakistan, Carlos Romulo of the Philippines, and Per Haekkerup of Denmark. (W. B. Edwards)

Disarmament was the issue at the United Nations when Max addressed the Ad Hoc Committee of the tenth special session of the General Assembly in 1978. (United Nations / Y. Nagata)

Max and Betty pose with two pieces of African sculpture nicknamed "Max" and "Betty" by University of Iowa art students. (Joan Liffring-Zug)

Max, February 1983.

Max became an honorary rector of the University of Dubuque in 1983. (Siebe Studio)

Max, sitting in his office in the Stanley Building (Stanley Consultants headquarters) in Muscatine, 1984.

folly."[10] In his last months he sent kind words to his friend Kosta Tsipis after reading his *Arsenals,* and to John Anderson for his *The American Economy We Need* and Linus Pauling for his *No More War.*

Stanley kept up with the best-selling novels, too, and he paid attention to regional works, such as the published version of William Randall's radio series, *Little Known Stories of Muscatine,* the *Des Moines Register's* tribute to cartoonist Frank Miller, and *Ding,* David Lendt's biography of an earlier *Register* cartoonist, Jay N. "Ding" Darling, for whom Sanibel's wildlife reserve is named. But the reading that probably delighted Stanley most were the whodunits — *Diamonds Are Forever,* by Ian Fleming, *Slay-Ride,* by Dick Francis, and anything by Agatha Christie and Rex Stout.

For a man so absorbed in public affairs, especially those of international importance, Stanley was not an avid newspaper reader. When he was home, he routinely read the *Des Moines Register,* the *Muscatine Journal,* and *Time,* but he left it to the staff of the Stanley Foundation to glean material for him from the *New York Times,* the *Washington Post,* and current affairs magazines. In later years he became a regular watcher of "The MacNeil-Lehrer News Hour" on public television.[11]

To get more from books, magazines, and sundry reports, Stanley once began a do-it-yourself speed-reading course. He did not stick with it, which is also what happened when he decided to learn French. He succumbed easily to enthusiasms, as he called them, or fads, as others might say. "Count your enthusiasms, not your birthdays," Jean Stanley remembered her father-in-law advising in old age.[12] In his midseventies he suddenly, but only briefly, took up jogging. Not long before he died, he brought home a personal computer on which he planned to catalog his magnificent collection of African art, a hobby that bloomed suddenly and ripened into an enduring pleasure.

Wine was a gratifying discovery for the teetotaling Methodist after he started circulating among the elite of the world federalist movement, especially at gatherings in Europe where wine, rather than cocktails, normally was offered guests. Once he took a liking to wine, he immersed himself in books on the subject so that he would feel competent to order high quality vintages in restaurants and to buy good selections for his table. At Sanibel he installed a cooling cabinet to keep his wines at a proper "cellar" temperature in a house without a cellar.[13]

As wealth accumulated, Betty and Max satisfied desires to travel to distant parts of the world. Some trips were made in conjunction with the foundation's conferences on the United Nations of the Next Decade and meetings of the World Association of World Federalists. When he had business to tend to in Africa, she occasionally went along. They went to Paris often enough to dispel her notion of it as a "city of sin," and she came to like it far more than London. An around-the-world trip in 1970 included a visit to the Philippines where Stanley accepted an honorary degree from the University of Manila.

Pakistan drew them in the fall of 1976 and the spring of 1978, when their daughter Jane Buckles and her children were there. Jane had business interests in Karachi since she was running a wholesale import business specializing in Pakistani goods in Denver, Colorado. These were other opportunities for the Iowans to come in touch with life in the Third World—shopping in the noisy bazaars, fishing for crabs, which were cooked on wooden boards, and visiting Jane's cook in a squatters' village ("Poverty at its worst," Stanley wrote in his journal).[14]

Later in 1978 Betty and Max joined a group of art lovers for a tour of Italian art treasures in Venice, Ravenna, Verona, and several other places. But seeing Paul Cezanne's studio was "not worth the visit," Stanley said, and a trip to the Palace of the Popes at Avignon was "wasted time."[15]

Five years later he had a somewhat similar reaction on a tour of the Middle East, which included a trip to Israel. He and Betty and their fellow travelers walked in old Jerusalem, drove along the Dead Sea, visited Bethlehem and Capernaum, and stood on the shores of the Sea of Galilee. But, unlike many Christians who return from the Holy Land with pious memories of walking in the footsteps of Jesus, Stanley wrote in his journal, "Tour very interesting and informative but it evoked little religious emotion."[16]

Another time they attended a series of concerts in Europe, and they took a cruise on the Mediterranean in a sailing vessel, on which they became acquainted with William Christopher, the actor who played Father Mulcahy on "M*A*S*H." One of their most pleasurable trips was in the summer before Max died. It was a relaxing, ten-day cruise through the Norwegian fjords to the North Cape, where they watched a sunset just before midnight. Spectacular scenery—snow-capped mountains, sweeps of pine forests, uphill meadows dotted with little farms, picturesque waterside villages—furnished a backdrop for the leisurely hours aboard ship. Stanley walked a mile or two around the deck each day, wrote letters to his grandchildren, read a couple of new books, and attended lectures on the Vikings and their impact on European history. He summed it up, "We have enjoyed cruise more than expected—few dull moments—genuine rest—good food—why not another?"[17]

New York, or midtown Manhattan specifically, was a magnet for the couple. From the Barclay Hotel (now the Inter-Continental) on Lexington Avenue, he fanned out to the United Nations, the offices of *World Press Review,* and numerous art galleries and museums where he and Betty nourished their fondness for painting and sculpture.

Their first trip together to New York was in January 1936 when Stanley was given the Collingwood Prize, an annual honor of the American Society of Civil Engineers to a promising young engineer. One evening they attended the society's banquet and ball ("some affair," said the young Iowan), and the next night they had tickets to see Helen Hayes in *Victoria Regina.*[18]

Al Balk, former editor of *World Press Review,* said New York was a place for Stanley to "unwind" from the work pressures he faced in Muscatine, an unusual twist on the customary weekend migration of big city executives to the countryside or the seashore. Max and Betty usually went to a play or a musical at least one night, and occasionally they attended a concert at Lincoln Center or Carnegie Hall. An evening at a playhouse frequently began with dinner at their favorite French restaurant, LeVert-Galant, where Max took delight in fresh oysters and soft-shell crabs. Occasionally, the Stanleys accepted invitations to receptions for art exhibitions, private dinners with art collectors, and social affairs connected with the United Nations. For the most part, though, they preferred quiet dinners with old friends, such as Balk and his wife Phyllis in their Upper East Side apartment. Stanley's "old-shoe nature," said Balk, "just didn't care for all the dressing up, the black-tie thing" that went with much of the social activity of the U.N. people.[19]

Closer to home the Stanleys found much of their entertainment at the University of Iowa, in Iowa City. Hancher Auditorium provided a variety of concerts, musicals, and ballets. The Museum of Art had a continuing series of exhibitions. And there was Big Ten football in Kinnick Stadium and basketball in the Fieldhouse and, in later years, at Carver-Hawkeye Arena.

Stanley was a *fan*. Normally a serious, intellectual sort, he could be as gleeful over a Hawkeyes victory on the gridiron as a little boy who got his Christmas wish. When he enrolled at the university in 1922, the football team was the scourge of the Big Ten. Under Coach Howard Jones, the Hawkeyes won twenty consecutive games, claimed the conference title after undefeated seasons in 1921 and 1922, and produced seven All-America players, including tackle Fred "Duke" Slater, quarterback Aubrey Devine, and fullback Gordon Locke, whose exploits took on legendary character among Iowa fans of that era.

So Stanley was elated by the revival of Iowa football under coaches Forest Evashevski in the fifties and Hayden Fry two decades later. Here is a journal entry for November 7, 1981: "Iowa 33, Purdue 7—First winning season (6–3 now) for 20 years, also first win over Purdue in 21 years. Great game—great day." The lean years had passed. It was a *"Big day"* two weeks later when Iowa was chosen to go to the Rose Bowl by defeating Michigan State while Ohio State was winning from Michigan. After first deciding he wouldn't go to the New Year's Day game, he went anyway, along with Dave, Jean, and their son Nate. They watched the Rose Bowl Parade before heading for the stadium, where they saw Washington trounce Iowa, 28 to 0. "Team flat," said Stanley. But more exciting times lay ahead.[20]

Likewise, the success of Iowa basketball teams coached by Lute Olson cheered Stanley, even though he often was on Sanibel as the Hawkeyes made their annual run for conference status, if not a championship, and a bid for the National Collegiate Athletic Association tournament. When he could, he listened to the games on WHO radio, the clear channel station in Des Moines, and sometimes he watched replays on ESPN, the sports television network, sitting up into the middle of the night. Then he bought a VCR and had Dave and, later, Kenton Allen send him tapes from the games shown in Iowa.

As the victories rolled up for the football, basketball, and several other teams at the university, Stanley wrote a letter commending Athletic Director Chalmers W. "Bump" Elliott. Observing that Elliott had "received few plaudits and honors," Stanley said many Iowa fans realize "the critically important role you have played in the upgrading of Iowa athletics. You have selected coaches who are not only able in their sports, but are gentlemen in the truest sense and are sympathetic to their responsibilities as part of an educational institution. . . ."[21]

Darrell Wyrick, executive director of the University of Iowa Foundation, remembered Stanley, wearing a black and gold jacket, striding across the campus toward the stadium where the Hawkeyes were about to play Iowa State in their 1984 meeting. Iowa won the game, 59 to 21, and Stanley was hopeful, enthusiastically so, about the season that lay ahead. But he would not know how Iowa finished the season. Two weeks later he was dead. In a letter of sympathy to Betty, Jack Rigler, a Muscatine banker, could not help mentioning "what a *Hawkeye fan* he was!!!" Betty thought so, too, and left a personal tribute with the fan: in the hands that lay folded across his lifeless chest she placed a gold mum with a black I.[22]

16

Visible Dissenter

When Ronald Reagan emerged as the darling of Republican conservatives, Max Stanley reacted sharply against what he saw as a threat to the moderate, progressive policies that were the touchstones of his political philosophy. Consequently, the last five or six years of Stanley's life turned into some of his most active in political affairs. He was particularly troubled by Reagan's foreign policy statements, studded as they were with anti-Communist rhetoric. After watching a Reagan television talk in 1976, Stanley tried to dismiss it as a "charismatic appeal to hard liners," although he doubtlessly realized that Reagan's popularity was broad enough to menace the continuity of U.S. foreign policy and relations with the United Nations. The actor-turned-politician severely tried the Iowan's political allegiance.[1]

Stanley always called himself a Republican and seldom disavowed the party's presidential nominees. He defected in 1964, preferring President Lyndon Johnson over Senator Barry Goldwater; he did it again in 1976, voting for Jimmy Carter rather than President Gerald Ford. Four years earlier, disenchanted with President Richard Nixon and dissatisfied with Democratic Senator George McGovern, he left his ballot for president blank.[2]

With Reagan, though, Stanley was not satisfied with a voting-booth protest. The former California governor represented too much of an abrupt turn, especially in international relations. Stanley had lost confidence in President Carter, and as the 1980 elections neared he began looking for a more suitable candidate. Late in 1977 he sent a campaign contribution to Republican Representative John B. Anderson of Illinois, whom he had gotten to know at a Stanley Foundation conference in Denmark in 1970. He enclosed a letter in which he said he shared the congressman's "concern over the thrust of the ultraconservative special interest groups within the Republican Party. As a lifelong Republican, I feel that I am threatened and that if the Party continues on the path being set by the national Republican leadership, I'll soon find myself an independent, rather than a Republican."[3]

Stanley's dismay was evident in letters he sent to Senate Republican Leader Howard Baker in 1979. He deplored the "hawkish approach" of GOP fund-raising appeals and warned that if "you succeed in your efforts to defeat ratification [of the SALT II Treaty], you will have done a great disservice to the United States and to the Republican Party."[4] (The treaty was not formally submitted to the Senate after the Soviet Union sent military forces into Afghanistan in December 1979; after taking office, the Reagan administration promised to abide by terms of the treaty if the Soviets did the same.)

Stanley began raising funds in 1978 for a presidential bid by Anderson, and in 1980 he plunged eagerly into the congressman's campaign (he and Betty each gave $1,000, the legal limit) and submitted suggestions on foreign policy positions. After Reagan won the Republican nomination, Anderson ran as an independent, and Stanley stayed with him. He sat on the national finance committee and the Iowa steering committee, and he was one of the most successful money raisers in the state.[5]

He teamed up with Nan Waterman, who had been chairwoman of Common Cause, the national citizens' lobby, to lead the Anderson campaign in Muscatine County. To a reporter for Davenport's *Quad-City Times* Stanley voiced his unhappiness with the nominees of the two major parties, saying that Carter was inept in foreign affairs and that Reagan tended to oversimplify the issues. He pointed out that Anderson understood the workings of government, both foreign and domestic, after serving twenty years in Congress.[6]

But Anderson's National Unity Campaign fell short, as political experts predicted it would, with the candidate getting only 7 percent of the national vote for president. In Iowa he received 114,000 votes while Reagan collected 672,000 and Carter 505,000. Anderson fared better in Muscatine County, a Republican stronghold, getting about 1,500 votes, 10 percent of those cast for president.

The day after Reagan's election, Stanley wrote in his journal: "Groggy from shock of Reagan & GOP landslide and a short night. A conservative trend is here. Desirable domestically but hazardous globally if Reagan pursues tough stance."[7] It was one voter's concession statement to the election day victor. After the shock wore off, Stanley did not wait to find out *if* Reagan would pursue his tough stance. He soon was active in attempts to correct what he saw as a dreadful mistake by American voters. He looked seriously at a third-party initiative, began an opinion-disseminating project at the foundation, and joined an effort by several U.N. leaders who hoped to outflank the new administration on a plan to spread economic and technological benefits to Third World nations.

Notes scrawled on a yellow legal pad prior to a visit with Tom Stoner in the summer of 1979 give clues to Stanley's political thinking as the 1980 elections drew nearer. Stoner, a Des Moines broadcasting executive, was the "moderate" candidate for the Republican nomination for the U.S. Senate seat held by Democrat John Culver. Stoner's conservative foe was Republican Representative Charles Grassley of the Third Congressional District. Stanley's notes show that he saw the Republican Party moving to the "right of public" while Culver was "left of public but right [correct] on arms control, etc." But Culver was also a "spender," a frequent complaint Stanley had about liberal Democrats. He urged Stoner to take a "positive not defensive posture" and occupy the middle ground.[8]

Recalling the conversation at Stanley's home, Stoner said his host put considerable stress on the importance of nonproliferation treaties. "I certainly subscribed to his views," Stoner added, "and subsequent events have shown how right he was." The two discussed a number of other international matters, such as human rights, the population explosion, environmental pollution, energy supplies, and economic development for the Third World. Stanley voiced doubt that nations could adequately manage such matters without "international mechanisms."

Stanley was concerned about the 1980 Senate contest lest it turn out as the 1978 race, in which Republican Roger Jepsen upset Democratic Senator Dick Clark. Stanley liked Clark's views on foreign affairs, invited him to foundation conferences, and supported him in his campaign against the conservative Jepsen.[9]

Stimulating trade was among the "pocket book issues" Stanley listed for Stoner, noting particularly Iowa's corn and farm machinery. (Grassley drew criticism the next year from Governor Robert Ray, a close friend of Stoner's, because he voted against a trade agreement with China.) World economic order and Third World development are dependent on stable international relationships, Stanley insisted.

Stoner said he found Stanley's political beliefs akin to his own — "traditional in outlook and progressive in perspective." In 1980, however, progressivism was not in fashion among most Republicans. Grassley easily defeated Stoner in the Republican primary in June and then dislodged Culver in the November election. The new senator later surprised Stanley and gained his respect by giving diligent attention to waste and excess in military spending and then objecting publicly.[10]

An incipient third-party overture—a prospect brightened by the seeming rise of a centrist movement in Great Britain—tempted Stanley in the first year of Reagan's presidency. He and about twenty other Iowans met in a Cedar Rapids motel on a fall Saturday afternoon, October 3, 1981, to talk about the future of John Anderson's National Unity Campaign. They agreed, among other things, that starting a new party should not be seen as launching another Anderson-for-President drive. They contended, though, that some Reagan programs were "ill-conceived, dangerous to the economy, and reckless as to the security of the nation and the world" and should be "seriously challenged—and soon."[11]

But the initiative waned. In August 1983 Anderson mailed some of his supporters "A Statement of Principles" that ended with an appeal to start a new political party. Stanley replied that he was "somewhat ambivalent" about the idea. He mentioned being "deeply distressed that the Republican Party has deviated so far from a number of fundamental principles which have given it strength in the past. . . . I now style myself an Independent rather than a Republican with Independent leanings." But before giving his support to a new party, he wanted a "tolerable chance of success" so that it would not suffer the fate of most third-party stirrings. He thought, however, it was too late to start an effective campaign for 1984 even though "Reagan must be defeated for a variety of reasons." A little over a month later, Stanley had breakfast with Anderson in Washington and went away with the impression that the congressman "seems determined to run again."[12]

While he waited for Anderson to make up his mind, Stanley sent a contribution to Senator Alan Cranston of California, a friend from the world federalist movement who was an early entrant into the race for the Democratic presidential nomination. Stanley also spurned an offer from

Harold Stassen to run the Iowa phase of another of his presidential excursions. After Anderson decided not to run for president in 1984, he endorsed the Democratic candidate, former Vice-President Walter Mondale. Stanley wrote to Anderson, commending his decision and indicating he would give financial support to "Independents for Mondale." He added that he believed "Mondale is more likely to check, if not reverse, today's insane arms race and bring more common sense into our foreign policy."[13]

Beginning early in 1982, the Stanley Foundation began mailing its president's opinions on various public issues to 185 newspapers across the country. Many of these op-ed articles for opinion pages were critical of Reagan policies: on the Star Wars project, Stanley suggested that the President "abandon fantasies of weapons that make us invulnerable" and concentrate on "working out peaceful means for resolving our differences with the Soviet Union"; on the CIA mining of Nicaraguan harbors, he said the United States "is behaving like an international outlaw"; on covert actions generally, he asserted that the government "has no right to interfere in the affairs of other nations even if we disagree with their policies and alliances"; on growing voter support of nuclear-freeze referendums, he said the people are "beginning to question the Reagan administration's moves to further expand the already multiple overkill of our nuclear arsenals."[14]

Stanley had become a visible dissenter. He was volunteering his political views to the people, not only to his fellow Muscatine Rotarians or to members of the 33 Club. Not since his days as a world federalist leader had Stanley appealed so broadly to the public, and then his messages on world government did not turn sharply on partisan arguments.

When he spoke at the Iowa Wesleyan College commencement in May 1983, his remarks on political and international matters were summarized in a story in the *Des Moines Sunday Register.* He was quoted as saying that the Reagan foreign policy was "domineering and arrogant" and that the human rights policy "has deteriorated from dynamic leadership to evasive disregard." He added: "No longer should we tolerate the mounting economic burden of the arms race. Overemphasis on military buildup diverts human and financial resources from critical domestic needs, detracts from our efforts to deal with global problems, and weakens our relations with other nations. . . ." The previous month Stanley addressed a convocation at the University of Dubuque, when he was installed as the school's honorary rector. There, too, Stanley criticized Reagan for neglecting the "leadership role" thrust upon the United States in international affairs by World War II. Five or ten years earlier such partisan comments would have been alien to a Stanley talk, especially one to a campus audience.[15]

As the prospect of a Reagan presidency heightened in 1980, many of Stanley's friends at the United Nations grew uneasy about the likelihood of drastic shifts in U.S. foreign policy. One of them, Baron Rudiger von Wechmar, who was presiding over the U.N. General Assembly, approached Stanley about arranging a special conference to help speed deliberations on Global Negotiations, a proposal to improve the economic and trade balance between rich and poor nations. Von Wechmar feared that a Reagan victory might stymie the U.N. initiatives on what he described as "the serious and sustained attempt to restructure the present world economic order." The veteran West German diplomat promised to line up conference participants if Stanley would provide the forum under foundation auspices. Von Wechmar recognized Stanley as a sympathetic ally, for the previous spring he had attended the foundation's annual conference on United Nations Procedures, which provided a preparatory exploration of Global Negotiations, the theme of the U.N. session later in the year.[16]

The U.N. proposal was given impetus after an international commission led by former West German Chancellor Willy Brandt tried to awaken the richer, industrialized nations of the Northern Hemisphere to the extraordinary danger lurking in the poverty, hunger, and economic chaos of the world's underdeveloped nations in the South. The commission report, issued in February 1980, called for an annual increase of $30 billion in aid to the Third World by the rich nations.

Six months later, as the United Nations opened a special session on the world economy, Secretary of State Edmund Muskie promised a broad range of U.S. economic help, including modern technology, financial aid, and a lowering of tariff barriers. But he added that the American people would weary of giving aid unless Communist countries and the oil-rich nations of the Middle East took part.

Ten days after Reagan's election victory, Stanley was at Arden House in Harriman, New York, for the opening of the foundation's special conference. Most of the thirty participants had U.N. connections; others included representatives of the State Department, the International Monetary Fund, the World Bank, and the Commission for the Economic Community. "The right people at the right time," Stanley wrote in his journal as the sessions began. After the conference, he entered a brief summation: "Near agreement on agenda items re energy & money & banking [items causing the most difficulty in the General Assembly]. Significant progress re procedures. Determination to start global negotiations before Reagan takes office."[17]

The conference report was typed immediately after the participants left; Xerox copies were made that night and, with von Wechmar's approval, distributed the next morning at the U.N. building to the representatives by Jack Smith and Jeff Martin of the foundation staff. The report concluded with the participants' concurrence on the "urgency of the need to begin negotiations on a sound footing in early 1981, given the severity of problems confronting the international economy and the developing countries. . . ." Unmentioned was the biggest obstacle: the probable unwillingness of the incoming Reagan administration to enter negotiations that smacked of a share-the-wealth plan to tap the resources of the industrialized nations to aid the Third World.[18]

For a few weeks, Stanley was euphoric about the maneuvering in which he had a chance to play a part. Four days after the conference ended, his journal contains this note: "Called von Wechmar—elated re Arden House conference—Stanley Fdn is the talk of the town, he says." A few days into the new year, von Wechmar and his wife Susie visited Max and Betty Stanley at their Sanibel Island beach house. It was a good time, but it didn't last.[19]

Late in January, in what amounted to a public appeal to the new administration in Washington, von Wechmar wrote in an op-ed page piece for *The New York Times* that "the key governments of the industrialized North and the developing South have virtually agreed on the rules of procedure and a time-frame for the Global Negotiations. They have agreed on 90 percent of an agenda for the conference." He asked then whether the administration would "examine the issue of North-South negotiations simply from a limited fiscal point of view or grasp the political dimensions of the global round [of negotiations]?" In the end, he closed, "it will be the United States that can make or break the exercise."[20]

Although the Reagan administration had no intention of letting the United Nations tamper with international trade, monetary practices, and energy policies, it preferred foot-shuffling to a firm stance. Reagan himself was more interested in a domestic tax-cutting measure than in boosting foreign assistance. As late as May, Jose Sorzano of the U.S. mission at the United Nations announced that the administration had not completed its review of relations with the developing countries. His statement caused widespread disappointment at the United Nations, where the U.S. lagging was seen as a retreat to an isolationist position. By summer von Wechmar was ready to concede defeat; Global Negotiations could not commence with any hope of success without U.S. participation, and the Reagan administration no longer bothered to hide its disinterest.

Reagan's appointees to key State Department and U.N. posts were not long in confirming Stanley's pre-election trepidation about right-wing shifts in policy. Stanley felt the chill of the changing attitudes on a trip to New York two months after the new administration took charge. After tending to some business at the United Nations on a March afternoon, Stanley and Foundation Director Jack Smith went to a reception at the U.S. mission. The socializing was interrupted so that Ambassador Charles Lichenstein, Sorzano, Marshall Brement, and George Saddler could explain how the administration planned to work with the United Nations. Smith recalled the discussion centering on "two U.N.s—the Security Council, which mattered, and the rest, the General Assembly and the various agencies, which apparently did not matter to the administration." Smith said he looked at Stanley and could tell he was "absolutely furious" about the downgrading of the United Nations. At such a function, Smith said, Stanley normally would ask questions or volunteer a few observations. "All he said that night was, 'Thanks for having us here.'" To his journal Stanley confided his opinion of the U.S. delegation: "Pathetic, naive and uninformed."[21]

As Stanley wrote later to a fellow world federalist, "Here at the foundation we have often said that the advent of the Reagan Administration set us back about ten years in achievement of the objectives which we share with you and many others."[22] For Stanley, they were years he would never recapture.

Lincoln P. Bloomfield, a political science professor at Massachusetts Institute of Technology, perceived a "growing disillusionment" in his old friend from Iowa after seeing him at a conference in the early eighties. "The miracle was probably that he stayed the course as long as he did, in a period when the U.N. was steadily declining in effectiveness as a political institution and the leadership to which Max had been steadily appealing turned away from the multilateral route."[23]

The last affront came in 1984, not many months before Stanley's death, when the State Department refused to grant visas to a political scientist from the Soviet Academy of Sciences and his wife to attend the foundation's summer conference on the United Nations of the Next Decade. The conference theme was, "Peace and Security: The United Nations and National Interests." It was the first time the U.S. government blocked Soviet guests from attending foundation affairs; it apparently was not a malicious act against Stanley, but merely a tit-for-tat reaction to a Soviet bar against an American professor. But Stanley's protests, and those of friends in Congress, were unavailing. The State Department insisted on upholding the kind of diplomatic pettiness Stanley considered ridiculous and reprehensible. Henceforth, he advised the foundation staff, if the State Department continued to cause difficulties for Soviet officials invited to the foundation conferences, then he would schedule such conferences outside the United States.[24]

17

An Artistic Feat

In the relatively brief span of ten years—the last ten years of his life—Max Stanley assembled a collection of African art that is judged among the finest in America. It has been valued at $5 million.[1] Such an accomplishment in so short a time did not surprise those who knew Stanley well. Once he had fixed on a goal, his nature was to strive relentlessly for it, which is how he satisfied his curiosity about the tribal arts of Africa. What did surprise many friends was his attachment to such an unusual hobby. His children found it difficult to imagine their practical-minded father becoming so captivated by such an esoteric diversion, especially when they saw their old playroom in the house on Sunset Drive remodeled into an in-home gallery where their parents displayed many of their favorite sculptures.

All this began with Betty Stanley. In the early years of the Stanley Engineering Company operations in West Africa, she frequently traveled with her husband when he visited the company outposts. While he tended to business matters, she arranged to visit Methodist missions and schools. During a trip to Liberia in 1960, she flew into the bush country to a mission station at Ganta, about 175 miles from Monrovia. She stayed with Dr. and Mrs. George Harley. He was a physician who took care of ailing Africans along with his church and school responsibilities. In his long service in Africa he had accumulated a large store of artifacts and had earned respect as an authority on the native arts. The American visitor was told that Africans who turned to Christianity often brought to the Harleys objects that had been used in tribal rituals. It was their way of renouncing the past. When Betty asked if she could buy a few pieces, the Harleys agreed since they were about to return to the United States to retire. Among the articles she chose was a carved wooden game board and a pair of metal anklets. She also liked a carved figure with two faces, representing a spirit with the ability to see everywhere at all times. It was a popular subject for African carvers. Harley did not want to part with his sculpture, so he promised to get a similar one to send to Muscatine.[2]

More than a decade passed before Max showed a purposeful interest in African art. His early disposition, as the Rockford Plans tests confirmed in 1946, was to slight aesthetic pursuits.[3] But Betty had long been attracted to the arts—to painting, sculpture, music, drama, dance, and literature—and through her he began to appreciate creative expression. The two of them became frequent visitors to the University of Iowa Museum of Art, where they struck up a friendship with Ulfert Wilke, the museum director from 1968 to 1975.

The walls of the Stanley home were a reflection of Betty's eclectic tastes. There she displayed several works by Wilke and by Mauricio Lasansky, the renowned printmaker who taught at the university. From a New York auction she bought an oil painting, "White Lotus," by Georgia O'Keeffe, which hangs in the dining room, always inviting the attention of dinner guests. She also obtained one of O'Keeffe's pencil drawings. Other of her purchases included two lithographs by Marc Chagall, one oil and two watercolors by Carl Mattern, an oil by Jean Marie Couillard, two intaglio prints by Virginia Myers, and several watercolors by Paul Norton, one of which was "Muscatine High Bridge," a long-gone landmark of the city. It was a modest collection, yet it bore witness to Betty's growing interest in the varied modes of contemporary art.

While on a European trip in 1972, the Stanleys went to Munich to meet Wilke, who once had lived in the old Bavarian capital. He guided them around the city, took them to the famous museums and the opera, and then brought them to the apartment of Ludwig Bretschneider, who was considered the pioneer German dealer in African art. As Wilke recalled, "It was here that Max and Betty Stanley each bought a 'souvenir' to remind them of Munich. Max selected a Yoruba rider and Betty a Cameroon clay pipe. Both were fine pieces . . ."[4]

Wilke cultivated Stanley's embryonic curiosity about African art, and the following year Stanley made his first purchase at Merton Simpson's gallery in Manhattan. That started what was to become almost a routine part of trips to New York—visiting galleries and then either suppressing or succumbing to the "temptation" (Stanley's word) to buy a piece or two or more. Early in 1975 Stanley went to Montreal to see the figures Norman Thorn had acquired during the time he was in Liberia managing the Stanley Engineering branch. Stanley liked what he saw and agreed to buy the lot for $4,000, plus packing and shipping.[5] Within a few years Stanley spent five to ten times that much for a single object.

"Spending some time most evenings on African Art," Stanley recorded in his journal in late summer. Two months later he admitted to being "hooked on African Art."[6] As he did when any subject gripped his mind, he began an intensive period of self-schooling: He read books and art journals, visited museums and galleries, talked at length with scholars, dealers, and other collectors. By the end of the year a few dealers bearing African art found their way to Muscatine to call on a prospective customer whose name was floating about in art circles. Others showed up on Sanibel Island when the Stanleys transferred to their winter home in 1976. In March alone they bought twenty-one pieces.

In April, on their way back to Muscatine, the Stanleys stopped at Bloomington, Indiana, to meet Roy Sieber and his wife Sophie. Sieber, an Iowa art school graduate who was professor of African art history at Indiana University, was recognized as a leading authority on the characteristic art from different regions of Africa. From Sieber the novice collector learned that he had made some poor purchases, information that was to make him more aware of the quality and aesthetic value of the objects dealers showed him. Sieber became a regular consultant to Stanley, along with Wilke (among friends Stanley took to calling the two his "hookers" because they had hooked him on his new hobby).[7]

Business trips to Chicago, Houston, Washington, and Los Angeles included detours to galleries and museums and, if possible, lunch or dinner with other collectors. The same happened on travels to Europe — to London, Berlin, Cologne (the curator even took him browsing in the storerooms), and Paris in 1976, to Amsterdam, Brussels, and Hamburg two years later. In Betty he had a kindred spirit. After she had selected three pieces in a Denver gallery, he wrote in his journal, not without some pride, "Betty more interested than she admits."[8]

In 1978 the Stanleys promised their collection to the University of Iowa, with the proviso that the School of Art use it as the foundation for courses and research in African art and the arts of other tribal cultures. By then they had bought about three hundred sculptures and other objects from all regions of Black Africa. Christopher D. Roy, who had studied with Sieber at Indiana, was appointed to the Iowa art faculty that year and was engaged by the Stanleys to prepare an exhibition at Iowa City for spring 1979.

Under Roy's leadership, the Stanley Collection has become a valuable addition to the art school's functions. Part of it is always on display at the museum for public viewing, for teaching purposes, and as a focus for student research projects. The collection's catalog has been used as a textbook in classes on African art. The collection has been a resource for the university's African Studies program, in which faculty members from eleven departments (anthropology, geography, and political science, to mention a few) have prepared courses.

It is understandable that an Iowan who had lived practically all of his life in an environment where farming was a dominant economic and social force would be drawn to the creative idiom of the agricultural villages of Africa. The day-to-day life, in a cycle of centuries, continued to inspire the craftsmen who made what their fellow villagers needed, from spoons and stools for mundane chores to the masks and magical figures for entreaties to supernatural beings. This was not art for art's sake—it was art for daily life, blending with a craft passed on for generations.

As Stanley's collection grew, he familiarized himself with the functions of different objects. Some were for religious or magical ceremonies while others were for group rites, such as the initiation of boys to manhood or the burial of a patriarch. Each new phase of life was marked by ritual. Stanley was taken with the magical objects used in such rituals. Masks were worn for dances in which departed ancestors were thought to be taking part in the performance; when a man wore the mask of a particular spirit, he believed he became the spirit temporarily. Other masks were meant to terrify strangers, especially women who encroached on male initiation rites or other secret rituals. Objects called fetishes usually contained substances consecrated by a "medicine man" and bore the features of revered ancestors.[9]

Broadly speaking, African art includes various crafts—pottery, textiles, basketry, metalwork, and musical instruments—as well as the prized wood sculptures, mural paintings, and rock carvings. With rare exceptions, Stanley purchased only sculptured works. He did not buy weapons, although he once bought a spear with a decorative handle, but only after being assured it was meant solely for ceremonial use as a symbol of political authority. He refrained from objects with an erotic purpose.

Stanley learned to easily identify the tribes from which certain objects came or in which recognizable styles developed—Dogon, Dan, Fang, Senufo, Yoruba, Luba, Bangubangu, Songye, Ibo, and many more. For generations the craftsmen in one community tended to carve a decorative comb or the figure of a woman as their ancestors had done.[10] The Stanleys were particularly fond of carvings from tribes in Zaire, once the Belgian Congo. These are, for the most part, fine, polished sculptures of delicate workmanship. The favorite material of African sculptors is wood. Since wood is perishable, little African art, other than ancient rock carvings, can be traced beyond 150 years. Most of the Stanley Collection predated World War II and doubtlessly was brought from Africa by civil servants of the European colonial governments and by Christian missionaries from western nations.[11]

The 1979 exhibition in Iowa City marked a turning point in Stanley's collecting. Many of the pieces attracted the attention of visiting scholars, collectors, and dealers. While the exhibition was a success, Stanley realized that he had a useful teaching collection for a state university. He wanted to do better than that, so he decided to improve the quality of the collection. Where he had been spending $3,000 or $5,000 for a single object, he began buying what he wanted, even if that meant outlays of $20,000 or $50,000 or more.[12]

While the Stanleys were at Sanibel in January 1984, Marc Felix appeared at their door. He was a Brussels art dealer who had become a trusted friend of the Iowa couple. He brought with him the figure of a Chokwe tribal chief, and Stanley bought it "at a bargain ($150M) price," as he put it in his journal. It must have been that, for the piece increased in value by about $100,000 within a few years. Heading home to Muscatine three months later, the Stanleys stopped in Bloomington to visit Sieber and his wife. "He drooled over our Chokwe Chief," Stanley wrote with delight after bringing out his new possession.[13]

The Chokwe chief was to become a popular attraction for students in Roy's classes and for visitors to a new exhibition of the Stanley Collection in 1985. Once home again in the spring of 1984, Stanley started focusing on plans for that exhibition, and soon he and Roy met to begin selecting the pieces to show (there were about 380 from which to choose). To help catalog the collection, Stanley bought a personal computer, which he set up at home to link with one in Iowa City on which Roy would work. He was prepared for an absorbing task, one he faced with enthusiasm and pride.

The second exhibition, which Stanley did not live to see, was testimony to his will to excel. What had been a respectable regional collection in 1979 had become one worthy of national attention. Stanley had done this by combining mature knowledge with judicious buying, selling, and trading. In a tribute written for the second exhibition, Ulfert Wilke said of Stanley's growing familiarity with African art: "My role and Max's became reversed. It was now I who asked the questions and he who gave the answers."[14]

The Stanley Collection is overshadowed, as are other collections, by the Rockefeller in the Metropolitan Museum of Art in New York. The Rockefeller, however, is not limited to African art, but also contains pre-Columbian (the Indian civilizations of South and Central America) and Oceanic (the South Pacific islands) materials. As a personal collection the Stanley is in the class of the Katherine White Collection in Seattle, and as a university collection it ranks with those at Indiana and the University of California at Los Angeles, both of which were drawn from many sources.[15]

But for Stanley there was more than art in art collecting. He learned about different peoples and how they lived, not only the black Africans but also a substrata of American culture that has the wherewithal to encourage artistic achievement. Stanley was touched by Africa in two ways, first by his engineering work and then by his interest in the native art. Both had an impact on his thinking when he championed proposals to provide various forms of economic and technological assistance to the developing countries of the Third World. The poverty of millions in Africa contrasted starkly with the extravagant, flamboyant lifestyles of many art collectors and dealers. The dour-looking midwestern businessman didn't seem to fit; yet he learned once again that he could move in fast company and earn respect because of his competence, integrity, and tolerance.

Kosta Tsipis, who teaches at the Massachusetts Institute of Technology, was pleasantly surprised when he saw the Stanley Collection on a trip to Iowa City. "I went from exhibit to exhibit, becoming more and more impressed. . . . At the end I told Max that I was overwhelmed by the beauty of the collection, and somewhat slyly, pulling my leg, he said, 'You see, Kosta, not everything beautiful and worthwhile is out in Cambridge. There are some good things in Iowa.' This was a thing he put up again and again — that, for example, he thought one could fight the good cause of arms control and peace from the shores of the Mississippi as well as from the banks of the Potomac, and that culture and taste and intellectual excellence can be found among the fields of Iowa as well as on the banks of the Charles River."[16]

18

Farewell

Max Stanley died September 20, 1984, in an emergency treatment room at Bellevue Hospital in New York City. He was taken there by ambulance after he was stricken with a heart attack in the editor's office at *World Press Review* on Park Avenue in Manhattan's Midtown. He was discussing magazine business matters with Al Balk, the editor, and key staff members when he suddenly slumped over in his chair, speechless and immobile.

Betty learned what had happened when a staff member at the magazine called her at the Barclay Hotel, where she was packing for the return trip to Iowa later in the day. She set out on foot for the magazine offices, only two blocks away, and arrived as the ambulance pulled up at the curb. She rode up in the elevator with the ambulance crew, then back down to watch as her husband was lifted into the vehicle. She got in and rode to the hospital as a paramedic worked over Max.

Balk and his wife Phyllis, a nurse, waited with Betty outside the room where Max was taken. A young priest sat next to her, offered comforting words, and took one of her hands in his. She felt confident that the doctors would revive Max because he seemed to be in such good physical condition for an eighty-year-old. Two months earlier the two of them had gone to the Mayo Clinic in Rochester, Minnesota, for a series of examinations and tests, and both had been pronounced fit. But on that September day in New York a young physician came out of the emergency room to say that Max's life had ended.

Three busy, happy days preceded the sad event of Thursday morning. Betty and Max flew into New York late Sunday afternoon. The next morning he went to the magazine offices to confer with Balk, and she went shopping. Together they went to lunch, joining Brigitte and Jacques Hautelet, an African art dealer they had met a few years earlier in Brussels. Then there was time to look at, but not to buy, some African art pieces before a late-afternoon reception to open a new exhibition at the Center for African Art, to which Max had pledged financial support. With several friends they saw there, the Iowans went to a late dinner at a nearby restaurant.

There were more gallery stops the next two days, including a return to the Center for African Art, and visits with friends from their art circle, including Ulfert Wilke, former director of the Museum of Art at the University of Iowa, and Marc Felix, the good friend who was an art dealer in Brussels. Dinner Tuesday evening was in an elegant home with about fifty guests, most of them art collectors. Wednesday's schedule included an appointment for Max at the Bachrach studio, where he sat for a photographic portrait that was to be the cover of *Consulting Engineer* when the editors announced his selection for the Steinmetz Award, given annually to recognize a distinguished career as a consulting engineer. While in the studio he received a telephone call from his daughter, Jane Buckles, who told him about her daughter Donna's plans for a December marriage to Frank Albert, her English friend. That evening Betty and Max had a quiet dinner with the Balks at LeVert-Galant, the French restaurant they enjoyed so much.

The news of Max's death stunned his friends and neighbors in Muscatine and soon cast a somber spell over the city where he had lived for a half century. "There was almost a sense of disbelief about it," said one resident. "It was quite an emotional time in Muscatine, especially for old-time employees of the [Stanley] companies," said a former HON executive. Mayor Donald Platt ordered flags at public buildings flown at half-staff, and he disregarded the complaint of an anonymous caller who insisted that only government officials and members of the armed services were entitled to such tribute. For four days Max Stanley was honored as the First Citizen.

Letters and telegrams expressing sorrow and extending consolation arrived in voluminous convergence from all parts of the country and from many parts of the world. From numerous diplomats, such as Alfonso Garcia Robles and Rudy von Wechmar; from Senator Alan Cranston, who remembered the heyday of world federalism; from directors of foundations dedicated to improving international relations—the Arms Control Association, the Institute of Cultural Affairs, the American Committee on East-West Accord, and many more; from Jack Rigler, who saluted a fellow Hawkeyes fan; from JoAnn Turner, who was grateful that Max and Betty "came to the rescue of the Corning Public Library. . . ." Bouquets and sprays of flowers multiplied, as did the donations given as memorials.

On Saturday evening and Sunday afternoon the friends and neighbors came, and stood in long lines, to see the family at the Ralph Wittich funeral home. Mary Jo Stanley, Dick's wife, remembered her daughter Lynne saying she "had never seen so many crusty, middle-aged men with tears in their eyes. We all heard for the first time," Mary Jo added, "of the many private acts of kindness he had done," thinking of the men and women who told how her father-in-law had provided money to help pay medical bills, or make a mortgage payment, or put a child through college.

A private burial, attended only by family members, in Memorial Park, near the city's western edge, preceded a memorial service in Wesley United Methodist Church. In addition to the Rev. Paul Williamson, four family friends were invited to speak.

Stanley Howe, president of HON Industries, mentioned Max's "human relations" emphasis in the jobs he provided through HON and SCI: "A profit-sharing program was developed before there was any profit. Cost-of-living programs, sick-leave programs, communications programs, all far ahead of their times, were developed." Max, he stressed, wanted the members of his companies to take pride in the way the businesses were run, not just in the financial returns of their labors.

Mayor Platt touched on Max's leadership of community efforts to attract more industry "to a dying old river town with a stagnated economy." Proudly he added that Muscatine "now enjoys a broad economic base, low unemployment . . . and is the envy and bright spot of the entire state of Iowa."

Darrell Wyrick, president of the University of Iowa Foundation, commended Max for his "good works for education" through service on the boards of the university foundation and Iowa Wesleyan College, generous gifts to schools and educational organizations, and the African art collection bequeathed to the university.

Congressman Jim Leach, whom Max considered a friend as well as a political ally, said: "No individual in America has given more of himself in time, financial assistance, and scholarly endeavor to the cause of advancing and strengthening international law and institutions. . . . There hasn't been a serious student of international organizations or ambassador to the United Nations in the last thirty years who hasn't known in one way or another the impact of Max Stanley."

Leach also read a message from U.N. Secretary-General Javier Perez de Cuellar, who wrote: "We shall always be particularly grateful for the encouragement and support that he provided to furthering the principles and objectives for the United Nations." He referred to the Stanley Foundation conferences as "a great, indeed unique, contribution to promoting international cooperation, and we shall always be in his debt for that."

Williamson spoke of his parishioner as a "global citizen" who recognized that where a person lived "has very little to do with allegiance of the heart. Whether in Soviet Russia, Tanzania, or his own country, Max found that loyalty to the whole world."

Then, before the benediction, the congregation sang, to the tune of Jean Sibelius's "Finlandia," verses so fitting with Max's beliefs that most in the sanctuary were moved to tears. The hymn was their farewell to a companion who, more than most, knew the world as home.

> This is my song, O God of all the nations,
> A song of peace for lands afar and mine.
> This is my home, the country where my heart is;
> Here are my hopes, my dreams, my holy shrine;
> But other hearts in other lands are beating
> With hopes and dreams as true and high as mine.
>
> My country's skies are bluer than the ocean,
> And sunlight beams on cloverleaf and pine.
> But other lands have sunlight too, and clover,
> And skies are everywhere as blue as mine.
> Oh, hear my song, thou God of all the nations,
> A song of peace for their land and for mine.
>
> This is my prayer, O Lord of all earth's kingdoms,
> Thy kingdom come; on earth thy will be done.

Let Christ be lifted up till all men serve him,
And hearts united learn to live as one.
Oh, hear my prayer, thou God of all the nations.
Myself I give thee; let thy will be done.

At Betty's request, the service ended with the choir singing "Hallelujah!" from Handel's *Messiah*.

Appendices

A

Global Citizenship

Max Stanley's address at the University of Dubuque,
April 27, 1983

Like it or not, our great country is an integral part of the spinning globe we call the world; many Americans wish it were otherwise. The comfortable isolation we enjoyed prior to and following World War I is but a happy memory. The Atlantic to the east, the Pacific to the west, and friendly nations to the north and the south no longer assure security. Our once comfortable resource self-sufficiency has eroded. Our economy relies heavily on imported raw materials including petroleum and on manufactured products such as communication equipment and autos. We also rely upon such exports as grain, machinery, and high technology products. Yes, not only geographically, but also economically and for security we are integrally tied to the rest of the world.

Ready or not, World War II thrust the United States into a leadership role from which there is no withdrawal. Too many Americans, including President Ronald Reagan, would reduce this role if not reject it completely. As the war ended, the United States was a leader in creating new international institutions – the United Nations, the World Bank, the International Monetary Fund, and a host of the U.N.'s special agencies – destined to emphasize a multilateral approach to peace, security, and other global problems. Then followed the Marshall Plan, the Truman Doctrine, the Cold War with intensified Soviet-American confrontation, and the frightening race for nuclear and conventional weapons superiority. Subsequent economic, political, and social developments have vastly complicated the critical issues and problems facing the world community. Today our world drifts towards economic chaos and international anarchy because it lacks both a coordinated multilateral response to its problems and determined, innovative leadership — leadership that the United States and other powerful nations fail to provide. We shy away from this role which involves both heavy responsibility and enormous opportunity because too many of our leaders and the great majority of their followers are inadequately informed and motivated to respond to the demands of global citizenship.

Global Problems

As a member of the world community and as a country from which leadership is properly expected, we have both a high stake and a heavy obligation in managing global problems. What are these problems?

By far the most serious global problem is assuring peace and security. An alternative security system must be developed to replace current dependence on the threat and use of national military force. Adequate procedures and institutions must be created and used to assure peaceful settlement of international differences, protect nations from overt or covert intervention, and thereby allow general and complete disarmament.

Economic order is a second issue. The various systems and mechanisms comprising the world economic order must be improved to better handle ever-expanding trade, commerce, and development.

Achieving an acceptable pattern and a tolerable pace of economic and social development for the less developed two-thirds of the world's population is a third critical issue.

A fourth issue concerns resource depletion and population growth. Use of the earth's finite resources and population growth must be balanced to achieve and sustain a quality of life compatible with human dignity.

Protecting and managing the biosphere is a fifth issue. Hazardous deterioration of the biosphere must be avoided while enhancing environmental and resource contributions to the quality of life.

The sixth and most fundamental global issue concerns human rights. Elemental human rights need to be extended to all people, and better systems must be structured to protect these rights.

While these six broad global problems are not new, they have grown in seriousness and complexity as the result of technological and political change, especially since World War II. Technology has compressed the world. Transmission of infections—human disease, terrorism, or economic inflation—has accelerated. Through television we vicariously experience the jubilation of a royal wedding in Europe, the pain and anguish of an earthquake victim in South America, or the terror of a soldier in combat in any one of too many global hot spots. No nation is an island unto itself. Local crises immediately become global concerns. Nations are more economically interdependent. Through the development of powerful nuclear and conventional weapons, technology has had a direct, and mostly negative, impact on international peace and security. Human desires and aspirations are expanding.

The management of the six critical issues is made more difficult by the proliferation of nation states; U.N. membership has grown from the 50 charter signers to 157 vastly diversified nations. It is further handicapped by the East/West or industrialized nation confrontation, the North/South or rich/poor confrontation, and power balances shifting from bipolar to multipolar.

I need not dwell on these six global problems. You are all well aware of their scope and the serious lack of progress in finding solutions. Global problems are not well managed.

Challenge

Is it possible for a world community of over four billion people represented by numerous sovereign nations varying in size, power, population, wealth, ideology, culture, experience, capability, and interest to manage critical global problems? Not, I believe, until their leaders face facts, restrain excessive nationalism, and cooperate to gain common objectives. Pursuit of short-term benefits must be subordinated to longer-range common goals. Better global and regional institutions must be structured and used. Progress must be made towards a world without war. Economic and political factors as elements of security must receive greater attention. These objectives will not be achieved, indeed will not be seriously pursued, without a greater sense of global citizenship.

Is it possible for the United States with its complex political structure, serious economic problems, expanding military establishment, and exaggerated fear of communism and Soviet military power, to provide better leadership in the management of global problems? Not, I believe, until our attitudes and approaches reflect a much greater sense of global citizenship.

If responsibility and opportunity truly parallel power and affluence—and I believe they do—the United States ought to be the world's leading advocate of a more ordered world without war and the most dedicated activist promoting wise management of critical world issues. Competence, technology, affluence, experience, and heritage all combine to equip us uniquely for leadership. The missing ingredient is a strong national will to provide such leadership. The development of national will depends upon vastly enlarging the American constituency supporting a stronger global leadership role.

Global Citizenship

Each of us—by virtue of our residence—is a citizen of the globe. Such global citizenship, however, is quite different from that enjoyed by citizens of a nation. As yet there is no central world authority or government to which one owes loyalty or from which one expects rights, privileges, and protection. (Parenthetically, I would suggest that difficult as achievement may be, global institutions with extranational, if not supranational, authority will, in the long run, be used to manage serious global problems and to provide rights, privileges, and protection to the inhabitants of the earth.) Therefore, global citizenship as the term is used here is not a formal legalistic status. Rather, it is some combination of beliefs, attitudes, and convictions concerning the policies and leadership of national governments regarding the management of global problems.

A global citizen, in conformity with this crude definition, would be both tolerably knowledgeable and positively concerned about global issues and the current inadequate efforts to manage them. One would understand the harmful impact of poorly managed global problems upon the security and economic well-being of one's own country and would have firm convictions about desirable national policy and leadership initiatives to deal with global issues.

If national policy and leadership in this or in any other nation are to be influenced, a stronger constituency of globally minded citizens must be developed at three interrelated levels. One essential is an expanded group of opinion shapers in the private as well as the public sectors who forcefully advocate more sensible governmental policy and more consistent innovative and intelligent leadership in the international arena. These opinion shapers would help to inform the public and also to prod decision makers. A second need is a better informed public committed to support the advocacy of opinion shapers and influence governmental officials. Finally, more globally minded persons must be advanced to decision-making positions in the public and private sectors. They must not only be fully aware of global problems but strongly committed to solving them in concert with other nations. Obviously, decision makers influence the public and opinion shapers. Dynamic guidance from the White House is essential for, as Theodore Roosevelt once said, it is a "bully pulpit."

How then can we increase the number of informed, concerned, and committed global citizens?

Education

Education has a great but largely unfulfilled role in stimulating global citizenship. More people must be motivated to influence US foreign policy toward better management of global problems. One's attitudes and beliefs are influenced by many factors: opinions of family, friends, and associates; judgments of prominent persons and leaders; events at home and abroad as reported or misreported by media; and value judgments which usually reflect one's early home, school, church, and community environments. Nothing, however, does more to shape one's attitudes and beliefs than knowledge and understanding of our world—its peoples and its problems.

While, for some, a unique or overseas experience may be a contributing factor, for most of us the educational process—informal as well as formal—is the primary source of knowledge and understanding. My sad lament is that our formal educational institutions from kindergarten to graduate level, including so-called adult education, fail miserably to provide the global perspective essential to global citizenship.

Through my work at the Stanley Foundation I am often in contact with some of our nation's brightest young adults. I am often appalled at how little these holders of B.A.s, M.A.s, and Ph.D.s comprehend or appreciate the United Nations, global problems, or the world itself.

At the other end of the scale, we were amazed several years ago to discover how little teaching to encourage global knowledge and understanding occurred in the primary, secondary, and, yes, in the community college of our city. Curricula were such that most high school graduates had only the faintest knowledge of the geographic and demographic nature of the world, and almost no perception, let alone understanding, of the global problems which would inevitably impact upon their lives. We responded with a program called "Project Enrichment," which provides teaching aids and assistance to instructors and sponsors extracurricular activities. This program has helped to overcome some deficiencies, but it is far from enough.

Preparation for global citizenship places two demands upon educators. First, traditional curricular patterns from kindergarten to graduate school should be modified and augmented to better prepare graduates for citizenship in the vast, complex, and ever-changing world. Particular attention should be given to curriculum and requirements at the collegiate and graduate levels where the leaders of the next generation are being prepared. Greater international and multidisciplinary emphasis will produce more global citizens and strengthen domestic citizenship as well.

Second, educators, along with media executives and NGO activists, must enlarge and improve the informal educational opportunities for the general public—those voters and the leaders who will influence U.S. foreign policy in the near future. Too few governmental officials, opinion shapers, and private sector leaders have yet developed a truly global perspective. Listening recently to congressional debate on foreign issues convinced me that many members of Congress are sadly lacking in knowledge and understanding of the world and its problems.

Constituency Building

Fortunately, a solid base of globally minded citizens exists in this country, but it must be enlarged and strengthened. A considerable number of nongovernmental organizations (NGOs) are actively dealing with issues related to global problems. The varied activities of these NGOs include research, education, advocacy, and lobbying. Some NGOs are membership organizations; others are institutes, centers, foundations, and departments of educational institutions. Many of these organizations focus on a particular area such as disarmament, development, human rights, or the environment. Others have a broader scope of activity. Whatever their scope or focus, these NGOs and the people involved in them recognize that multilateral action is necessary to manage global problems. Hence, they think and act as global citizens.

Numerous individuals are influenced towards global citizenship by participation or contact with these NGOs. Additionally, many other persons reason their way to a global outlook as a result of education, experience, travel, or study. During the past few years, increasing numbers at home and abroad, alarmed by the potential hazards of nuclear war, have recognized the urgency of managing global problems—at least those related to peace and security. Some, but far from enough, governmental and private sector leaders have already joined the ranks of convinced global citizens.

The complications of influencing public opinion on global issues is illustrated by an educational program to enlarge the disarmament constituency which was suggested at a recent Stanley Foundation–sponsored conference on public opinion and disarmament priorities.

To attract more people, education must be on a large scale with an emphasis on activities that:

1. Demonstrate in understandable terms that the military power, particularly nuclear, of the United States and its NATO allies and that of the Soviet Union and its Warsaw Pact allies, is essentially balanced
2. Counter the misconception that a major buildup of U.S. nuclear weapons must occur before there can be a nuclear freeze or negotiated limitations and reduction
3. Moderate the unreasonable fear of the Soviet Union by clear presentations of its security problems and its economic, social, and diplomatic difficulties
4. Explain the harmful domestic impacts of excessive military spending and significant economic, social, and political benefits of freeing financial and human resources to cope with vital domestic problems

Similar want lists could easily be prepared for the other major global problems.

Building upon foundations such as those just cited calls for effort in two areas. The first, largely educational in nature, as already discussed, involves increasing people's knowledge of the world and its problems and making them more aware of the urgency of better management. Otherwise, few people will be motivated to advocate and support changes in U.S. policy and leadership. The second effort concerns changing some of our approaches to international affairs and modifying some of the widely held opinions that now handicap U.S. leadership in the international arena.

Style and Approach

While an expanding constituency of global citizens is essential to more effective U.S. leadership in the international arena, changes must also be made in the way we deal with other nations.

Many of our current operational patterns reflect conditions prevalent during the period before World War II when we enjoyed isolated security or the decade of unparalleled U.S. power just after World War II. Others are strongly influenced by widely held value concepts and attitudes. Both our philosophic approach and *modus operandi* must be modified if the United States is to be an effective leader in managing global problems.

NATIONALISM – The United States as well as most nations is afflicted by excessive nationalism. It is the major block to effective management of global problems. We need not abandon warranted pride and strong belief in our country. We need, however, to moderate our nationalistic spirit with a greater sense of global concern.

COOPERATION – The name of the game in managing global problems must be cooperation among nations. We need to overcome our tendency to unilaterally make a decision or take some action and then expect others to agree. This domineering and sometimes arrogant approach is usually counterproductive; witness the recent confrontation with our Western allies over the Soviet pipeline and intermediate range nuclear force negotiations.

MULTILATERALISM – Bilateralism, the diplomacy of the past, will never be eliminated, but only multilateralism can solve most global problems. Even in the area of disarmament, where some nuclear issues involve only the Soviet Union and the United States, the multilateral approach such as the two U.N. Special Sessions on Disarmament is essential.

LONG-RANGE THINKING – Americans are oriented to expect instant results whereas managing global problems is slow and tedious. Eleven years were required to negotiate the U.N. Convention on the Law of the Sea. While short-term national benefits are not to be overlooked, the United States must exhibit more concern for the long-range objectives beneficial to both the world community and our country.

POWER—National power and influence do not depend on military strength alone; economic and political strength are fully as important. Overemphasis on military buildup diverts human and financial resources from critical domestic needs, detracts from our efforts to deal with global problems, and weakens our political relations with other nations. A better balance of the three elements is needed.

NATURE—Only within the last fifteen years has the world community been shocked into realizing that we must protect and enhance our environment. Adjustment of U.S. policy to this reality is only partially accomplished. We should emphasize better management of the biosphere. Joining the rest of the world by ratifying the U.N. Convention on the Law of the Sea would strengthen the U.S. approach in this area.

SECURITY—To achieve secure peace with freedom and justice, nations must break the mental shackles imposed by centuries of reliance on the threat and use of national force. A world without war requires an alternative security system with mechanisms to resolve peacefully controversies among nations, comprehensive disarmament, and international techniques to deter imminent aggression and to deal effectively with breaches of peace. Until our country gives more than lip service to this concept, we will be severely handicapped in dealing with the most critical global issues of peace and security. For much too long, our emphasis has been on planning war rather than on preparing for peace. Our efforts to negotiate disarmament agreements pale in comparison to our efforts to develop and amass ever greater weapons of mass destruction. Too many of our leaders, as well as those of other countries, are crippled by a near paranoiac obsession that only unlimited armaments assure peace and security. This narrow mindset severely restricts the possibility of radically changing the way we think about security and defense.

HUMAN RIGHTS—The status of human rights throughout the world is an important yardstick for determining how well other critical issues are being managed. The U.S. approach to human rights worldwide has deteriorated from dynamic leadership to evasive disregard. Rhetoric, yes, but refusal to ratify numerous U.N. human rights conventions and continued support of dictatorial governments which are disregarding human rights are deeds that speak louder than words.

We value political and human rights — freedom of worship, speech, assembly, and movement, and rights of equal treatment, privacy, dignity, fair trial, and property ownership. We need to expand our definition of human rights to recognize the rights of food, shelter, health care, employment, and education — the needs of those suffering from extreme poverty and malnutrition. We need to include the most elemental and inalienable human right to which every citizen of this globe is entitled — the freedom from the insecurity and trauma of war, terrorism, and barbarism.

Conclusion

I will conclude these remarks by mentioning another element essential to better management of global problems. Wisdom and intelligence, cooperation and coordination, innovation and determination are all necessary, but they are not enough. We need greater compassion. Understanding, respect, and love are needed to accommodate our differences and unite our efforts to enhance the livability and grandeur of this tiny ball spinning in space.

U Thant, a quiet, thoughtful man from Burma, who served as Secretary-General of the United Nations for ten years, repeatedly stressed the moral and spiritual aspects as important elements of the human approach. In a farewell speech to the Planetary Citizens he said:

What was my basic approach to all problems? . . . I would describe it as the human approach or the central importance of the human element in all problems: political, economic, social, colonial, racial, etc.

The problems we face are global in proportion, but their solution begins with individuals. I challenge each of you to think and act as global citizens and to commit yourselves to educating your friends, family, associates, and students for a greater sense of responsibility concerning this fragile planet we call home.

B

C. Maxwell Stanley:
Service, Honors, and Awards

Max Stanley's scholastic achievement was recognized by his election to Tau Beta Pi, the engineering scholastic honorary fraternity, during his college years.

Throughout his career, Max Stanley was active in professional engineering societies. He attained the membership level of Fellow in the American Consulting Engineers Council, the American Society of Civil Engineers, the American Society of Mechanical Engineers, and the Institute of Electrical and Electronic Engineers.

He was a registered professional engineer in twenty states and the District of Columbia. He held a Certificate of Qualification from the National Council of Engineering Examiners.

In addition, Max Stanley received many recognitions and awards and held numerous leadership positions throughout his distinguished career. These included:

1933	The Alfred Noble Prize from the American Society of Civil Engineers for a technical paper of exceptional merit.
1935	The Collingwood Prize from the American Society of Civil Engineers for a paper describing an engineering work or investigation contributing to engineering knowledge.
1943	The John Dunlap Memorial Award from the Iowa Engineering Society, in recognition of an outstanding paper presented to IES.

1947	The Anson Marston Award, recognizing outstanding service to the Iowa Engineering Society.
1949	Served as president of the Iowa Engineering Society.
1951–1965	Served as trustee, Iowa Wesleyan College.
1954–1956	Served as president of the United World Federalists.
1957–1964	Served as president of the Muscatine Development Corporation.
1958–1965	Served as chairman of the Council of the World Association of World Federalists.
1960–1968	Served as a member of the General Board of Christian Social Concerns of the Methodist Church
1961	Awarded the honorary degree Doctor of Humane Letters from Iowa Wesleyan College.
1962	The Distinguished Service Award from the Iowa Engineering Society, honoring outstanding service to the engineering profession.
1963	Decorated with Grand Commander, Star of Africa, by the government of Liberia in recognition for engineering work and achievement in the Republic of Liberia.
1963–1965	Served as chairman of the Board of Trustees of Iowa Wesleyan College.
1964–1966	Served as president of the United World Federalists.
1965	Award for Outstanding Service to the Engineering Profession, from the National Society of Professional Engineers.
1965–1984	Served as honorary trustee, Iowa Wesleyan College.
1966	The Edwin B. Lindsay Peace Award for contribution to world peace from the United World Federalists.
1966–1976	Served as director, University of Iowa Foundation
1967	Distinguished Service Award from the University of Iowa, recognizing graduates for meritorious service to their community, state, and nation.
1967	Decorated with the Order of African Redemption by the government of Liberia for service to the Republic of Liberia.
1970	Awarded the honorary degree Doctor of Humanities Honoris Causa from the University of Manila, Republic of the Philippines.
1971	The Hancher-Finkbine Medallion, from the Univer-

sity of Iowa, recognizing outstanding alumnae leaders who have demonstrated leadership, learning, and loyalty and mutual concerns for the traditions and vitality of the university.

1971–1975	Served as president of the University of Iowa Foundation.
1972–1975	Served as trustee of Garrett Theological Seminary.
1973	Served as member of the Board of Governors of the American Institute of Consulting Engineers.
1975	The Distinguished Service Award for service to the private practice of engineering from the Professional Engineers in Private Practice division of the National Society Professional Engineers.
1975	Awarded honorary membership in the Iowa Engineering Society for high professional attainment and exceptional service to the engineering profession and Iowa Engineering Society.
1975–1976	Served as chairman of the Committee of Fellows of the American Consulting Engineers Council.
1976	Named Paul Harris Fellow of Rotary International.
1976–1984	Served as lifetime honorary director, University of Iowa Foundation.
1978	Awarded the honorary degree Doctor of Humane Letters from Augustana College.
1979	The Herbert Hoover Humanitarian Award for the Iowa Engineering Society, awarded once every five years to an individual who has demonstrated exceptional concern for the condition of mankind and has translated that concern, through personal actions and deeds, to improve the intellectual as well as physical conditions of the world in which we live.
1980	First recipient of the Oscar Schmidt Iowa Business Leadership Award from the College of Business of the University of Iowa, recognizing achievement by an Iowa business person.
1983	The Past Presidents Award of the American Consulting Engineers Council, awarded by the ACEC past presidents in recognition of specific accomplishments or service to the profession or to ACEC.
1983	Named Honorary Rector, University of Dubuque.
1984	The Steinmetz Award, recognizing a distinguished

career in consulting engineering, from *Consulting Engineer* magazine.

1985   Posthumous presentation and recognition by the United Nations Association of the U.S.A. at their national convention in honor of contribution toward the cause of peace.

1986   The Eisenhower Tribute Award from the Business Executives for National Security (posthumous).

Notes

Chapter Notes will contain the following abbreviations:

AES — Arthur E. Stanley
CMS — C. Maxwell Stanley
DMS — David M. Stanley
EMS — Elizabeth M. Stanley
HON — HON Industries and Home-O-Nize
JSB — Jane Stanley Buckles
RHS — Richard H. "Dick" Stanley
RJ — the author
SCI — Stanley Consultants Incorporated
SF — Stanley Foundation
U of I — University of Iowa

Chapter 2

1. Much of the material about the Stanleys in Corning is drawn from interviews with AES, Dec. 3, 1986, and his cousin Byron Stanley, Oct 23, 1986, who still lives in Corning.

2. Donna Buckles, one of CMS's granddaughters, has collected material on the Stanley ancestors; Laura Stanley, CMS's mother, once provided him with hand-written records of the Stephenson and Emmons lines from which she was descended.

3. School grades provided by Ken Mallas, superintendent of schools in Corning.

4. From copies of news stories in the *Adams County Free Press,* supplied by Ken Mallas.

5. Ibid.

6. Claude Stanley recounted his wartime exploits for Ruth S. Beitz, whose article "Somewhere in France" appeared in the *Iowan* (Summer 1965).

7. CMS, occasional correspondence and journal, July 2, 1965. Files are held by SCI or E & M Charities, Muscatine, Iowa.

8. Leland L. Sage, *A History of Iowa,* (Ames: Iowa State University Press, 1974), 265.

9. Arnold Garson, "The Stanley Touch from Moravia to Monrovia," *Des Moines Sunday Register,* Oct. 31, 1982; Marilyn Jackson and Charles W. Roberts, "Citizens of the World: The Stanleys of Muscatine," the *Iowan* (Spring 1980).

10. Biographical material on CMS is held by SCI, Muscatine, Iowa.

11. EMS interview, Aug. 28, 1986; CMS biographical material.

12. CMS talk, "Memorial to Floyd A. Nagler," U of I College of Engineering, Apr. 14, 1934.

13. EMS interview, plus Jackson-Roberts article.

14. EMS interview; AES interview; Garson, "Stanley Touch."

15. AES interview; CMS biographical material.

16. RHS conversation with RJ, Feb. 23, 1988.

17. CMS talk, SCI annual conference, Apr. 28, 1962.

Chapter 3

1. EMS interview, Aug. 23, 1986.

2. Robert A. Caro, quoted in *Extraordinary Lives,* ed. William Zinsser (New York: American Heritage, 1986; distributed by Houghton Mifflin).

3. Richard A. Pence, *The Next Greatest Thing: 50 Years of Rural Electrification in America* (Washington, D.C.: National Rural Electric Cooperative Association, 1984). The section "Finding the Way" traces the development of the New Deal electrification plan.

4. Ibid.

5. Carl Hamilton, "Former REA Official Remembers . . . Dream Times," *Iowa REC News,* Iowa Association of Electric Cooperatives, May 1985.

6. CMS journal, Aug. 5, Nov. 18, and Dec. 12, 1936. Journals are held by SCI, Muscatine, Iowa.

7. Jill Tubbs and Jim Sayers, "A Leader in Rural Electric Development," *Iowa REC News,* July 1985.

8. Sanford K. Fosholt interview, Sept. 24, 1986.

9. CMS journal, Mar. 31, 1945.

10. CMS journals, Apr. 14, May 12, June 1, 1945, and Mar. 28, 1946.

11. Fosholt interview, Oct. 1, 1986.

12. CMS journals, Apr. 12, 1952, June 2, 1953, Dec. 14, 1966.

13. Ron Barrett interview, Jan. 26, 1987.

14. Fosholt interview, Sept. 24, 1986; AES interview, Dec. 2, 1986; RHS conversation with RJ, Feb. 23, 1988.

15. CMS talk, "Iowa Rural Electric Power Supply: Past, Present and Future," Iowa Rural Electric Cooperative Association managers' meeting, May 31, 1956.

16. CMS, "Time for Change: An Argument for Less Confusion in the Rate Making Process," *Public Utilities Fortnightly,* June 1959.

17. Carl Hamilton, *In No Time At All* (Ames: Iowa State University Press, 1974), 17, 18.

18. CMS, "Design of Rural Electric Systems," paper distributed by American Institute of Electrical Engineers, Dec. 1950.

19. CMS talk, "Change," Finkbine dinner, University of Iowa, Apr. 25, 1963, U of I *Extension Bulletin,* June 1, 1963.

Chapter 4

1. CMS journal, Dec. 7 and Dec. 16, 1941. Journals are held by SCI, Muscatine, Iowa.

2. Various journal entries from summer 1941 and into early 1942 record the effects on CMS and the company of the war atmosphere.

3. EMS interview, Sept. 12, 1986.

4. DMS interview, Jan. 7, 1987.

5. Kenton Allen telephone conversation with RJ, Apr. 2, 1987.

6. DMS interview, Jan. 1, 1987.

7. Wendell L. Willkie, writing in "We, the People," *Fortune,* Apr. 1940, quoted in *Never Again: A President Runs for a Third Term,* by Herbert S. Parmet and Marie B. Hecht (New York: Macmillan, 1968) 85.

8. CMS journal, Mar. 14, 1942.

9. Day by day the journal entries tell of the progressing work at Sioux Falls.

10. CMS to AES, Apr. 17, 1942. Files are held by SCI or E & M Charities, Muscatine, Iowa.

11. CMS to AES, May 2, 1942.

12. Ibid.

13. CMS to AES, Sept. 1, 1942; AES to CMS, July 22, 1942.

14. CMS journals, Dec. 12, 1942, Aug. 26, 1943.

15. AES interview, Dec. 2, 1986.

16. Claude M. Stanley to CMS, Aug. 12, 1946.

17. CMS journal, Dec. 29, 1942.

Chapter 5

1. Company reports, employee publications, and sales brochures are sources of much of the data used in this chapter. See SCI files, Muscatine, Iowa.

2. Ron Barrett interview, Jan. 26, 1987.

3. CMS journal, Dec. 31, 1946; Sanford Fosholt interview, Sept. 24, 1986. Journal and CMS occasional correspondence are held by SCI or E & M Charities, Muscatine, Iowa.

4. Interviews with RHS, Oct. 1, 1986, Gregs Thomopulos, Oct. 29, 1986, Barrett, Oct. 16, 1986, and Fosholt, Sept. 24, 1986.

5. CMS journal, Mar. 4, 1957.

6. AES interview, Dec. 2, 1986; Barrett interview.

7. Interviews with RHS, AES, Barrett, Fosholt.

8. CMS journal, Feb. 10, 1966; AES interview.

9. CMS journals, Apr. 28, 1969, Mar. 30, 1970; AES note to RJ, Mar. 1988.

10. CMS talk, SCI officers dinner, Feb. 22, 1971.

11. CMS journal, May 15, 1971, Dec. 31, 1971.

12. CMS, "The Engineer and Environment," *Civil Engineering* (July 1972).

13. CMS report, "Stanley Consultants and Environmental Activities," SCI document, Jan. 4, 1973.

14. Milton Carlson to RJ, Nov. 18, 1986.

15. Hunter Hughes, review of *Consulting Engineer,* by C. Maxwell Stanley, *Mechanical Engineering* (July 1961).

16. CMS articles in *Consulting Engineer:* "Nonprofessional Ownership," (May 1970); "Curb Nonprofessional Ownership?" (June 1971); "To Bid or Not to Bid" (Jan. 1972); "The Client and Price Competition" (Feb. 1973); "Discipline, Disclosure and Dedication" (Jan. 1974); "A Jekyll and Hyde Approach" (response to "I Gave Up Ethics—To Eat") (Dec. 1975).

17. Interviews with Henry M. Black and A. F. Faul, Oct. 10, 1986.

18. CMS journal, Mar. 31, 1955; Fosholt interview.

19. Barrett interview.

20. RHS and Fosholt interviews; CMS memo to staff, Dec. 3, 1969.

Chapter 6

1. Robert L. Carl interview, Sept. 4, 1987.

2. Arnold Garson, "Slam-bang Production Helps HON Stay Strong," *Des Moines Register,* Nov. 7, 1982.

3. CMS manuscript, "The HON Story," Chap. 1, pp. 1–3. See text, p. 80, for background on this forthcoming volume.

4. Ibid., Chap. 1, p. 5.

5. Ibid., Chap. 2, p. 10.

6. AES interview, Dec. 2, 1986.

7. EMS interview, Sept. 10, 1986.

8. CMS manuscript, "The HON Story," Chap. 4, pp. 16, 17.

9. CMS manuscript, "The HON Story," Chap. 8, p. 1; James H. Soltow, "HON Story," Unpubl. manuscript, p. 80.

10. CMS manuscript, "The HON Story," Chap. 7, pp. 3–6.

11. Ibid.

12. CMS manuscript, "The HON Story," Chap. 11, pp. 17–19; Carl interview.

13. Soltow, "HON Story," p. 55.

14. CMS manuscript, "The HON Story," Chap. 1, p. 5, and numerous journal entries on HON matters; Soltow, "HON Story," 3. CMS journal and correspondence on file, SCI or E & M Charities, Muscatine, Iowa.

15. Soltow, "HON Story," 12; Garson "Slam-bang Production," Nov. 7, 1982.

16. "Stanley Will Leaves Funds for Foundation, Charities," *Muscatine Journal,* Sept. 27, 1984.

17. Stanley M. Howe, from remarks in a tribute to CMS at a HON Recognition Dinner, recorded in a letter to EMS, Apr. 27, 1977.

18. Arthur E. Dahl interview, Dec. 15, 1986.

19. Interviews with Edward E. Jones, Dec. 4, 1986, and Howe, Dec. 8, 1986.

20. Howe interview.

21. CMS manuscript, "The HON Story," Chap. 11, p. 8.

22. Ibid., Chap. 4, p. 17.

Chapter 7

1. Emory Reves, *Anatomy of Peace* (New York: Harper, 1945), 279.

2. Jacques Leprette to RJ, 1986 (translated from French by Mary Gray and Matthew Carey).

3. CMS journal, Oct. 31, 1947.

4. George W. Neill, "United World Federalists Ask Arms Control to Curb Aggression," *Christian Science Monitor,* Apr. 2, 1955.

5. Ibid.

6. CMS journal, Dec. 31, 1947.

7. CMS journal, various entries from early 1948.

8. AES interview, Dec. 2, 1986.

9. Neill, "United World Federalists," 11.

10. Marilyn Jackson and Charles W. Roberts, "Citizens of the World: The Stanleys of Muscatine," *Iowan* (Spring 1980), 9.

11. CMS journal, Dec. 9, 1950.

12. CMS journal, May 21, 1955.

13. *Seattle Times,* report of CMS interview, Dec. 14, 1954; *St. Petersburg Times,* report of CMS talk, Jan. 29, 1955; *Berlingske Tidende,* Copenhagen, report of CMS interview and talk, Jan. 15, 1957 (translated from Danish by Willard R. Garred).

14. CMS talk, "Report to the Twentieth General Assembly, United World Federalists, Inc.," Washington, D.C., June 17, 1966.

15. William L. O'Neill, *Coming Apart: An Informal History of America in the 1960's,* (Chicago: Quadrangle Books, 1971), 7.

16. Ronald Berman, *America in the Sixties: An Intellectual History,* (New York: Free Press, Macmillan, 1968), 164, 165.

17. CMS talk, "Report to Twentieth General Assembly," UWF.

18. *Muscatine Journal,* CMS will filed for probate, Sept. 27, 1984.

19. Jack Smith interview, Dec. 18, 1986.

20. CMS talk to World Federalists USA assembly, Boston, Sept. 11, 1971.

Chapter 8

1. Willard D. Archie, "Remarks Prepared for the Dedication of an Addition to the Corning Library," June 7, 1981.

2. Bill Wickersham to RJ, Fall 1986.

3. Lauren Soth interview, Oct. 26, 1986.

4. James M. Towers, *Foundations in International Education: A Case Study of the Stanley Foundation, 1956–1983* (Ph.D. diss., University of Iowa, 1985), 48, 50, 139.

5. Ibid., 53, 54.

6. Jack Smith interview, Dec. 18, 1986.

7. CMS journal, Feb. 7, 1976. On file, SCI, Muscatine, Iowa.

8. Towers, *Foundations,* 80, 81.

9. CMS, "President's Letter," *World Press Review,* May 1984, 4.

10. CMS, memo to attorney Roger Lande, Dec. 24, 1974. Office files, SCI or E & M Charities, Muscatine, Iowa.

11. Alfred Balk interview, Nov. 10, 1986.

12. CMS, "President's Letter."

13. Balk interview.

14. SF budgets; Balk interview, Nov. 12, 1986; Towers, *Foundations,* 105.

15. Balk interview, Nov. 12, 1986.

16. Towers, *Foundations,* 100, 101; Jeffrey Martin interview, Nov. 19, 1986.

17. Martin interview.

18. SF budgets; Jim Berard interview, Nov. 24, 1986.

19. Martin and Berard interviews.

20. CMS journals, year-end 1966, Apr. 7–11, 1968, Sept. 16–24, 1968. On file, SCI or E & M Charities, Muscatine, Iowa.

21. Exchange of correspondence between Thomas Manton, July 10, 1971, and CMS, Aug. 24, 1971.

22. Smith interview.

23. CMS, *Waging Peace: A Businessman Looks at United States Foreign Policy,* (New York: Macmillan, 1956), 205, 206.

24. Ibid., 6.

25. CMS, *Managing Global Problems* (Muscatine, Ia.: Stanley Foundation, 1979), 241.

26. CMS journal, Jan. 16, 1969 (Dartmouth); EMS interview, Aug. 20, 1987.

27. CMS, *Managing Global Problems,* 4ff and Chaps in Part II deal specifically with the problems listed.

28. CMS, *Managing Global Problems,* 237.

Chapter 9

1. William B. Buffam interview, Nov. 12, 1986.
2. Ibid.
3. Jeremy J. Stone to RJ, Sept. 29, 1986.
4. John Redick interview, Jan. 26, 1987.
5. Burns H. Weston interview, Jan. 27, 1987.
6. James M. Towers, *Foundations in International Education: A Case Study of the Stanley Foundation, 1956–1983* (Ph.D. diss., University of Iowa, 1985), 141; Homer A. Jack to RJ, Oct. 5, 1986.
7. Jack Smith interview, Dec. 18, 1986; similar comments came from others, both on the foundation staff and at the United Nations.
8. Smith interview, and others on specific negotiations.
9. Jacques Leprette to RJ, 1986 (translated from French by Mary Gray and Matthew Carey).
10. "Final Document of Assembly Session on Disarmament," May 23 to July 1, 1978, distributed by Office of Public Information, United Nations.
11. Kosta Tsipis, taped recollections of CMS, Feb. 1987.
12. "Multilateral Disarmament and the Special Session," SF report, 12th United Nations Next Decade Conference, June 19 to 25, 1977, San Juan del Rio, Mexico, 36–38.
13. Leprette to RJ, 1986.
14. CMS testimony, House of Representatives Subcommittee on International Organizations and Movements Regarding Status of International Law of Sea Conference, Apr. 26, 1972.
15. "Ocean Management and World Order," SF report, 7th United Nations Next Decade Conference, July 9 to July 16, 1972, South Egremont, Mass., 4.
16. Garry Wills, *Reagan's America: Innocents at Home* (Garden City, N.Y.: Doubleday, 1987).
17. T. T. B. Koh to RJ, Sept. 29, 1986.
18. Rikhi Jaipal expression of thanks to CMS at Lake Mohonk conference in 1977.
19. Redick interview.
20. CMS journal, Feb. 2, 1980. On file, SCI or E & M Charities, Muscatine, Iowa.
21. "The United Nations Peace and Security," SF report, 18th United Nations Next Decade Conference, June 25 to 30, 1983, Burgenstock, Switzerland, 11; Jeff Martin and Jack Smith interview, Jan. 23, 1987.
22. CMS to Buffum, then assistant secretary of state, Nov. 20, 1975; CMS journal, Feb. 2, 1976.
23. Louis B. Sohn to RJ, Nov. 6, 1986.
24. Smith interview, Dec. 18, 1986.
25. Rudiger von Wechmar to RJ, Nov. 10, 1986.

Chapter 10

1. *Muscatine Journal,* editorial, Sept. 21, 1984.
2. Ibid.
3. EMS interview, Sept. 12, 1986.
4. CMS journal, Jan. 14, 1946, Mar. 25 and Apr. 4, 1946. Journal and CMS occasional correspondence on file, SCI or E & M Charities, Muscatine, Iowa.
5. CMS to William F. Angell, Muscatine I Club president, May 25, 1982.
6. Jonathan Raban, *Old Glory: An American Voyage* (New York: Simon and Schuster, 1981; Penguin Books, 1982), 192, 193, 198.
7. Ibid., 202.
8. *Muscatine Journal,* special section for Muscatine Industry Appreciation Week, Feb. 26, 1957; Harold Ogilvie interviews, Sept. 25, and Oct. 3, 1986.
9. Ogilvie interview: Iowa Development Commission, "Local Manufacturing Characteristics [for Muscatine]," 1985.
10. Delbert White, Muscatine Chamber of Commerce, interview, Jan. 16, 1987.
11. White interview; Ib Petersen, Muscatine Chamber of Commerce, interview, Jan. 16, 1987; Darrell Wyrick, University of Iowa Foundation, interview, Jan. 27, 1987.
12. Burns Weston, University of Iowa, interview, Jan. 27, 1987; Jack Smith interview, Dec. 18, 1986.
13. RHS conversation with RJ, Feb. 23, 1988.
14. Mark Twain, *Life on the Mississippi* (New York: H. O. Houghton, 1874, 1875; Harper and Row, 1917, 1951), 467, 468.
15. CMS journal, Mar. 26–29, 1968.
16. CMS, *Compass,* SCI, 1, 1961.
17. *Compass,* 8, 1967.
18. *Des Moines Register,* Sept. 4, 1982.
19. *Des Moines Register,* Mar. 25 and Mar. 29, 1977.
20. CMS journal, Apr. 26 and May 1, 1980; Dan Clark interview, Nov. 18, 1986.
21. Susan Koehrsen interview, Nov. 18, 1986.
22. Ogilvie and Petersen interviews.
23. AES interview, Dec. 2, 1986; Ron Barrett interview, Oct. 16, 1986; Jack Smith interview, Dec. 8, 1986; John Redick interview, Jan. 21, 1987.
24. EMS interview, Sept. 12, 1986.
25. Roger Lande interview, Jan. 15, 1987.
26. CMS journal, May 28, 1958; Byron Stanley interview, Oct. 23, 1986.
27. JoAnn Turner interview, Oct. 24, 1986.

Chapter 11

1. The material in this chapter, unless otherwise noted, is drawn from interviews and conversations with Betty Stanley, her sons and their wives, Dave and Jean Stanley and Dick and Mary Jo Stanley, and her daughter, Jane Stanley Buckles. These talks took place at various times between the summer of 1986 and the spring of 1988.

2. CMS journal, Oct. 3, 1972.

3. *Des Moines Register,* Aug. 25, 1974.

4. CMS journal, Apr. 18, 1944.

5. CMS journal, Jan. 4, 1953.

6. CMS journal, May 26, 1984.

Chapter 12

1. DMS memo to RJ, Feb. 21, 1988.

2. *Des Moines Tribune,* Oct. 16, 1968; Ed Failor interview, Jan. 8, 1987.

3. RHS to RJ, July 6, 1988; Failor interview.

4. Failor interview; James C. Larew, *A Party Reborn: The Democrats of Iowa, 1950–1974* (Iowa City: Iowa State Historical Department, 1980), 122, 123; various news accounts of the campaign in the *Des Moines Tribune* and *Des Moines Register.*

5. *Des Moines Tribune,* Oct. 15, 1968; CMS journal, Oct. 17, 1968; Failor interview; DMS interview, Jan. 30, 1987. CMS journal and correspondence files are held by SCI or E & M Charities, Muscatine, Iowa.

6. CMS journal, Nov. 3–6, 1968; Larew, *Party Reborn.*

7. CMS journal, Nov. 19, 1968.

8. CMS journal, June 2, 1970.

9. CMS journal, May 9, June 30, and July 12, 1974; *Des Moines Tribune,* Nov. 28, 1974.

10. CMS journal, Aug. 8, Sept. 8, 9, and 15, and Oct. 6, 1974.

11. CMS journal, Oct. 25, Nov. 3 and 6, 1974.

12. RJ conversations with former colleagues at the *Des Moines Register,* including Lauren Soth, Gilbert Cranberg, James Flansburg, and George Mills, and with Gerald Bogan, a news reporter who became a legislative lobbyist and an analyst of Iowa political trends; Kenton Allen, administrative director of SF and a former executive director of the Iowa Republican Party; DMS and Failor.

13. *Des Moines Register,* editorial, Jan. 14, 1970.

14. *Des Moines Register,* Sept. 2, 1974.

15. CMS journal, Aug. 31, 1974; Roger Lande interview, Jan. 15, 1987.

16. DMS memo to RJ.

17. Walt Shotwell interview, Oct. 10, 1986; Failor interview.

18. CMS journal, Nov. 17, 1971; Dan Clark interview, Nov. 18, 1986; DMS interview, Jan. 30, 1987.

19. CMS journal, Sept. 11, 1984, and notes for conference with Ray; interviews with DMS, Clark, and Allen, Nov. 25, 1986; Jack Smith interview, Dec. 18, 1986.

Chapter 13

1. Ron Barrett interview, Oct. 16, 1986.
2. RHS interview, Dec. 18, 1986.
3. CMS journal, Sept. 6, 1972; *Muscatine Journal,* Sept. 11, 1972; Burns Weston interview, Jan. 27, 1987. CMS journal and correspondence files are held by SCI or E & M Charities, Muscatine, Iowa.
4. Kosta Tsipis, taped recollections of CMS, Feb. 1987.
5. Willard Boyd to RJ, Jan. 21, 1987; Christopher Roy interview, May 26, 1986.
6. Darrell Wyrick interview, Jan. 27, 1987; U of I Foundation reports, 1971–1974; CMS report to foundation board, Oct. 3, 1975.
7. James M. Towers, *Foundations in International Education: A Case Study of the Stanley Foundation, 1956–1983* (Ph.D. diss., University of Iowa, 1985), 81; Weston and Wyrick interviews.
8. John Redick telephone conversation with RJ, Jan. 21, 1987; Kenton Allen interview, Nov. 25, 1986.
9. Jack Smith interview, Jan. 6, 1987.
10. David Doerge interview, Nov. 19, 1986.
11. CMS talk, U of I Center for World Order Studies, Nov. 22, 1974.
12. CMS talk, "Change," U of I Finkbine dinner, Apr. 25, 1963, published in U of I *Extension Bulletin,* June 1, 1963.
13. CMS talk, "The Library in the Modern World," Iowa Wesleyan College, June 7, 1969.
14. CMS talk, "The University and World Peace," University of Manila, March 11, 1970.
15. CMS talk, "The USA in a Revolutionary World," Wesleyan Associates, Iowa Wesleyan College, Mar. 31, 1967.
16. CMS to Jeremiah Milbank, Jr., Oct. 22, 1970; Rogers C. B. Morton to CMS, Nov. 13, 1970.
17. CMS, "The Best Advice I Ever Received," *Des Moines Sunday Register,* Picture magazine, Nov. 15, 1970.

Chapter 14

1. Many persons interviewed by the author touched on Stanley's religious faith and how he gave expression to it in his life.
2. CMS, *Waging Peace* (New York: Macmillan, 1956), 199, 200.
3. CMS, SF videotape, June 1983.
4. EMS interview, Sept. 12, 1986; DMS interview, Jan. 7, 1987.

5. DMS interview.

6. Ibid.

7. John Schenkel conversation with RJ, Jan. 28, 1987.

8. DMS interview.

9. Ibid.

10. RHS conversation with RJ, Feb. 23, 1988.

11. Summary of E & M Charities activities supplied by DMS, the foundation's president.

12. EMS interview, Oct. 6, 1987.

13. CMS talk, "The United Nations and the United Methodists," Council of Bishops, United Methodist Church, New York, Mar. 4, 1971.

14. Ibid.

15. CMS talk, "Methodologies of Peace Programs for the Laity," Garrett Theological Seminary, Evanston, Ill., Feb. 27, 1974.

16. CMS videotape, June 1983.

17. "Our Faith Compels Us to Speak . . .", issued by the Iowa Inter-Church Forum, Des Moines, published by SF, 1984.

18. CMS talk, "United Nations and United Methodists."

19. CMS talk, "A Christian Foreign Policy?", Wesley United Methodist Church, Muscatine, June 8, 1980.

20. See Chap. 9 for CMS role in Global Negotiations.

21. Paul Williamson at CMS memorial service, Wesley Church, Muscatine, Sept. 24, 1984.

Chapter 15

1. Harold Ogilvie interview, Oct. 3, 1986.

2. CMS journals, Aug. 29, 1967; Feb. 25, 1976. CMA journals and occasional correspondence held by SCI or E & M Charities, Muscatine, Iowa.

3. Ogilvie interview; CMS journal, Aug. 2, 1961.

4. Harold Bragg interview, Nov. 3, 1986; CMS journals, Mar. 23, 1982, Mar. 1, and Mar. 19, 1984.

5. Bragg interview; CMS to G. O. Jones, Feb. 17, 1969; Edward E. Jones interview, Dec. 4, 1986.

6. Byron Stanley interview, Oct. 23, 1986.

7. CMS journal, Mar. 14, 1976.

8. CMS talks at Stanley Consultants annual conference, May 13, 1972.

9. EMS interview, Sept. 12, 1986.

10. CMS to Don Wooten, Aug. 22, 1984.

11. Jack Smith interview, Jan. 6, 1987.

12. Jean Stanley interview, Jan. 20, 1987.

13. EMS interview, Aug. 28, 1986; CMS journal, Feb. 12, 1972.

14. CMS journal, May 23, 1978.

15. CMS journal, various entries, Sept. 1978.

16. CMS journal, Sept. 14, 1982.

17. CMS journal, various entries, July 5 to 21, 1984.

18. CMS journal, Jan. 15 and 16, 1936.

19. Alfred Balk interview, Nov. 10, 1986; EMS interview, Sept. 10 and 11, 1986.

20. CMS journals, Nov. 7 and 21, 1981, and Jan. 1, 1982.

21. CMS to Chalmers "Bump" Elliott, Jan. 13, 1983.

22. Darrell Wyrick tribute at CMS memorial service, Wesley Church, Muscatine, Sept. 24, 1984; CMS journal, Sept. 8, 1984; John B. Rigler to EMS, Sept. 20, 1984; Mary Jo Stanley interview, Sept. 30, 1986.

Chapter 16

1. CMS journal, Mar. 31, 1976.

2. Donald J. Mitchell to CMS (Johnson), Oct. 26, 1964; CMS journals, Nov. 2, 1976 (Carter); Nov. 7, 1972 (Nixon/McGovern). CMS journals and occasional correspondence on file, SCI or E & M Charities, Muscatine, Iowa.

3. CMS to John B. Anderson, Dec. 28, 1977.

4. CMS to Howard Baker, May 8 and Sept. 24, 1979.

5. CMS journals, Nov. 20, 1978 and July 1, 1980; CMS to Mike Mc-Cloud with contributions, July 8, 1980; Ben Gibson interview, Apr. 22, 1987.

6. "Anderson Gets Prominent Support," *Quad-City Times,* Davenport, Aug. 9, 1980.

7. CMS journal, Nov. 5, 1980.

8. CMS notes, Aug. 25, 1979; Tom Stoner telephone conversation with RJ, Apr. 28, 1987.

9. CMS journal, Nov. 7, 1978; Kenton Allen interview, Nov. 25, 1986; DMS interview, Jan. 30, 1987.

10. Allen interview; DMS interview, Jan. 30, 1987.

11. Gibson report to Cedar Rapids meeting participants, Oct. 3, 1981.

12. Anderson, "A Statement of Principles," Aug. 22, 1983; CMS to Anderson, Aug. 30, 1983; CMS journal, Oct. 6, 1983.

13. CMS journals, Mar. 24, 1983 (Cranston) and Jan. 23, 1984 (Stassen); CMS to Anderson, Aug. 31, 1984.

14. SF files, "op-eds," Feb. 10, 1984 (Star Wars), Apr. 13, 1984 (CIA mining), June 8, 1984 (covert actions), and Nov. 5, 1982 (nuclear freeze).

15. *Des Moines Sunday Register,* May 22, 1983; CMS talk, "Global Citizenship," University of Dubuque, Apr. 27, 1983.

16. Jeff Martin and Jack Smith interviews, Jan. 23, 1987; Rudiger von Wechmar, "On the Need for Global Negotiations," *New York Times,* Jan. 24, 1981; SF, "Global Negotiations and Economic Development," May 1–4, 1980.

17. SF, "Global Negotiations on International Economic Cooperation for Development," Nov. 14–16, 1980; CMS journal, Nov. 15 and 16, 1980.

18. Martin and Smith interviews; SF, "Global Negotiations."

19. CMS journal, Jan. 5, 1981; Von Wechmar to RJ, Nov. 10, 1986.

20. Von Wechmar, *New York Times,* Jan. 24, 1981.

21. CMS journal, May 27, 1981; Smith interview, Jan. 15, 1987.

22. CMS to Maclean W. McLean, Dec. 2, 1981.

23. Lincoln P. Bloomfield to RJ, Oct. 22, 1986.

24. CMS journal, June 7 and 14, 1984; SF, op-ed article, July 13, 1984; RHS conversation with RJ, Feb. 23, 1988.

Chapter 17

1. Christopher D. Roy interview, May 26, 1987.

2. EMS interview, Sept. 12, 1986; Roy, "To Max Stanley," *Art and Life in Africa: Selections from the Stanley Collection,* the University of Iowa Museum of Art, 1985.

3. See reference to Rockford Plans tests in Chap. 1, 11.

4. EMS interview; Ulfert Wilke, "In Memoriam," *Art and Life in Africa.*

5. CMS journal, Mar. 4, 1975. CMS journal and occasional correspondence held by SCI or E & M Charities, Muscatine, Iowa.

6. CMS journal, Aug. 22 and Nov. 16, 1975

7. CMS journal, Apr. 14, 1976; Roy interview.

8. CMS journal, Apr. 24, 1976.

9. Elsy Leuzinger, *The Art of Black Africa* (Greenwich, Conn.: New York Graphic Society, 1972), 11, 12; Margaret Trowell and Hans Nevermann, *African and Oceanic Art* (New York: Harry N. Abrams, 1967), 21–23.

10. Leuzinger, *Art of Black Africa,* 13; Trowell and Nevermann, *African and Oceanic Art,* 10.

11. Roy interview.

12. Ibid.

13. CMS journal, Jan. 19 and Mar. 24, 1984.

14. Wilke, "In Memorium."

15. Roy interview.

16. Kosta Tsipis, taped recollections of CMS, Feb. 1987.

Index